IMPARTIAL REASON

Stephen L. Darwall

IMPARTIAL REASON

Cornell University Press

ITHACA AND LONDON

Fordham University
LIBRARY
AT
LINCOLN CENTER
New York, N. Y.

First published 1983 by Cornell University Press.
Published in the United Kingdom by Cornell University Press Ltd.,
Ely House, 37 Dover Street, London WIX 4HQ.

International Standard Book Number 0-8014-1560-8
Library of Congress Catalog Card Number 82-22046
Printed in the United States of America
*Librarians: Library of Congress cataloging information appears
on the last page of the book.*

The paper in this book is acid-free and meets the guidelines for permanence and durability of the Committee on Production Guidelines for Book Longevity of the Council on Library Resources.

To the memory of my father

Contents

Acknowledgments 9

1. Introduction 13

PART I. DESIRE AND REASONS: PLACING THE WEDGE

2. The DBR Thesis and Its Four Roots 25
3. Desire and an Agent's Reasons 35
4. Coherentism 43
5. Humean Internalism 51
6. Reason and Preference 62
7. Retrospective and a Framework for Reasons 78

PART II. REASON AND PERSONAL GOOD

8. Rational Consideration: An Initial Account 85
9. Unified Agency 101

PART III. REASON AND INTERSUBJECTIVE GOOD

10. Nagelian Objectivity 117
11. Objective Reasons and Intersubjective Value 130
12. The Pervasiveness of Intersubjective Valuation 146

7

Contents

PART IV. REASON AND RIGHT

13. The Hobbesian Approach   171
14. Normative Rationality   201
15. Impartial Reason   218
16. Caveats and Consequences   240
    Works Cited   251
    Index   257

8

Acknowledgments

The ideas expressed in this book have taken shape slowly over a period of years. Their final contours bear the imprint of many people, but three philosophers in particular have influenced my thought.

While I was a graduate student at the University of Pittsburgh and interested in other things, Kurt Baier attracted me to the study of ethics and kindled in me a passion to understand its basis. What follows owes no small debt to his own work.

On leaving Pittsburgh I had the good fortune to come to Chapel Hill, where I have had the opportunity to learn from David Falk, through whom I have come to appreciate the force of internalism in practical philosophy and the importance of Kant. Although Falk would almost certainly reject the theory I offer here, much of its inspiration derives from him.

Finally, John Rawls's theory of justice and, most important, its Kantian interpretation provided me with a perspective to see that the standpoint that serves in Rawls's theory to assess principles of justice, his original position, should also serve, when suitably modified, to assess principles of rational action. The present work is an attempt to provide Rawls's theory of justice with a theory of practical rationality to anchor its Kantian interpretation.

Acknowledgments

In addition to these three I am very much indebted to many others. In years past, while I was groping toward the views I present here, Arthur Kuflik, Allen Buchanan, and Richard Grandy provided much philosophical stimulation, and Nora Faires, intellectual and emotional companionship. Of those who have read or heard portions of various drafts I am especially grateful to Kurt Baier, Marcia Baron, William Frankena, Stephen Hudson, Conrad Johnson, Willard Mittelman, Gerald Postema, Jay Rosenberg, Gregory Trianosky-Stillwell, the philosophy departments of Rutgers and Columbia universities, and an informal circle of moral philosophers in the Raleigh–Durham–Chapel Hill area, who met as a reading group in 1979–1980.

The first draft of the manuscript was written in New York in 1978–1979 while I held a fellowship for independent study and research from the National Endowment for the Humanities. The philosophy department at Columbia University generously extended to me the privileges of a visiting scholar during that time. I am very pleased to be able to express my thanks to both.

My thanks also go to Joanne Ainsworth, who edited the final manuscript; to Carolyn Shearin, who produced an earlier typescript; to Muriel Dyer, who typed the final version; and to Claire Miller, who often was able to find money tucked in departmental cubbyholes for copying expenses.

Finally, my wife, Rosemarie Hester, saw me through the writing of this book and by her example taught me the patience needed to work out ideas carefully.

STEPHEN L. DARWALL

Chapel Hill, North Carolina

IMPARTIAL REASON

CHAPTER 1

Introduction

Contemporary discussion of rationality in action has produced two widely divergent and contending camps. One takes the view that practical rationality is wholly self-centered. Any reason to act, it holds, can arise only from an agent's own desires, preferences, interests, or good. If to ignore the welfare of others or considerations of morality is not contrary to their own desires or interests, people may do so without acting contrary to reason in any way.

Members of the opposing camp deny this. They believe that the person who acts without consideration either for others or for morality ignores an important class of reasons. Indeed, many would add, to ignore morality is to ignore reasons that are often, if not always, weightier than self-centered ones.

Philosophers who believe in the self-centered theories are perhaps justified if they look upon the ardor with which their opponents have maintained the connection between morality and reason as based rather more on optimism or moral enthusiasm than on dispassionate argument. One moralist after another has sought to demonstrate that it is contrary to reason to flout ethics. And although no particular attempt has been found compelling, indeed not even by a consensus of the moralists themselves, they continue to assert what they feel in their bones: that it must be so.

Introduction

It is only fair to point out that the other group has not been long on compelling arguments for its view either. Even if everyone agrees that self-centered considerations are among the reasons for persons to act, further argument is required to show that they are the only ones. Nonetheless, unlike the moralists, these theorists have been in the enviable position of claiming a consensus that their favored considerations are indeed reasons. Not having to argue constructively for this point, they have taken an essentially critical posture, defeating the arguments of the moralists as they have been advanced.

Still, consensus is ultimately no substitute for argument. Indeed, we should be especially skeptical of the idea that practical rationality counsels exclusive concern for our own ends as such. Whatever consensus exists at present for that point of view is as likely to be the result of political-economic factors as it is to be a reliable indicator of the truth. Moreover, defenders of a self-centered conception of practical reason have traditionally enjoyed an important source of support to which they are not really entitled.

It has seemed to many that to deny a self-centered point of view is to deny virtually uncontestable assumptions about practical reason. As an example, consider Kant's hypothetical imperative: a person who wills an end must, insofar as he is rational, also will "the indispensably necessary means to it" (Kant 1785/1959, p. 34).[1] Who would deny that it is in an important sense contrary to reason not to take the means necessary to one's ends? This is perhaps the clearest example, but because we have a plurality of ends we may go further. Since in achieving one end we may utilize means that make it possible for us to achieve others, we may conclude that we should choose, other things equal, the most efficient means—the one with the least "opportunity cost," as economists say. Or consider the formal theory of decision under

---

1. *Preussische Akademie*, vol. 4, p. 417 (further references will be cited as *Ak.*, with page number). I follow Thomas E. Hill, Jr., here in referring to this principle as "*the* Hypothetical Imperative." While Kant himself refers only to different specific hypothetical imperatives, they stand to this fundamental principle as the different specific categorical imperatives stand to the Categorical Imperative in its various formulations. See Hill 1973.

risk. It counsels that we take account of our beliefs regarding the likelihood that various consequences will ensue from alternative acts and that we choose the act that has the highest expected utility (where utility is a measure of our relative *preferences* for the various possible outcomes). Like the hypothetical imperative, and other principles of "means-end rationality," the theory of decision under risk seems undeniable. Moreover, all are self-centered principles. They counsel action that bears a certain relation to the *agent's own* ends and preferences, and thus they have been thought to support self-centered theories of practical reason.

Nevertheless, the moralists really have nothing seriously to fear from these principles. Insofar as they are uncontestable they provide no support at all for exclusively self-centered theories of practical reason, if we understand the latter to include views about what considerations are *reasons* for agents to act. To think otherwise is to overlook a crucial distinction between what it is for action to be *consistent* or *coherent* with certain ends or preferences, assumed as fixed, and what it is for ends or preferences to give an agent *reasons* to act on them. To mark this difference, we may call the principles in question principles of *relative rationality*, since they tell us what it is rational to do relative to holding the rationality of certain other conditions fixed.

Consider, for example, the difference between saying, "If you want to kill Jones in a particularly violent way you should use a cleaver," and saying, "If you want to kill Jones in a particularly violent way you should see a psychiatrist," or "If you really want to play tennis this afternoon, you should do so." The first statement *may* simply express the judgment that using a cleaver is the act most consistent with the avowed end, without any comment on whether having that end is any *reason* at all to hack at Jones with a cleaver. The last two sentences, however, express the judgment that the person's having the end is indeed a reason for the recommended acts.[2]

The sense in which principles of relative rationality are uncontestable is as principles of coherence. They tell us what we must do

2. R. M. Hare (1971) makes this point.

to act most coherently with our ends, preferences, and beliefs,[3] but they are silent on the question of what *reasons* there are for action. The hypothetical imperative does not counsel us to take the means *because* (that is, for the *reason* that) we have the associated end. Taken strictly, it counsels us *either* to take the means *or* to give up the end—on pain of incoherence. Likewise, the theory of decision under risk tells us what act is most consistent with our preferences and subjective probability assignments. It counsels us either to act or to change one of the latter.

Principles of *relative rationality* describe the *transfer* of reasons. Reasons for me to make something my end are, owing to the hypothetical imperative, equally reasons for me to take the necessary means to it. Likewise, if my preferences and beliefs about likelihoods are supported by reasons, it follows from the theory of decision under risk that the act that maximizes expected utility is equally supported. Even if they delineate the paths along which reasons flow, however, principles of relative rationality do not entail anything at all about which considerations *are* reasons for agents to act. Any support that those believers in self-centered theories have derived from them is, therefore, illusory.

It is, of course, possible to maintain that there is nothing more to rationality than coherence and that if coherence entails nothing about reasons to act, then there simply are no reasons at all to do one thing rather than another—something rather than nothing. This would at least be an honest rendering of where the view of practical reason as coherence should end up. After all, the radical skeptic who holds that there is no reason to believe anything about the world is certainly willing to admit that one belief may be rational relative to a set of beliefs if it is entailed by them. But practical reason cannot wholly consist in pursuing coherence. As I shall argue in Chapters 6 and 9, coherence of preference is itself

---

3. This statement must be qualified. The theory of decision under risk is a theory of practical coherence if we understand expected utility to be constructed from our preferences and *beliefs* about the likelihood of alternative outcomes. If, however, we use some more objective interpretation of probability, it ceases to be simply a theory of coherence.

best understood if we can distinguish between desires and preferences that have some *basis* in reasons and those that do not.

As its title suggests, this book seeks to vindicate the feeling of the moralists that considerations other than self-centered ones are reasons to act, indeed, that moral requirements, suitably understood, provide reasons for any agent that generally *override* those based on the agent's own individual preferences. It maintains that practical reason is, at its base, *impartial* rather than self-centered. More specifically, it argues that reasons to act are grounded in principles that it would be (relatively) rational to choose were a person to adopt a perspective impartial between agents and to select principles for all to act on. This ties practical reason to principles of the right, conceived as those that would be chosen in a Rawlsian original position.[4]

It may seem not a little presumptuous to attempt such a project. What could be a more obvious and ominous portent than the many impressive, but ultimately unconvincing, efforts that the moralists have produced to date? My defense to this charge is that while no particular attempt by these philosophers has been successful, different important parts of the puzzle have been placed on the table. My own solution draws from the work of a number of such thinkers: philosophers with views as disparate as Kurt Baier, David Gauthier, David Richards, and Thomas Nagel. By working through their various insights and, crucially, by viewing them from an internalist and Kantian perspective, I believe that an argument emerges for the fundamental impartiality of practical reason.

Certain aspects of my approach are shared by three other approaches. A growing number of philosophers, including John Rawls (1980), contend that the willingness to be guided by considerations whose force as reasons can be appreciated from an impar-

---

4. John Rawls (1971) maintains that principles of justice and, more generally, of right conduct can be justified as objects of rational choice from a hypothetical perspective he calls the original position.

Introduction

tial or intersubjective standpoint is what defines the *reasonable* person. [5] An agent who considers matters only from his own standpoint and acts accordingly cannot be faulted, they believe, in terms of his conduct's *rationality*, but he can be characterized as unreasonable. And practical reason, they think, demands reasonableness as well as rationality.

But why does it? The defenders of reasonableness typically despair of any more telling answer to this question than pointing out that such a conception of reasonableness is our own. But, then, why does reasonableness, so conceived, have anything to do with practical *reason?* Perhaps we must believe it does if we call it *reasonableness*, but why should we do that? If reasonableness is distinct from rationality, why should we suppose that they are both aspects of the same thing? Why not think that reasonableness is simply a category of moral appraisal rather than one of practical reason?

While agreeing with the defenders of reasonableness that practical reason includes guidance by considerations that one could recommend to all from an impartial standpoint, the present approach attempts to anchor that claim with argument. In this respect it converges with two other approaches.

The kinds of argument that have been given for the rationality of moral conduct may be roughly divided into two groups, those that give a central role to what are held to be formal or necessary features of rationality and those that focus on the contingencies that face rational beings. The arguments of Thomas Nagel (1970) and Alan Gewirth (1978) typify the former. Each author attempts to show how philosophical reflection on formal aspects of rational action itself, regardless of the circumstances of life, is sufficient to demonstrate the untenability of a self-centered view of practical reason. Nagel believes that he can demonstrate on such a basis that *no* reason to act could be ultimately self-centered. Gewirth seeks to show that any rational agent implicitly recognizes a *right* of every person to noninterference and basic well-being. In each case the

5. This view has been given its most systematic expression in Richards 1971. It is also maintained in Harrison 1971, p. 395; Held 1977; Rescher 1954; and Sibley 1953.

18

argument proceeds by drawing out entailments of notions that constitute the core of our idea of rational action.

The other approach is typified by Kurt Baier (1958, 1978a) and, recently, by David Gauthier (1975). Baier has argued for years that the conclusion that moral requirements provide (overriding) reasons to act follows from Hobbesian reflections regarding a world in which everyone takes only self-centered considerations as reasons to act. Since everyone benefits if everyone regards considerations of right and wrong as the weightiest reasons for acting, Baier argues, they must indeed be the weightiest reasons.

Gauthier, while an earlier critic of Baier, has now come around to a similar view. He holds that although there is nothing inconsistent with a self-centered view of practical reasons, such a theory cannot be self-supporting as a theory of rationality should be: it would not be rational in the theory's own terms for a person to choose to act on it. This follows, he believes, for the sorts of reasons that Baier cites.

Like this third approach, ours will advert to the benefits for everyone (viewed from a suitable perspective) of everyone's acting on principles of right conduct. But this is not sufficient to make the case. As I shall argue in detail in Chapter 13, both Baier's and Gauthier's arguments ultimately fail to convince. Baier's conclusion follows from his premises only if we assume a questionable background theory of practical reasons. And Gauthier simply assumes that whether it is rational to choose to act on a principle is to be decided by considering what it would be like to act on it if everyone knew which principles everyone else was acting on.

As I argue in Part IV, what must be added to Hobbesian reflections to demonstrate the overriding rationality of right conduct is a consideration of additional, more formal aspects of practical rationality. But, again, the argument offered will differ substantially from those given by Nagel and Gewirth, respectively. For neither of these is convincing either.

The added formal element is what I shall call the *normativity* of reasons to act. The normative aspect of reasons consists in just this: reasons for a person to act bear on what he or she *ought* (rationally) to do. Reasons are guides to action we *recommend* as rational.

Introduction

Once the normative aspect of reasons to act is made explicit, it may perhaps be objected that there are none. An extreme skeptic might deny that any material considerations bear on the rational appraisal of conduct. He might hold that practical rationality is wholly a formal matter; for example, that it involves no more than coherence of preference and the maximizing of expected utility. As I mentioned above, and as will become clear in Chapter 6, I do not believe that this view can be maintained. I shall argue there that preferences can be coherent or incoherent only if they admit of criticism by material considerations—by reasons.

An appreciation of the normative character of reasons provides the perspective from which to see the relation between rationality and ethics. Premises derived by reflection on the normativity of reasons to act, when taken together with Hobbesian considerations regarding the results of all agents acting to pursue their individual preferences, entail the overriding rationality of morally required conduct.

We begin in Part I by considering arguments that have been given on behalf of the most popular self-centered theory of practical reason: the thesis that any reason must be based in the agent's own desires. Far from demonstrating that considerations relating to an agent's desires are the *only* reasons, however, these arguments do not demonstrate even that they *are* reasons to act.

Still, Part I is not wholly destructive. For what underlies many of the arguments for self-centered theories of rationality is a deeply attractive view about the relation between reasons and motivation: the *internalist* view that reasons for a person to act are considerations capable of *motivating* the person (when considered in the right way). Those who have held self-centered theories have been right, I think, to embrace internalism. Their mistake has been to suppose that internalism supports a self-centered theory of practical reason. In Chapter 5 we see why internalism is so appealing. At the end of Part I, I develop a general internalist characterization of reasons that will serve us throughout the rest of the book: a fact is a reason for a person to do something if he would be motivated to do it, other things equal, were he to consider that fact rationally.

Part II begins with an initial account of what rational consideration itself consists in. To consider something rationally, whatever else it involves, is to reflect on it fully, to make oneself vividly aware of it. This initial account enables us to demonstrate what the arguments of Part I could not: that considerations relating to what an agent prefers for its own sake are indeed reasons for him to act. But there is a crucial difference. What provides reason is not the simple fact of preference itself. Rather, considerations that when reflected upon *motivate* a preference for an act, other things equal, are reasons for the agent so to act. We then extend this insight: first, by considering how an agent can rationally settle conflicts between his intrinsic preferences and then by developing a notion of the best life for an agent (other things equal) as constructed out of what he or she would intrinsically prefer, all things considered, under certain ideal conditions.

Parts III and IV add to the initial account of rational consideration. In Part III we see how certain kinds of facts can be considered only if one makes oneself aware of them from a perspective that abstracts from one's own personal relation to what one considers: what Nagel has called the *impersonal standpoint.* Considerations that motivate us from such a perspective are, therefore, reasons for us to act.

Finally, in Part IV, we unpack the normativity implicit in the idea of *rational* consideration: that is, consideration that an agent ought (rationally) to give relevant information. This crucial idea leads us ultimately to the conclusion that principles of rational conduct are principles on which it would be chosen from an impartial standpoint that all agents act.

Far from leading to a self-centered theory, then, internalism actually supports a view of practical reason as fundamentally impartial.

Part I

Desire and Reasons:
Placing the Wedge

CHAPTER 2

The DBR Thesis and
Its Four Roots

1. The idea that practical reason is wholly self-centered pervades much recent philosophical and social scientific literature. One finds there an easy movement from theoretical models of decision that encapsulate a notion of rationality as maximizing expected individual utility to the general identification of practical reason with selecting the most efficient means to accomplishing our ends, desires, or preferences, whatever they may happen to be. A common way of stating this received doctrine is to claim that the only reasons for a person to act are provided by his *desires*.

The main purpose of Part I will be to argue that the connection between reasons and desires is much looser than this view supposes. If successful, the argument will place a wedge between reasons and desires in two ways. First, it will demonstrate that the usual arguments that are given for thinking that *any* reason to act must be based in the agent's desires do not show this. Second, it will suggest that these arguments do not even establish that considerations relating to an agent's desires actually are themselves reasons.

So the primary purpose of Part I is destructive. We must begin by loosening the connection ordinarily thought to exist between desires and reasons. Indeed, we may come at one point to think that connection so loose as not to exist at all. The constructive task of showing that considerations relating to an agent's desires actually are reasons must await Part II.

There is, however, an important constructive goal to be pursued in this first part. Appreciating what is compelling and profound about the view of practical reasons that underlies the supposed connection between reasons and desires will enable us to develop a framework for understanding practical reasons that will aid us in the constructive task of the rest of the book.

2. When it is claimed that all reasons for an agent to act are based in her[1] *wants* or *desires*, these terms are used interchangeably, and in an artificially broad sense, to mean the most general motivating condition of any intentional action. Whenever a person acts intentionally, he does so in order to accomplish something wanted (in this broad sense), even if only to perform the action itself. So understood, desire need not be felt, like the thirsty man's desire for a cool drink, nor be an enthusiasm, like the opera lover's desire to see the latest production at the Met. We may want to do something in this sense though we expect no pleasure and view the task as sheer drudgery.[2]

It is tempting to suppose that if we interpret desire this broadly the thesis that all reasons are based in the agent's desires becomes empty, but this is a mistake. Though Sarah might intentionally go out of her way to be kind to Luis, and therefore want to do so, without looking forward to it or getting any pleasure from it, in the view under consideration there would be no reason for her to do so unless she did in fact want to. It is her wanting to be kind to Luis, as expressed in her uncoerced kindness toward him, that provides whatever reason there is for her so to act. If Harry is not similarly concerned about Luis, if he would not freely act to aid him, then there is no reason for him to do so.

1. I shall alternate, more or less, the gender of third-person personal pronouns so as generally to avoid the more unwieldy 'he or she' or 'she or he'.
2. In this connection see J. C. B. Gosling's interesting discussion of this broad sense of 'want' as contrasted with its more ordinary sense in which we often intentionally do things we do not want to do (1969, p. 97).

Let us call the doctrine that the only reasons for an agent to act are those which, in the words of one adherent, "have their source in" the agent's desires (Harman 1975, p. 9), the Thesis of Desire-Based-Reasons, or for short, the *DBR Thesis*. It is doubtful that this designates a specific view because of the vagueness of the phrase "have their source in," and below I shall sort out different ways in which we might understand the DBR Thesis. Nevertheless, it is generally understood to be a single, coherent view, and I shall for the moment treat it as though it were.

There are at least four different sources, or roots, of the DBR Thesis. First, it can be maintained that it follows from the role of reasons in *explaining* rational action that reasons must have their basis in desires. One sort of explanation that is peculiarly appropriate for actions renders them intelligible by giving the agent's reasons for having acted, but we also characteristically explain actions by reference to the agent's beliefs and desires. So it might be thought that a person's action could not be explained by a reason, a consideration could not be that person's reason for acting, unless the consideration were somehow related to his desires. Indeed, some writers, most notably Donald Davidson (1963), simply identify the agent's reason with a complex consisting of the agent's relevant desires and beliefs.

There is, of course, a conceptual distinction, which we shall explore below, between an agent's reasons for acting and reasons for an agent to act. The former serve to explain conduct, the latter to recommend it. Nonetheless, it is reasonable to suppose that the set of reasons to act must be a subset of the considerations on which it is possible for an agent to act—of what can be his reasons.

A second source of the DBR Thesis is a general view of rationality as a kind of coherence. Reasoning about what to believe, for example, is a matter of making our beliefs more coherent. Some writers, in attempting to extend this view to the practical realm, have maintained that intention and desire play there a role analogous to that played by belief in the theoretical realm (for example, Harman 1976). Practical reasoning becomes, then, a matter of making our intentions, beliefs, and desires a coherent whole. And that suggests support for the DBR Thesis.

A third source of the DBR Thesis combines the view that practical reasons must have motivational efficacy with the Aristotelian and Humean doctrine that the mere perception, judgment, or belief that something is the case is in itself motivationally inert. From these two propositions together it is concluded that a mere statement of fact cannot be a reason for anybody to do anything. The only considerations that can be are those connected to the agent's desires.[3]

The fourth source of the DBR Thesis is especially widespread and influential. It is the notion that the DBR Thesis is required by well-entrenched formal theories of rational decision. These are typically formulated in terms of the decision maker's *preferences*.[4] Since a preference for A over B is ordinarily understood as a disposition to choose A rather than B, there seems little difference between saying that an agent prefers A to B and saying that she desires A more than B in our broad sense. Because formal decision theories base rational decision on the agent's own preferences, they appear to entail the DBR Thesis.

In the next four chapters we shall consider each of these arguments for the DBR Thesis. Our aim will not simply be to show they are unsound. Since widely held views are rarely without any foundation at all, our aim will also be to discover what grains of truth about practical reason they contain, unsound though they may be. What we learn will provide us with a basis for our constructive task in the rest of the book. Before we consider these arguments, however, we must be clearer on what the DBR Thesis itself says.

4. It is important to distinguish three different ways in which the notion of a reason may be related to action. We speak variously of the *reasons why* someone did something, of that *person's reasons* for so acting, and of the reasons that there were *for* the person so *to* act.

3. A particularly pristine example of this point of view is found in Meikle 1974.

4. For an account of these various decision theories see Luce and Raiffa 1957, pp. 12–38, 275–326.

The sorts of reason indicated in the first instance, the reasons why someone did something, include any fact that serves to explain the act. There are many things, however, that explain behavior, and that are therefore included among the reasons why someone acts in an omnibus explanatory sense, but that are not part of *the person's reason(s)* for acting. For example, it is an interesting fact that people who are conversing together tend to mimic the postures of each other so that, for example, a particular change in posture by one of the conversants may be explained by giving as a reason the slightly earlier similar change in posture by the other. To say, however, that the "mimicking" *conversant's reason* for changing posture was that the other person had changed and he wanted to bring their bodily postures back into harmony suggests a degree of self-consciousness that is usually absent from such behavior. Indeed, when this regularity is pointed out he may, like Dostoyevsky's Underground Man, strive to controvert it simply because it is *not* based in his own reasons.

Even more obviously, someone might cite as among the reasons for a person's action such things as ignorance or prejudice, suggesting that if the person had not been ignorant of some fact or prejudiced in some particular way he or she would have acted differently. But neither ignorance nor prejudice can be a person's reason for acting. For one thing, a person's reason must be something of which he is aware in at least some way. Thus, that Mary does not know that maraschino cherries are carcinogenic cannot be her reason for eating them, though it is a reason why she does if she would not eat them if she knew.

If not every reason why someone acts is included among that person's reasons for so acting, how do we distinguish those that are from those that are not? To answer this question we need first to consider the third way in which reasons are related to action.

Since reasons of both the first and second kind are explanatory, they seem to depend for their existence on the occurrence of what they explain. If no action occurs, then there is obviously no reason why it occurred, nor could the person himself have had a reason for so acting, in the sense that it explains his doing so, since he did not. This way of putting the point is not quite right, however, for even if an action did not occur, it may be the case that a reason of the first kind existed. Thus, given our understanding of human behavior, we may say on seeing one of our two conversants change posture that the other *should* change to a coincident posture now. And even if he does not, we may still say, "Well, he should have." Here we mean roughly the same thing as when, on checking out a reluctant car's electrical system, we judge that it should have started: given what we know about auto mechanics there was reason to expect that it would (see Wheeler 1974, p. 235).

When we judge, however, that the conversant should have changed posture, we do not employ the 'should' of evaluation or criticism. We do not judge that there was reason *for* him *to* have changed posture in the sense that there existed a balance of considerations that *recommended* or *justified* that act. This is the crucial contrast between reasons of the third kind, or *justificatory reasons* as they have come to be called, and reasons of the first two, explanatory kinds. [5] Justifying reasons do not depend for their existence on the occurrence of that for which they are reasons, nor does their existence necessarily give rise to a reasonable expectation that that for which they are reasons will occur. We may know an act to be the one there is preponderant reason for the agent to take even as we know that it will not occur or that it is not even thereby likely to occur. [6]

Reasons of the third kind are things that can be said or thought in favor of, or against, an action. Rational choice, as opposed to random selection, is made on some basis or other. This idea of a *basis* for rational choice is the root idea of a reason *for* someone *to* do something. Justifying reasons are considerations that recommend or disrecommend one alternative rather than another. They

---

5. The distinction between 'justifying' and 'explaining' reasons is often marked by philosophers. In the eighteenth century, Francis Hutcheson distinguished "justifying" reasons from what he called "exciting" reasons: that "Truth [which] shews a quality in the action, exciting the Agent to do it" (Hutcheson 1728/1964, p. 404). For a modern account that reintroduced this distinction to philosophical discussion, see K. Baier 1958, pp. 148–156.

6. These features of justification and explanation lead Carl Hempel to reject the view maintained by Dray and others that to explain action is to justify it and, therefore, that its explanation cannot be causal. See Hempel 1965, p. 469.

are grounds for the practical judgment of what it would be best, or what there is reason, on the whole, to do.

The crucial mark of reasons of the third kind, then, is their role as considerations relevant to the evaluation of alternative acts in order to make the best choice. Moreover, since actions are what are being evaluated, these reasons are relevant to the *guidance* of conduct and are, in the broad sense, *normative*. We may say, therefore, that reasons of the third kind have a *normative aspect*. The full elaboration of the normative aspect of reasons for a person to do something must await Part IV, but at this point we may say that what there is reason on the whole for a person to do is what he, rationally speaking, *ought* to do. By 'ought' here we need mean nothing stronger than the course of action reason recommends. (See K. Baier 1973.)

What sorts of things are reasons for someone to act? Since they are what people are to take account of in evaluating choiceworthy alternatives, they must be the sort of thing that can be thought or said on behalf of an act. Accordingly, they must be propositional in form and expressible with a 'that' clause.[7] While a person may cite the weather or the reluctance of her car as a reason for her to take the subway across town, it is because these items figure in what might be said or thought in favor of her taking the subway, such as *that it is raining cats and dogs* or *that her car will not start*.

Most generally considered, reasons for someone to do something are a subclass of the things that can be said, asserted, considered, judged, thought, and so forth. To have a convenient tag to refer to such items, and to preserve the association of reasons with things that can be said on behalf of acting, I shall say that reasons for someone to do something are *dicta*.

This notion appears to conflict in more or less serious ways with views that other writers have presented of the matter. For example, Thomas Nagel identifies a reason with a property or predicate R such that "for all persons p and events A, if R is true of A, then p has prima facie reason to promote A" (Nagel 1970, p. 47). This difference is only superficial, however. It is the fact, or true dic-

7. On this point see Richards 1971, p. 59.

tum, that R is true of A that gives the person reason to do A.[8] Indeed, when Nagel himself refers to examples of reasons he does so with 'that' clauses.[9]

When speaking of justificatory reasons I shall generally follow English usage and speak of reasons *for* a person *to* do something. Only reasons of the third kind can be referred to by this form of words. We may speak of someone's reasons (of the second kind) for doing or for having done something, but the phrase 'so-and-so's reason to do, or for him to do', has no meaning.

Having said something about justificatory reasons we are now in a position to distinguish the subset of reasons of the first kind, purely explanatory reasons, that is comprised of *agents' reasons* for having acted, reasons of the second kind. The notion of an agent's reason brings the idea of justificatory reasons essentially into play. Something may be somebody's reason for having acted without having been a reason for him so to have acted (a reason of the second kind without being a reason of the third kind), but it must nonetheless be a consideration that *he regarded* (or perhaps would regard under certain conditions) as a reason for him so to act. What characterizes explanation of action in terms of the agent's reasons is that it explains it as an expression of the agent's own conception of what reasons there were for him to act.[10] To take the metaphor involved seriously, we make certain considerations *our own* reasons by deciding to act on their basis.

Since something is somebody's reason for having done something only if he regarded it as a reason for him to do it, reasons of the second kind must be dicta also. A person's reason for acting is something he thought favored his action.

8. I want to avoid the issue of whether *p* can be a reason for S to do A only if *p* is true. Ordinarily, the person who takes *p* to be a reason for him to do A does not simply believe there to be a *relation* between *p* and his doing A: that his doing A is *reasonable relative to p*. Rather, he has some tendency to detach the conclusion that his doing A is supported by reason because he believes *p* to be true.

9. See, for example, Nagel's examples (1970, p. 91).

10. This view is urged by Kurt Baier (1978c, p. 711), Don Locke (1974), and D. E. Milligan (1974).

5. We shall be concerned almost wholly with reasons for acting of the third or justificatory sort.[11] Our guiding question will be: what considerations, in general, are reasons for a person to act? The thesis that all reasons for acting must be related in some (yet to be specified) way to the agent's desires is an attempt to answer that question. It is a thesis about what considerations can be reasons for a person to act.

One way in which it has been asserted that reasons are "provided by" the agent's desires is that they are *identical* with those desires. If it is being asserted only that desires figure among the most general explanatory reasons (of the first kind) of any action no problem arises. Desires themselves, however, are not of the appropriate ontological category to be identical with reasons of either the second or third kind. In the view of the matter I am suggesting, reasons for someone to do something, or what a person could regard as such reasons and accordingly act on, are *dicta* or considerations that could be thought to favor the action. Insofar as one can consider one's desires as such, it is in virtue of considering such *dicta* as *that I desire to do A, that my desire to do A is stronger than my desire to do B,* and the like. An initial version of the DBR Thesis, that any reason for a person to do something must actually *be* a desire of his, is therefore a nonstarter. Let us call this Version I:

A reason for a person to act just is a desire of that person.

If we are to take the DBR Thesis as a claim about what reasons there are for agents to act we must understand it to assert that the only reasons are provided by dicta relating to the agent's desires. One way of understanding this is as asserting that there is ultimately only one reason for a person to act: that acting will enable her to accomplish what she desires. Let us call this rendering of the DBR Thesis, Version II:

11. When 'reasons' appears subsequently in the text, it will refer to justificatory reasons unless otherwise noted.

The only reason to act is that doing so will enable the satisfaction of one's desires.

6. We may now sum up: 'Reasons for action' is ambiguous as between:

(a) reasons that are purely explanatory, including anything that serves to explain an action (reasons of the first kind);
(b) reasons that are purely justificatory in that they include any consideration that serves to render an alternative choiceworthy (reasons of the third kind); and
(c) reasons that are explanatory but explain action as the expression of the agent's conception of what considerations made the alternative choiceworthy (reasons of the second kind). Though explanatory, these reasons engage considerations that seemed recommendatory in the agent's own view.

To be a thesis about what reasons there are for persons to act, the DBR Thesis must hold that only dicta relating to the agent's own desires can be reasons for him to act. We turn now to considering what has led people to maintain this thesis.

CHAPTER 3

Desire and an
Agent's Reasons

Reasons to act are considerations that guide rational action. It is a necessary condition of something's being a reason, then, that it can play this guiding role; it must be possible, that is, for a person to act for that reason, for the consideration to be a *person's reason* for acting. If the class of considerations that can function as an agent's reason is limited in a certain way, then the class of reasons for an agent to act must be similarly limited. Nothing can be a reason for someone to do something if it is impossible for it to be a person's reason.

If it could be shown that whatever can be a person's reason for acting must always be based in his or her desires, this would have important consequences for the question of what facts are reasons for a person to act. It would be significant support for the DBR Thesis.

1. Such an argument would begin by noting that any intentional action can be explained as resulting from the agent's desires (and beliefs). This much follows directly from the characterization of desire we have been using: the most general motivating condition of any intentional action. If I intentionally flip a switch, I must

have some desire to do so, though not necessarily to do so for its own sake.

So an action can be explained by an agent's reasons only if it can be explained by his desires. Similarly, something can be an agent's reason for acting only if he has some desire that would also explain his so acting. Thus, it can be argued, the only considerations that could possibly be among a person's reasons for acting are those that are related in some way to his desires; for he can act on that reason, that reason can explain his act, only if the act is also explainable as the result of his desires.

When we add this result to the considerations in the first two paragraphs, we seem to get some version of the DBR Thesis: a consideration can be a reason for a person to act only if it is based in his desires. Because this argument trades on the role of reasons in explaining, as well as in recommending, conduct, we may call it the Argument from Explanation.

To evaluate this argument we must consider in more detail the way in which an agent's reasons must be related to his desires. Donald Davidson, for example, seems simply to identify an agent's reason for acting with a complex consisting of a desire (or "pro attitude" as he calls it) and a belief. The relevant desire and belief are the desire to perform an act having a certain property and the belief that the act, under the intended description, has that property (1963, p. 69). That is, whenever we do something intentionally, there is something we want to do, and we believe that what we are doing is indeed what we want to do. The desire and belief taken together comprise our reason for acting.

This view of the matter, however, fails to distinguish what must be kept distinct if we are to understand rational action. Specifically, it fails to distinguish what we called in the last chapter reasons of the first kind from reasons of the second kind. To view any intentional action as explainable by a desire and belief complex is simply to suppose that the latter are reasons in the omnibus explanatory sense. Nothing directly follows about the relation of an agent's desires to *his* reasons for acting; that is, to reasons of the second kind.

Indeed, as we saw in the last chapter, desires are not the sort of

36

thing that could be an agent's reason. Reasons of the second kind, like reasons that recommend or justify, are dicta. An agent's reason is a consideration awareness of which leads him to act and something he regards as a reason for him to act. The only way, therefore, in which an agent's desires can explicitly be contained in his reasons is if his reasons are considerations that explicitly refer to his desires; for example, the consideration that acting in a certain way will satisfy this or that desire. This is just to say that the Argument from Explanation cannot support Version I of the DBR Thesis ("A reason for a person to act just is a desire of that person"); Version I is unsupportable.

But if Version I is unsupportable in itself, neither can Version II ("The only reason to act is that doing so will enable the satisfaction of one's desire") derive support from the Argument from Explanation. From the fact that any intentional action must be explainable by the agent's desires it does not follow that the agent's reason for acting must itself make reference to his desires. Usually when we act as we desire we are not moved to act by our awareness of the fact that we desire. Rather, a desire itself partly consists in a disposition to be moved by certain facts connected with its *object*.[1] A thirsty person lost in the desert is moved to run toward the horizon by her awareness that there is an oasis just now within sight, not by her awareness that she desires to drink. To desire is not necessarily to have one's attention fastened on the fact that one desires, but to have one's attention on the object of desire. The thirsty person views the world from the perspective of her desire to drink, scanning it for potables.

This line of thought undermines the inference from the fact that any intentional act must feature a desire among its explaining reasons (of the first kind) to the proposition that any agent's reason (of the second kind) must itself refer to the fact of desire. Moreover, it suggests that the latter proposition is false. Desires are for their objects, and the locus of the desiring person's concern is most typically the object itself and facts connected with it rather than the fact that she has the desire.

1. On this point see Abelson (1969), Falk (1952), Gosling (1969), and Locke (1974).

2. There is, however, another way in which it might be claimed that an agent's reason for acting must itself be "provided by" the agent's desires. It might be suggested that a consideration could not be an agent's reason for acting unless he took that consideration to be connected in some way to something he in fact desires. Even if it is false that a person's reasons for acting are restricted to facts about his desiring things, it might still be true that they are restricted to facts about the objects of his desires. This would appear to support yet a further version of the DBR Thesis. Let us call this Version III:

> Something is a reason to act only if it evidences the act to promote something the agent desires.

Version II of the DBR Thesis held that there is ultimately only one reason for any agent to act: that doing so would promote a desired state of affairs. According to Version III, however, there is a multitude of reasons for an agent to act, many not referring directly to desires as such. Nevertheless, all reasons for acting are still held to have their source in the agent's desires in the sense that a necessary condition of their existence as reasons for her to act is that she have the coordinate desire.

The Argument from Explanation for Version III must establish, then, that a consideration can be someone's reason for acting only if she takes it to be connected to something she desires. Now there is, as Thomas Nagel has pointed out, a sense in which it simply follows from the fact that a person is motivated by a consideration that she has, at that moment, a relevant desire (Nagel 1970, p. 29; see also Foot 1972b, p. 204). In this sense, if I am motivated to move my arm by the knowledge that unless I do so I will be stung by a bee, it follows that I desire not to be stung by a bee.

From this truism, however, Version III will not follow. Though that one desires follows from the fact that one is motivated by a consideration and, hence, that the consideration is one's reason for acting, that one desires does not follow from the fact that one *can be* motivated by a consideration. This is what the Argument from Explanation would have to establish to demonstrate Version III.

Desire and an Agent's Reasons

The Argument from Explanation trades on the thesis that a necessary condition of something's being a reason for a person to act is that it can be a person's reason for acting. Consistent with the truism that a person is motivated by a consideration if, and only if, he has a relevant desire, is that a consideration could become a person's reason for acting though he does not now have the relevant desire. Indeed, it might be the case that his simply becoming aware of the consideration (in a particularly vivid way) would give rise to motivation, and hence to the relevant desire. (See Nagel 1970, p. 29.)

3. At issue here is whether an agent can be motivated by a consideration without his motivation's being itself explained by the prior existence of a desire. We may concede that whether a person can be moved by some consideration is determined by what we might call, in the broadest sense, his motivational capacities as well as by other factors. Put least tendentiously, a person cannot be moved by some consideration unless he is such that, under certain considerations, he *would* be moved by it.

What we should not concede, however, is that the agent's current *desires* function as a filter that determine which considerations can move him and which cannot, for a person's motivational capacities, in the broadest sense, are not constituted simply by his desires but also by capacities of imagination, sensitivity, and so on. To appreciate how it is possible for a person to be moved by awareness of some consideration, without that being explained by a prior desire, consider the following example. Roberta grows up comfortably in a small town. The newspapers she reads, what she sees on television, what she learns in school, and what she hears in conversation with family and friends present her with a congenial view of the world and her place in it. She is aware in a vague way that there is poverty and suffering somewhere, but sees no relation between it and her own life. On going to a university she sees a film that vividly presents the plight of textile workers in the southern United States: the high incidence of brown lung, low wages, and long history of employers undermining attempts of workers to organize a union, both violently and through other extralegal means. Roberta is shocked and dismayed by the suffering she sees. After the film there is a discussion of what students might do to help alleviate the situation. It is suggested that they might actively work in promoting a boycott of the goods of one company that has been particularly flagrant in its illegal attempts to destroy the union. She decides to donate a few hours a week to distributing leaflets at local stores.

Roberta may have had no desire prior to viewing the film that explains her decision to join the boycott. And whatever desire she does have after the film seems itself to be the result of her becoming aware, in a particularly vivid way, of considerations that motivate her desire and that she takes as reasons for her decision: the unjustifiable suffering of the workers.

Of course, it could have been the case that she had some such general desire as the desire to relieve suffering prior to seeing the film, saw this as an opportunity, and formed the desire to relieve *this* suffering, as per an Aristotelian practical syllogism. But this need not be what happened. To suppose that is to suppose that Roberta had already formed the abstract desire to relieve suffering, and she might never have done that even if she had been moved in the past by the suffering of family, friends, and pets. For her to come to a general *desire* to relieve suffering she would have had to become actively concerned about the fact of suffering itself, conceived independently of who suffers, and she may never have done that. That she was moved by their suffering does not entail a prior desire to relieve suffering or even a sensitivity to suffering in the sense that she was likely to notice it without its being brought to her attention.

A desire consists not simply in the capacity to be moved by awareness of facts regarding its object. It is both more active and more focused than that. It includes dispositions to *think* about its object, to *inquire* into whether there are conditions that enable its realization. For example, it may be true of me that were the aroma of fresh apple pie to waft past my nose I would be moved to discover its source and perhaps to try to wangle a piece. It does not follow from this, however, that before I smell the pie I desire to eat it or to eat anything at all. Without my encountering its aroma, apple pie,

Desire and an Agent's Reasons

or food in general, might be the farthest thing from my mind or cares.

It is instructive to consider here Hume's distinction in the *Treatise* between sympathy, on the one hand, and love of mankind or desire for their well-being, on the other. Human beings are, Hume believed, sympathetic; we are capable of empathy with the feelings of others and of being moved by our empathic understanding: "'Tis true, there is no human, and indeed no sensible creature, whose happiness or misery does not, in some measure, affect us, when brought near to us, and represented in lively colours. . . . (1739/1962, p. 481). But this does not mean that we have a general love for mankind, a general desire for human welfare. In addition to the reasons that Hume cites, we might add that such a desire would include a disposition to bring to mind the welfare of others and not simply to respond to it when the thought is vividly imposed on us.[2]

Not only does Roberta's deciding to join the boycott for the reasons she does (considerations with which she is presented in the film) not require explanation by the presence of a desire. In addition, she need not, and likely would not, view the *cogency* of her reasons as dependent on her actually acquiring the desire to aid in the effort. Most likely she thinks, mistakenly or not, that the considerations adduced in the film provide reasons for others to join the boycott, whether they are in fact so moved or not.

4. We earlier conceded that whether a person can be moved by some consideration is partly a matter of what might be called, broadly speaking, his motivational capacities. We have also implicitly granted that whether a consideration can be a reason for someone to do something depends on whether it can be his reason for acting, and hence, on whether he can be moved by consideration of it. It follows from this that whether a consideration is a

2. The reasons that Hume gives for refusing to recognize the general love of mankind as such, even though we are sympathetic, are (1) sympathy is a capacity to be moved by the plight of "sensible creatures" in general, and (2) our loves vary with the "personal qualities," "services," and "relation to ourself" of the person in question.

41

reason for someone to act depends, at least partly, on his motivational capacities—whether he is such that he would be moved by it were he to consider it in a certain way under certain conditions. We need not shrink from this conclusion. Indeed, we should be happy to embrace it. As we shall see when we examine the Humean roots of this internalist thesis in Chapter 5, it enables us to make sense of rational motivation. What we should resist, however, is the supposition that a person cannot be moved by some consideration without the existence of a prior desire. That seems an implausible account of what happens in Roberta's case. Nonetheless, if we insist that Roberta would not be moved by her learning of the plight of southern millworkers unless she already had, say, the desire to relieve suffering, then the notion of desire invoked is so weak that it will simply turn out to be the case that a person does indeed have the relevant desire if it is true of him that were he to consider certain things in certain ways under certain conditions he *would* be appropriately moved. So conceived, the filter of desire on possible reasons has just the same strength as the filter provided by an agent's motivational capacities. Since we shall accept the latter, the former poses no special problem.

The Argument from Explanation, then, can establish none of the versions of the DBR Thesis we have canvassed to this point. At most, it can establish that something can be a reason for a person to act only if it is possible for the person to be motivated by it. For the latter to be true it need not be the case that the person actually have a relevant desire in any stronger sense than the capacity to be motivated by the consideration.

CHAPTER 4

Coherentism

A second line of thought that some find persuasive on behalf of the DBR Thesis begins with a basically coherentist view of reason. Ordinarily, this view is taken with respect to rational belief, but it can also be extended to rational action. And some who have sought to extend it to action have apparently thought it to entail some version of the DBR Thesis. [1]

1. Reasoning about what to believe, according to this view, is a matter of making our beliefs more coherent. For example, reason requires that our beliefs be consistent, that they not conflict with each other. Coherence is not, of course, simply a matter of lack of conflict. To cohere, our beliefs must hang together as a systematic whole. We can organize our beliefs further by adopting new beliefs that enable us to explain what we already believed. We tentatively adopt hypotheses and theories, and our reason for believing them is that they support and make sense of previously held beliefs that we could not otherwise satisfactorily explain.

Especially relevant to our purposes is that in an exclusively coherentist conception of theoretical reason, any reason to believe

1. Most notably, Gilbert Harman (1976).

some proposition can apparently be provided only by something else one already believes. This seems like an analogue of the DBR Thesis for belief: any reason for an agent to believe something must be anchored in his beliefs. And indeed at least one writer, Gilbert Harman, has sought explicitly to extend this view of theoretical reason to desire and action: "Reasoning is . . . a process in which antecedent beliefs and intentions are minimally modified, by addition and subtraction, in the interests of explanatory coherence and the satisfaction of intrinsic desires" (1976, p. 442).

An exclusively coherentist conception of theoretical reason is by no means unproblematic in itself. For one thing, why should the process of canvassing reasons for and against believing a proposition be restricted to seeing how the proposition fits in with what one already believes? Should not rational inquiry also include the gathering of *new* information? When we look to see what reasons there are to believe a proposition we do not simply reflect; we look outward to see what might bear on it. It would seem, therefore, that we must think that reasons to believe propositions are not provided simply by what we already believe.

The coherentist may reply that he does not mean to restrict rational inquiry to reflection and that his view is only that no proposition can be a reason to believe something until that proposition is believed. But that seems artificial, for what explains our inquiry, our search outside the circle of our present beliefs, if not our curiosity about what reasons there *are* to support a hypothesis? In any case, we need not decide here the acceptability of a coherentist conception of theoretical reason. What will concern us in this chapter is the attempt to extend that view to support the DBR Thesis.

2. A natural way to begin such an extension is to note that committing ourselves to ends creates the possibility of an incoherence similar to the incoherencies that can arise when we are committed to inconsistent beliefs. It is incoherent, for example, to intend to do A, to believe that A cannot be done unless B is done, but to intend not to do B. Or, as Kant put it, "Whoever wills the end, so far as reason has decisive influence on his action, wills also the

indispensably necessary means to it that lie in his power" (1785/ 1959, p. 34; *Ak*. p. 417). That we intend to take means necessary to our ends or, at any rate, not intend not to take necessary means seems, then, to be a demand of acting coherently and, accordingly, of reason.

We can explain this incoherence in more than one way. Harman points out that since an intention to do something involves a belief that one will do it, intentions can be incoherent, either among themselves or with beliefs, if their associated beliefs are. Thus the intention to do A involves the belief that one will do A, and the intention not to do B involves the belief that one will not do B. When we conjoin these beliefs with the belief that A will not be done unless B is, we get an incoherence (1976, p. 432).[2]

Or, we may note, with Kant, that to be committed to an end is not simply to desire it but to be prepared to accomplish it, that is, to take the means necessary to bring it about oneself (1785/1959, p. 34, A*k*, p. 417). It is, therefore, incoherent to say, "I intend to do A, but not to do what is necessary to do A." And the corresponding intentions are themselves, therefore, incoherent.

From the fact that reason requires that we intend to take the means necessary to our ends, no version of the DBR Thesis follows, however. It is true that in our broad sense of 'desire', any agent who intends to do something can be said to desire to do it. Since reason demands that one intend the necessary means to ends, it might appear to follow that the fact that one desires to act becomes, therefore, the only reason for an agent to act. But this would be a mistake on two counts.

Most obviously, the inference would be mistaken because it requires that coherence of the sort described be not only a demand of reason but its only demand or recommendation. Someone might, of course, hold the former and reject the latter; Kant is the

---

2. Robert Binkley (1965) has derived the hypothetical imperative from a set of axioms that, on their face, seem weaker than Harman's thesis that if one intends to do A, one believes that one will do A. Along with other plausible assumptions, Binkley supposes that if one intends to do A, then one withholds belief that one will not do A; and that if one believes that one will do A, one withholds a decision not to do A.

prime example. His allegiance to the hypothetical imperative is by no means inconsistent with his contention that reason also makes "categorical" demands.

Second, even if reason's practical task were simply to achieve means-ends coherence, no version of the DBR Thesis would follow. It is worth taking some pains to see why this is so. First, even granting that it follows from the rationality of intending means to ends that one's intention to do something is a reason to take the means necessary to do it, this does not entail that one's *desires* provide reasons to act. Though it is incoherent to say, "I intend to do A but intend not to do what is necessary to accomplish A," there is nothing at all incoherent in saying, "I desire to do A but intend not to do what is necessary to accomplish A." Ends and intentions are rationally committing in a way that desires are not.

Moreover, it is by no means clear that it does follow from the incoherence of intending not to take necessary means to ends that one's ends provide *reasons* for one to take the means. Let us consider this point in the language of intention. Is the intention to do A a reason for one to do B, if B is the necessary means to A? Well, it would be if the intention to do A were a reason to do A, for if there is a reason to accomplish an end, then there is a reason, other things equal, to take the means necessary to accomplish it. This much follows from the fact that to commit oneself, even provisionally, to an end is rationally to commit oneself, provisionally, to taking the necessary means.

So let us ask whether the intention to do A provides a reason to do A. Ordinarily, the reasons for a particular action are no more and no less than the reasons that exist to intend that action. Deliberation about whether or not to do A proceeds before intention has been fixed or after it has been suspended. The intention does not provide a further, independent reason into the bargain.

Admittedly, there are cases in which we take the fact that we have already decided a question as itself a consideration in favor of going ahead and not reopening the issue of what to do. In such cases is not the intention to act itself a reason to do so? Ordinarily, when we are disinclined to reopen deliberation it is because we suppose that our current intention is already well-enough supported by reasons; or, perhaps, that though further deliberation may uncover other reasons against acting as we intend, they are not likely to be sufficiently weighty; or that the time and energy required to reopen the issue do not warrant doing so; or that we should generally abide by our decisions unless there is some compelling reason not to; or some combination of these. Quite possibly, the general truth of many of these considerations amounts to a case for generally regarding the fact of intention as a reason for acting.[3] But two points must be borne in mind. First, this case for regarding an intention as providing a reason for acting depends on the assumption that people generally have reasons, and reasons enough, for their intentions. It follows that if this is why intentions provide reasons, they cannot provide the *only* reasons. They provide reasons only if there are generally other reasons for the intentions people actually form. Were I convinced that I had absolutely no reason for intending to do something, my bare, unsupported intention could hardly provide a reason itself.

Second, that intentions provide reasons cannot follow from the hypothetical imperative alone. We can infer that an intention to do something gives some reason to employ means necessary to do it only if we know something about whether intentions are themselves based on reasons. When we regard an intention as adding some rational weight of its own because of the considerations in the last paragraph, we make the substantive assumption that there are *other* reasons for acting on which people's intentions are themselves often based. The idea behind the hypothetical imperative is not that our intentions provide us with *reasons* to employ means to our intended acts. The point is rather that the force of reasons is, as it were, transferred back and forth along the line connecting an

3. I am indebted to Gerald Postema for impressing this point on me. Recently a number of philosophers have argued that intentions do provide reasons. These include Aune (1977), Bratman (1981), and Raz (1975). Bratman, for example, argues that our capacity to plan and form intentions enables us better to satisfy desires. But this case for regarding intentions as generating reasons supposes that our intentions are themselves generally based on reasons (desire-based, or "desiderative," reasons, as he calls them). In this view, intentions generate derivative reasons. Were there generally no reason for us to intend one thing rather than another, intentions could not provide reasons by themselves.

end and its necessary means in the same way that the rational force of a deductive argument is transferred between premises and conclusion. If certain considerations provide me with reasons to intend to do something, then they provide me with reasons to employ means that are necessary to it. Likewise, if certain considerations provide me with reasons not to take the necessary means to something I intend, then they provide me with reasons not so to intend. If there are no reasons to intend to do A, then there is nothing to be transferred to the intention to take the necessary means to A.

3. It seems, then, that we can extract no argument for the DBR Thesis from a view of rationality as means-end coherence. It might be thought, however, that the analogy with coherent belief can be extended not simply to means-end coherence but explicitly to desire, as Harman suggests when he writes, "When planning what to do, one's plan should be not only internally coherent but should also, as far as possible, promote one's intrinsic desires" (1976, p. 443).

But what warrants this extension? What sort of incoherence is involved in failing to act in accordance with one's desires? It seems that this is precisely the *difference* between intentions and desires; while it is incoherent to intend to do A and not to do B, if one believes that to do B is necessary to do A, the associated desires are not incoherent. Nor is it necessarily contrary to reason to maintain conflicting desires as it is to maintain conflicting intentions or beliefs.

In the end, all that Harman can do to support the extension to desire is to note: "Practical reasoning that affects intentions . . . also affects desires. Even if there is nothing one can do about a situation, moreover, the belief that a given event would promote a desired end can lead one to desire that event." But the fact that we are often led to desire that which promotes the satisfaction of a desire does not itself warrant calling that movement of the mind a bit of reasoning; it does not warrant the conclusion that the desire provides a reason to do what will enable satisfying it.

Yet another coherentist approach is that involved in the formal theory of decision under circumstances of risk. This is the theory that holds that an agent ought to maximize his expected utility, where utility is measured by a function defined on his preferences, and the utility of various possible outcomes is discounted by what he believes to be the probability of their occurrence. This approach is coherentist in two senses. First, it recommends conduct that is rational for an agent relative to his preferences and probability assignments, or, as we might also say, the act that is most coherent with his beliefs and preferences. Moreover, because it is impossible to define either a cardinal utility or probability function without assuming that the agent's preferences and probability assignments satisfy certain formal constraints, there is a further sense in which the theory articulates a conception of coherent action. For example, it is assumed that the rational agent's preferences are transitive. If he prefers A to B, and B to C, then he must prefer A to C. As a theory of critical rationality, formal decision theory must assume that intransitive preferences are incoherent or irrational. Or again, if an agent assigns a probability p to a given proposition q, then he must assign probability $1-p$ to not-q. The theory must suppose probability assignments to a proposition and its contradictory that do not sum to 1 to be incoherent.

Because formal decision theory takes the basis for rational decision to be the agent's beliefs and preferences it has often been thought to support the DBR Thesis. I shall argue in much more detail in Chapter 6 that this is a mistake. Like any theory of relative rationality, the hypothetical imperative for another example, formal decision theory can indicate the rationality of conduct only relative to the conditions it assumes, the beliefs and preferences of the agent. This by no means entails that beliefs and preferences are not themselves open to rational criticism. Indeed, a much more striking result will emerge from Chapter 6. It will turn out that we can make sense of the transitivity constraint as a condition of rational preferences only if we do suppose that individual preferences are criticizable in terms of reasons that exist for and against them.

4. The view that is required by the position that reason's only role with respect to conduct is to achieve a coherence with intentions, beliefs, desires, and/or preferences is not, in fact, any version of

the thesis that our desires, and only they, provide reasons to act. On the contrary, a strict coherentism, because it is purely formal, implies that there are no reasons to act at all, no substantive considerations that recommend action as rational. What will emerge from Chapter 6 is that the conception of coherent conduct elaborated in formal decision theory cannot be the whole of the picture of rational conduct. It cannot because the formal constraints on preference presupposed by the theory cannot be made intelligible unless it is supposed that preferences are supportable and criticizable by reasons. A purely coherentist account of practical reason is, in short, incomplete and must be supplemented by an account of substantive rationality: of reasons to act. Moreover, as no conception of coherent conduct itself implies any particular substantive theory, it follows that none can support the DBR Thesis.

CHAPTER 5

Humean Internalism

Crucial to each of the arguments for the DBR Thesis we have
considered thus far is the idea that reasons must be capable of
motivating. Practical reasoning is practical not just in its subject
matter but in its issue. Its question is what *to do*, and its product is,
at the least, a judgment about what to do, and more characteristically, an intention or decision to act. In countering these
arguments I have suggested that, while it is indeed plausible to
suppose that reasons must have a motivating capacity, this supposition does not entail any of the versions of the DBR Thesis that
we have considered. A person's being moved by a consideration
may not be due to the presence of an antecedent desire.

1. In granting the motivating capacity of reasons, however, it may
be thought that too much is unnecessarily given away to propo-
nents of the DBR Thesis. After all, reasons to act are considerations that justify or recommend action. And action may be justified even if the justification does not motivate and, it may be held,
even if it is not capable of motivating. The issue here is that which
divides externalists and internalists. [1] The externalist believes that

---

1. This distinction is from Falk 1952. It is discussed in Frankena 1958. See
also K. Baier 1978c, pp. 724–725; Nagel 1970, p. 7; and Smith 1972.

reasons are guides to action; they are guides to the judgment of what action is best supported by reasons. What he denies is that something can be such a guide only if it is capable of motivating the agent.

The externalist may even grant the premise of the argument of Chapter 2, that a reason for a person to act must be something that could be that person's reason. But, he will say, something can be a person's reason without *its* moving him or even being such that it can move him. What may move him is simply the thought that it is a reason, where its being a reason, indeed his judging it to be a reason, is independent of its motivating capacity.

Internalism maintains, on the other hand, that there is indeed an intimate relation between a consideration's being a reason and its capacity to motivate, if only under certain more or less ideal conditions. When we judge that some consideration is a reason, therefore, part of what we judge is a condition of our will—that we are motivated by an awareness of that consideration, perhaps under certain ideal conditions. It follows that for the internalist the recognition of something as a reason is already tied to its capacity to motivate. Rational motivation is not due simply to a desire to act for reasons but is ordinarily internal to the judgment that a consideration is a reason for one to act.[2]

What I propose to do in this chapter is to examine the case made for internalism in the writings of David Hume. Hume is the philosophical ancestor most ardently claimed by internalists, especially by those who would seek to derive the DBR Thesis from their internalism. A close examination of Humean internalism will repay us in two ways. First, it will demonstrate that a defensible internalism does not entail the DBR Thesis. Hume is a prime example of a philosopher who embraces internalism but who is not committed to any version of the latter. Second, it will lay bare the good sense of internalism and provide us with a foundation for adopting a broadly internalist framework throughout the constructive parts of the book.

2. Compare here Nagel's idea that practical judgments have "motivational content." We shall examine this and the role that it plays in Nagel's argument for the rationality of altruism in Chapter 10.

2. It is somewhat curious that Hume is cited in defense of the DBR Thesis. He himself would have denied that speaking "strictly" and "philosophically," desires provide *reasons* to act, or that anything else does for that matter. In his own idiosyncratic conception, reason is a faculty that solely enables us to judge truth and falsehood. In a "strict and philosophical sense," actions, as "original existences," can be neither in accordance with nor contrary to reason, neither reasonable nor unreasonable.[3] Accordingly, for Hume the failure to be guided by any considerations in taking action is not contrary to reason.

Nonetheless, Hume did hold that conduct can be *evaluated*: judged as good or evil, right or wrong, something one ought or ought not do. Consider, for example, the evaluation of conduct within moral categories. Hume held that moral judgments "go beyond the calm and indolent judgments of the understanding" and are "forcible and obligatory" (1739/1967, pp. 457, 466). The "force" of morality is, Hume believed, an *internal* one, a force on (or more properly, within) the moral agent. In addition, the very existence of moral distinctions themselves consists at least partly in an internal motivational condition: "when you pronounce any action or character to be vicious, you mean nothing, but that from the constitution of your nature you have a feeling or sentiment of blame from the contemplation of it" (ibid., p. 469).[4]

3. Technically, for Hume the reasonableness or unreasonableness of a belief is no different from its truth or falsehood. What makes belief subject to rational appraisal is its "representative quality." The object of belief is a purported representation, either of the relations between ideas or of real existence. Reason enables us to judge the accuracy of that representation, most properly with respect to the relations of ideas but in an extended sense with respect to real existence. It should be noted how different a view of rational appraisal this is from our own. The reasonableness of belief in Hume's view has nothing to do with its evidentiary basis or with how it was formed. Indeed, speaking strictly, the object of reason is not the believing at all but what is believed. So conceived, reason has nothing to do with canons of inquiry; its sole rule is the unhelpful "believe the true and eschew falsehood" (Hume 1739/1967, p. 458).

4. Note here that the moral judgment, for Hume, is internal to the moral judge. Since he believed that there would be general agreement in moral sentiment within a society, a sentiment within the moral judge would, he thought, generally be present in the agent also, were he to be placed in the appropriate reflective circumstances.

53

The intimate relation that Hume contended to exist between moral judgment, indeed between the very moral quality of acts and characters, and motivation seems even more plausibly asserted to obtain between judgments about reasons to act, indeed reasons themselves, and motivation. The language of motivational force runs throughout our talk about reasons. We speak of reasons as compelling, strong, and forceful in a way that suggests that what makes a consideration a reason is at least partly the way in which it impresses us and moves us toward action. But what lies at the root of the internalist view of reasons? To understand that we would do well to examine Hume's case for internalism in ethics.

3. There are two different positions ordinarily referred to as internalist. Some internalists hold it to be a necessary condition of a genuine instance of a certain sort of *judgment* that the person making the judgment be disposed to act in a way appropriate to it. We may call this position *judgment internalism*. R. M. Hare holds (1968, pp. 163–179), for example, that a person cannot be said genuinely to have judged that he ought to forbear an act unless he is disposed to forbear it.

A different internalist position is the thesis that something is a ground of an act's actually having a certain property (being right, for example, or having the support of reasons) only if it is capable of motivating the agent. This sort of internalism places a constraint on the *existence* of grounds for an act's rationality or rightness, and thus, on the act's being either rational or right. In other words, it articulates a necessary condition of a consideration's being either a reason or a right-making consideration. We may call this position *existence internalism*. [5]

The sort of internalism assumed by both of the arguments for the DBR Thesis canvassed thus far is an existence internalism with respect to reasons. Both assume that a condition of a considera-

5. A judgment internalist such as Hare may not be an existence internalist if, like Hare, he believes that the kind of judgments involved are not about the existence of any sort of properties at all. Thus, Hare holds that moral judgments are entirely prescriptive, and therefore that there is no question of whether the act really has the moral quality or not.

tion's actually being a reason is its capacity to motivate. Since Hume believes that "moral distinctions" themselves, as well as genuine moral judgments, are tied to motivation, it is appropriate to examine his case for ethical internalism. We will, again, be interested in two things: what can be said on behalf of an internalist view of reasons and the relation between it and the DBR Thesis.

4. One clear source of Hume's internalism is his thoroughgoing naturalism. If something's being a right-making consideration is not a complicated sort of motivational property, a disposition to be impressed in certain ways by that consideration in certain circumstances, then what sort of property is it? The only alternative view seems to be a doctrine that requires both metaphysical and epistemological mystery: nonnatural properties and a special sort of intuition or insight to discern them. Hume thought that considerations that are themselves morally relevant or right-making are unproblematic enough. They are plain matters of fact about the object of judgment. But what about the moral quality itself? That is, what about the property of the fact's *being* a morally relevant or right-making one? Hume believes that property to be distinct from any natural property about the act on which a judgment about its moral quality might be based. Is the moral quality, then, some further metaphysical property of the act that is directly noticed or intuited by a person? A nonnatural property, perhaps, as Moore would have said.[6]

Hume finds that position untenable. When we judge the moral quality of an action, the only properties of the action of which we can take note in making the judgment are natural matters of fact about the act that are themselves morally relevant. We cannot take note of their property of moral relevance in the same way; it is not there in the object of consideration to be found. Their being morally relevant is not itself the object of cognition in the process of consideration. It is rather a complicated fact about how facts about the thing considered, the considerations themselves, weigh

6. Moore (1962) maintained that the property of goodness is a simple, unanalyzable, nonnatural property.

with, impress, or move us when we consider them under certain conditions. Hume gives us an example: "Take any action allow'd to be vicious: Wilful murder, for instance. Examine it in all lights, and see if you can find that matter of fact, or real existence, which you call *vice.*. . . The vice entirely escapes you, as long as you consider the object" (1739/1967, p. 468). But what else is there? Hume is loath to allow that the viciousness of the act might be a further, though nonnatural, property of it to be considered. Not finding the act's viciousness among those aspects of it that have real existence external to him he turns inward: "You never can find it, till you turn your reflexion into your own breast, and find a sentiment of disapprobation, which arises in you, towards this action" (ibid., pp. 468–469).

We can imagine a parallel argument with respect to reasons for acting. The considerations said to be reasons are themselves simply matters of fact of which we can take notice and consider. But in what does their property of being reasons itself consist? The internalist answer is that their status as reasons consists in their capacity to move agents when contemplated under certain conditions. Again, the internalist move seems the only alternative to treating the property of being a reason as a further, nonnatural property that is itself the object of a special sort of cognitive act. But when one considers whether there are better reasons to do or not to do something, the only things one can consider are those facts about the act that *are* reasons. It is not as if their property of being reasons can come before one's notice for rational weighing in the same way. It is, rather, something that is rightly judged by assessing the considerations *themselves* under certain conditions and noting (on reflection) a condition of one's own will.[7]

This is half of the Humean case for internalism. The other half has to do with the intelligibility of moral and rational motivation. If we were to suppose that an act's being right is a nonnatural property of it, we would have no deeply satisfying account of why a person would characteristically be moved to want to perform an

---

7. For an excellent discussion of these points in Hume, see Falk 1975 and 1976.

action on judging it to be the right thing to do. Hume remarks that "morality is . . . supposed . . . to go beyond the calm and indo-lent judgments of the understanding. And this is confirm'd by common experience, which informs us, that men are often govern'd by their duties, and are deter'd from some actions by the opinion of injustice, and impell'd to others by that of obligation" (1739/1967, p. 457). We can, of course, appeal to a desire to act rightly to explain this phenomenon. Hume himself must presup-pose such a desire to explain much moral action and to explain the willingness of persons to place themselves in the appropriate con-ditions of moral judgment so that their motivations are in harmo-ny with what they would judge right and wrong. But this explana-tion is not a deeply satisfying one. It does not make the desire to act rightly *intelligible* to us. That desire is presented as something that is superadded to our nature rather than deeply expressive of it. It is a desire from which we may easily alienate ourselves; it is not integral to us.

Hume argues that this view flies in the face of how we view morality and its relation to ourselves. He challenges the external-ists of his time who held morality to consist in certain relations of fitness and unfitness that can be known by proof or by direct intuition to demonstrate any connection between the existence or recognition of such relations and conduct: "In order, therefore, to prove that the measures of right and wrong are eternal laws, *obliga-tory* on every rational mind, 'tis not sufficient to shew the relations upon which they are founded: We must also point out the connex-ion betwixt the relation and the will; and must prove that this connexion is so necessary, that in every well-disposed mind, it must take place and have its influence" (1739/1967, p. 465).

This case for internalism is especially compelling when we apply it to reasons. If something's being a reason is simply a non-natural property of it of which we take notice in judging the con-sideration to be a reason, then the desire to act for reasons is in no sense integral to the self. It is a fascination with a nonnatural property that one may have or lack without any change in the self. So understood, the desire to act for reasons is not in itself intelligi-ble. We cannot see it as essential to us. But this seems incoherent.

Our disposition to look for reasons and to act on those we find compelling cannot be so easily separated from us. In fact, I shall argue in Chapter 9, the very existence of the self depends upon it. These, then, are Hume's arguments for internalism. It is required both to avoid a nonnaturalist metaphysics, together with its accompanying epistemological problems, and to give a deeply satisfying account of ethical motivation. If anything, these arguments appear even stronger when we consider them with respect to reasons for acting.

5. While these are powerful grounds for favoring some sort of internalist account of reasons, they do not support any version of the DBR Thesis that we have considered to this point. That a consideration can be a reason for someone to act only if she could be moved by it does not require either that the consideration explicitly refer to her desires as such or to an object of her desires. The considerations that Roberta takes to be reasons for her to aid in the boycott satisfy internalist demands: there are circumstances under which she can be moved by them, even if they neither refer to her desires nor to objects of her desires.

We might, however, isolate yet a further version of the DBR Thesis that would seem more tenable and indeed be required by an internalist account of reasons for acting. Let us call the following position Version IV of the DBR Thesis:

> A consideration is a reason for someone to do something only if his being aware of it would give rise to a desire to act.

This position does not make the reasons for an agent to act dependent on his or her current desires, though it still relates reasons to desire. Accordingly, we may regard it as yet a further version of the DBR Thesis.

If internalism does indeed entail this fourth version we should expect Hume to be committed to an analogous view about moral considerations. That is, we should expect that in his view something can be a morally relevant consideration only if the person would be given some desire to act (or would forbear from acting) on becoming aware of it. But Hume's internalism regarding morality is in actuality not so simple as I have described it to this point. Once we see its full complexity we shall see that the considerations that support it give no support by analogy even to Version IV of the DBR Thesis.

According to Hume, not every response we have to our contemplation of an action is a moral sentiment, that is, one in the evocation of which an act's moral quality consists. He is anxious to point out that the moral sentiment is a feeling of a "peculiar kind," one that "pleases after such a particular manner" (1739/1967, pp. 472, 471). Moreover, it is possible that an act is wrong even if it is false that a particular person will be moved to feelings of disapproval, or to forbear action, on contemplating it. This may occur for a variety of reasons. To begin with, the moral sentiment purports to be from a point of view that "makes us form some general unalterable standard." Just as perspective may make an "object, at a double distance," seem half its size, so are our sentiments and motivations in response to a consideration influenced by the circumstances under which we view it. Moral judgment must correct for peculiarities of perspective:

> A statesman or patriot who serves our own country in our own time has always a more passionate regard paid to him than one whose beneficial influence operated on distant ages or remote nations. . . . We may own the merit to be equally great, though our sentiments are not raised to an equal height in both cases. The judgment here corrects the inequalities of our internal emotions and perceptions, in like manner as it preserves us from error in the several variations of images presented to our external senses. [Hume 1751/1957, p. 54]

The moral sentiment that a moral quality evokes is not simply one that arises in *any view* of it but only in a view that is balanced, that corrects for proximity of time and place and for the special passions of the moment. Moral sentiments are perhaps the paradigm of what Hume means by a *calm* as opposed to a *violent* passion: one that is felt in a dispassionate, judicious view. The moral sentiment is felt as the result of a process of consideration in which "nice distinctions" are made, "just conclusions drawn, distant comparisons formed, complicated relations examined, and general facts fixed and ascertained" (Hume 1751/1957, p. 6).

Indeed, Hume holds that an act may have a given moral quality even if it is not possible for a person to feel the coordinate moral sentiment. Thus he writes that Nero may contemplate just what we do when he considers his killing Agrippina, but his not feeling disapprobation does not tell against the wrongness of his act. Our disapproval takes precedence over Nero's lack of it, even if based on no further considerations, since "from the rectitude of our disposition, we feel sentiments against which he was hardened, from flattery and a long perseverance in the most enormous crimes" (1751/1957, p. 109).

Finally, someone may fail to feel a sentiment of disapproval when contemplating an act that is wrong because he or she considers it from his own, or from some other particular person's, *personal* perspective, rather than from an impartial standpoint: " 'Tis only when a character is considered in general, without reference to our particular interest, that it causes such a feeling or sentiment, as denominates it morally good or evil" (Hume 1739/1967, p. 472). A moral sentiment arises, or at least purports to arise, from an impartial standpoint.

Hume's considered view, then, is that the internal character of morality does not consist simply in an act's capacity to cause a feeling, or to impress the will, on its mere contemplation. It consists, rather, in the act's capacity to cause such a sentiment when all of the relevant facts are considered in a way that allows them to have a full and balanced effect *and* from a disinterested point of view.

It follows that Hume is not committed to any analogue of Version IV with respect to moral qualities. An act may have the quality of being wrong even if either the agent's or some judge's contemplation of it does not provide any motivation to forbear from it. For example, the contemplation may not be sufficiently dispassionate, or it may not be from an impartial standpoint.

This last point is of special importance. The positive thesis about reasons for which I shall argue is that they are grounded in principles on which one would will, from an impartial perspective, all agents to act. There may be many things that one wants to do but that one would not want one (or others) to do were one to consider the matter from an impartial standpoint. Or, as regards Version IV, a fact may be such that awareness of it from a purely personal point of view might lead one to act but may also be such that were one to consider it from an impartial point of view, one would not favor one's acting; and conversely.

Hume's own complicated internalism regarding morality, and the arguments that underlie it, give no support by analogy to the DBR Thesis in any of the four versions we have considered. Certainly Hume's own position regarding morality does not commit him to the view that moral considerations must be based on desires in a way analogous to that claimed in any of the four versions of the DBR Thesis. And most important for the view of reasons I shall defend, he regards the internality of morality as consistent with its being essentially *impartial*. Motivation is, in his view, internal to moral judgments even if it is motivation from an impartial standpoint. That one is moved when considering a matter from a particular point of view does not make one any the less moved.

If there are no further grounds for a different kind of internalism with respect to reasons, we must take it that holding them to be grounded in principles on which one could *will*, from an impartial standpoint, all to act is consistent with a defensible internalist view of reasons.

CHAPTER 6

Reason and Preference

An especially influential line of thought that is supposed to support the DBR Thesis is the notion that various formal theories of rational decision appear to entail it, since these theories are articulated in terms of the decision maker's *preferences*. I shall argue that this appearance is exceedingly misleading. Indeed, the most coherent interpretation of the notion of preference they presuppose is at odds with the DBR Thesis.

1. Actions change the world, but precisely how they do depends on what else is going on in the world. If we know with precision what will happen when we act, then the problem of rational decision is to decide, on the basis of this knowledge, which action to take.

As complex as rational choice is when all the consequences of possible actions are known, this is almost never the case. Within the set of cases in which one is not certain of the outcomes of all available actions, we may focus on two important subsets.

First, there are cases where all possible outcomes of all alternative acts are known, as are the respective probabilities that those outcomes would occur were the various alternative acts to be performed. To take an oft-cited example, suppose one is deciding whether or not to take an umbrella to work. Though one does not know whether doing so will result in protection from rain or merely having a burden to carry on a rainless day, one may still know the likelihood of these outcomes. The theory of decision *under risk* is a theory of how rationally to take such probabilities into account.

In some cases, however, there is no basis, or at any rate little legitimate basis, on which to make such probability estimates.[1] Here we know the possible outcomes of actions but have no basis to judge how likely any of them are. These situations are said to be instances of the problem of decision *under uncertainty*.

Both theories of decision, under risk and under uncertainty, take the notion of preference as primitive. For their purposes, preferences may be thought of as given by an agent's choices between outcomes and hence between acts if their outcomes are known with certainty. It is assumed that the agent can order all the alternatives with the relation 'is not preferred to' in a way that satisfies certain formal constraints, including transitivity. If A is not preferred to B, and B is not preferred to C, then A is not preferred to C. Once such a preference ordering is given, the problem of decision making under uncertainty is to specify an act to be performed given the possible outcomes of each act. Likewise, in decision making under risk, the problem is to specify an act to be performed given a preferential ordering of possible outcomes together with estimates of how likely they are to occur if a given act is performed.

One further assumption, in addition to transitivity, must be made in order to define a "preferability" metric, analogous to the probability metric, to provide a mathematically elegant way of taking both factors into account. It is assumed that a preference ordering is *continuous* in the following sense. Suppose that one has ordered alternatives A_1 through A_r so that for any A_i, A_1 is not preferred to A_i and A_i is not preferred to A_r. Then for any A_i it is assumed that there exists p ($1 \geq p \geq 0$) such that one is indifferent

---

1. In this discussion I abstract from the vexed philosophical question of the proper interpretation of probability.

between A_i and a "lottery" in which there is a p chance of outcome A_l and a $(1 - p)$ chance of A_r. This assumption, together with transitivity and some others, enables the definition of a preferability metric or, as it is called, a *utility function*, up to a linear transformation.[2] This gives a cardinal measure, rather than a mere ordinal ranking, of the agent's preferences.

The theory of decision under risk is then quite simple. It selects as the most rational act the one that *maximizes expected utility*, where the expected utility of an act is the sum of the products of the utility of each possible outcome and its probability of occurrence if that act is performed.

The theory of decision under uncertainty is not nearly so uncontroversial and widely received as the theory of decision under risk, however. A variety of candidates have been proposed for the rational principle to follow when deciding between alternative acts whose possible outcomes are known but whose probabilities are not. Indeed, if we count all the possible Hurwicz rules there is a nondenumerable infinity of them.[3]

Assume again that we can assign utilities to the various possible outcomes of the alternative acts available in the choice situation. The *maximin rule* states that it is rational to choose the act whose lowest possible outcome is higher than (or at least as high as) the lowest possible outcome of any alternative act. It is often remarked that this is an extremely conservative or pessimistic rule in that it counsels one to act as if the worst possible outcome will issue from action whatever one does. The *maximax* rule, by contrast, urges one to perform the act whose highest possible outcome is higher than the highest outcome of any alternative act. It is an extremely optimistic decision principle. Hurwicz has proposed a compromise between these two extremes. He defines a "pessimism-optimism index", α, between o and 1, associating with each alternative act the sum of the product of α and the utility of the act's lowest possible outcome and the product of $(1 - \alpha)$ and the utility of the

2. See Luce and Raiffa 1957, chap. 2. They maintain (p. 27) that the continuity assumption is necessary only to simplify the presentation of the theory.
3. See Luce and Raiffa 1957, chap. 13, for a discussion of these various proposals.

Reason and Preference

act's highest possible outcome. The recommended act, then, is the one with the highest sum.

A very different approach is to treat the problem of decision under uncertainty as a case of decision under risk by simply supposing that each possible outcome is equally likely. Then one just maximizes expected utility.

What all the theories of decision under uncertainty share, both with each other and with the theory of decision under risk, is a relativization of rational decision to the agent's preferences. This is true whether we suppose that preferences admit of a cardinal utility measure or merely consider them in an ordinal way. Indeed, even nonmaximizing theories of rational choice such as Simon's "satisficing" proposal relativize rational decision to the agent's preferences (Simon 1957).

2. This relativization is perfectly understandable and legitimate if we keep in mind precisely why it must be made; namely, to deal with special problems of rational decision posed by uncertainty and by risk. Nevertheless, many philosophers have argued that the *only* questions about what it is rational to do are those to which the theories of decision making under risk and under uncertainty are addressed. Thus Amartya Sen has written: "Rationality, as a concept, would seem to belong to the relationship between choices and preferences, and a typical question will take the form: 'Given your preference, was it rational for you to choose the actions you have chosen?'" (1974, p. 55). Plainly, if we understand preference in terms of how someone would choose between different outcomes, then this question can be posed only in a situation of risk or uncertainty. If the agent knows the outcomes of all alternative acts, then his choices entail his preferences. There can be no such question as "Given that you preferred the outcome of act B, was it rational for you to have chosen act A?" A person's having freely chosen act A, together with his awareness of the outcomes of A and B, entails that he preferred the outcome of A to the outcome of B.

Sen goes on to draw the consequence of this in his view: "There is no immediate reason why it [rationality] should discriminate between one type of preference and another" (1974, p. 55). Along these same lines, Patrick Suppes writes, "the sole maxim to be followed by the rational man is: maximize expected utility" (1966, p. 287).

Thus, some have taken the relativization of formal decision theories to the agent's preferences to show that the *only* questions of rational choice are those that can be raised relative to such preferences and, therefore, that there is no role for reason to play in the critical assessment of preferences themselves.

If we understand preference in terms of dispositions to choose, there seems to be a clear connection between it and the broad notion of desire. In the sense of 'desire' in which a person's intentional action entails that he desired or wanted to act, it seems that it must be true that if an agent intentionally chooses to do one action over another, then he desires to do the one thing more than he does the other. In his article on weakness of the will Donald Davidson contends that the following is a framework principle in terms of which we understand this broad notion of want or desire: "If an agent wants to do x more than he wants to do y and he believes himself free to do either x or y, then he will intentionally do x if he does either x or y intentionally" (1970b, p. 95). When a person knows himself to be free to do either x or y and does x intentionally, we infer a stronger desire to do x than to do y as explaining his action. Our inference to the stronger desire is an inference to the best explanation in accordance with the framework principle.

So it seems that we may speak alternatively of a person's ordering various alternative outcomes in terms of preference or in terms of which he wants or desires more than others. And just as a utility measure gives an index of strength of preference, likewise it would seem to give an index of strength of desire in this broad sense. It appears, therefore, that decision theory judges the rationality of an action by its relation to the agent's desires.

3. If the DBR Thesis were required to give a suitable interpretation to the formal theories of decision under risk and uncertainty, that would be a strong argument for it. It is not so required,

however. It is more natural to regard these theories as exactly what their names suggest: theories about how it is rational to decide *given the special complexity* introduced by risk and uncertainty. These theories simply are not addressed to the issue of how one should select between alternative acts when their outcomes are known.

The rationale for relativizing to preferences is the same as that for abstraction in any theory: namely, to illuminate matters with which the theory is concerned by abstracting from those with which it is not. It is simply assumed that one knows what one would do (we might as easily say, what it would be *rational* to do) if the outcomes of one's acts were known, and it is supposed that what it is rational to do in the nonideal case in which the outcomes are not known must depend on what one would do in the ideal case in which they are. Such an abstraction for purposes of dealing with the special problems of risk and uncertainty does not require us at all to suppose that there are not legitimate questions about what it is rational for one to do when the outcomes of one's actions are known. To raise these questions is to raise questions about the rational assessment of preferences themselves.

This demonstrates that neither the theory of decision under risk nor any of the theories of decision under uncertainty require anything like the DBR Thesis or the doctrine that rationality has no role to play in criticizing preference. And that suggests that these theories are neutral on the DBR Thesis; they neither require it nor do they rule it out. I think, however, that reflection on the notion of *preference* suggests something rather different. The interpretation of preference most appropriate to the conditions that it is supposed by these theories to satisfy is itself in tension with the DBR Thesis.

4. Since a utility function cannot be defined unless preferences are assumed to be transitive, the theory of rational decision under risk must suppose that *sets* of preferences, at least, are subject to rational criticism. It must suppose that intransitive preferences are contrary to reason. As will become evident, this is by no means a

trivial requirement. More important for our purposes, it is only an *intelligible* requirement if preferences are construed in a way that casts doubt on the DBR Thesis.[4]

How must *preferences* be interpreted in order for it to be intelligibly maintained that intransitive preferences are contrary to reason? We cannot construe them as felt attractions. Something can be contrary to reason only if it is susceptible to rational regulation. Nor can we understand a preference for A over B as simply a behavioral disposition, say, to *select* A instead of B if given an option between them. For example, suppose that we are given choices among three dish detergents (A, B, and C) that *we judge equally choiceworthy*, taken two at a time. When given the option of A and B, we select A; between B and C, we select B; but between A and C, we select C. Our selections and, we are supposing, our preferences, are consequently intransitive. Are they contrary to reason? It is difficult to see why they must be. Though we do not think any one better than the other two, the packaging of A, B, and C might be such that the color combination of A and B makes A more salient, that of B and C makes B more salient, but that of A and C makes C more salient. This would explain dispositions to make these selections when presented with the packages, and habit might explain similar selections when the packages are not present. There seems nothing irrational about these behavioral dispositions.

In a recent paper, Sidney Morgenbesser and Edna Ullman-Margalit distinguish between what they call *picking* and *choosing* (1977). These are both species of the more general activity of *selecting*. The difference between picking and choosing is that the latter, but not the former, is an expression of the chooser's *judgment* that the chosen alternative is better or more choiceworthy in some crucial respect (that is, that it is better supported by reasons of at least some sort) than what is not chosen.

Even when one has considered the merits of all alternatives and narrowed them down to those than which none is better, there is

4. It is important to note here that the sort of coherence of preference required by decision theory, transitivity, is importantly different from the sort of coherence between one's intentions and beliefs required by the hypothetical imperative.

no reason to think that this will always be one. When there are more than one there is still a problem of selection—"Which one to pick?" This is especially true in contexts where all that matters is that an alternative be good enough in some way. There may be many such from which one must be picked.

Our pickings may well be intransitive without being contrary to reason. There is nothing rationally untoward about the intransitive cycle of dish-detergent pickings imagined above. Note that while in such cases there will be a reason why one picks as one does, it will not generally be one's reason for so picking. To select for reasons is to choose rather than simply to pick.[5]

What about choosings? Is a set of three choices—A over B, B over C, but C over A—contrary to reason? This question is especially important, since, as I remarked earlier, preferences are ordinarily understood as dispositions to choose.

What appears to distinguish choosings from pickings is that the former express the chooser's *judgment* that the chosen alternative is *better* in some crucial respect: that there is some *reason* to select the alternative chosen rather than the alternatives forgone. If intransitive choosings are contrary to reason it is most natural to suppose that it is because they express judgments that cannot

5. Some selection situations may appear to be pickings but turn out to be choosings. For example, when faced with a variety of toothpastes, all of which seem equally good, I may decide to take the one nearest to me to save time. Here the action of taking this toothpaste rather than that one is chosen rather than picked, though one would not judge the toothpaste any better. Often, of course, even the particular action is not chosen when, as in our detergent example, one simply responds to some salient cue. Needless to say, this will be a difficult distinction to make at the margin. Leonard Savage gives an initial, "loose" analysis of preference in terms of dispositions to select one alternative instead of another. He notes, however, that this account cannot "be wholly adequate because it does not sufficiently distinguish preference from indifference [choosing from picking]" (Savage 1954, p. 17). His suggested remedy is to distinguish these cases by seeing whether the addition of an "arbitrarily small bonus" to either of the alternatives always gives rise to a selection of it over the other. If it does for both alternatives, then the selection is a picking and not a choosing—a case of indifference rather than preference. There is no way, however, to understand the idea of an "arbitarily small bonus" independently of the agent's own judgments about what makes something better. Thus in this solution, preferences must be tied to judgments about what is better.

simultaneously be rationally maintained. The three judgments, then, are the judgments that there is some reason to favor A over B, some reason to favor B over C, and some reason to favor C over A.

Now it does not appear in itself contrary to reason to hold these three judgments simultaneously. It may be the case that A *is* better than B in *some* respect and thus that there is some reason to favor A over B, at the same time that this is also true for B over C and for C over A. What does seem incoherent, however, is that A could be, *all things considered*, better than B; B, all things considered, better than C; and C, all things considered, better than A. While there may be *some* reason for favoring A over B, B over C, and C over A, respectively, it seemingly cannot be the case that the relevant reason in each case makes the choice of A, B, and C within each pair, best supported by *reasons, all things considered*. What does appear contrary to reason, then, is a set of intransitive judgments about the support of reasons, all things considered: that, on the whole, A is better than B, B better than C, and C better than A.

Now it is well known that people sometimes choose acts that they believe to be better in some relevant respect than the alternatives, and for which, therefore, they have some reason, but that they also believe to be worse, all things considered, than at least some alternative. That is, it is well known that people not only sometimes act contrary to their better judgment but that they sometimes choose to do so. When they do so, they act contrary to reason, at least by their own lights, for they act contrary to their own judgment of which act is best supported by reasons. It appears, then, that a person who makes intransitive choices cannot be choosing according to reason. He is faced with a dilemma. Either his judgments about the support of reasons appear to be incoherent or he is not choosing in accordance with his own judgment of which alternatives are best supported by reasons. If intransitive choices are contrary to reason, the explanation must be that they appear incapable of expressing coherent judgments about the support of reasons, all things considered.

The perhaps startling conclusion is that if preferences are to be regarded as contrary to reason when they are intransitive, then this is because they are criticizable in the light of the agent's judgments about which alternatives are best supported by reasons, all things considered. That is, the supposition that preferences are contrary to reason if intransitive is most intelligible if preferences are themselves to be based on judgments about the support of reasons, and therefore, on reasons themselves. Far from assuming that preferences themselves are not rationally criticizable, formal theories of decision seem to require that they be.

It might be objected at this point that I have simply assumed that what distinguishes choosings from pickings is that the former, but not the latter, express the agent's judgment that the chosen alternative is better, for some reason, than others. Surely we need to distinguish pickings from choosings, the objector will grant, but we do not need to bring in judgments to do that. Why not say that what distinguishes choosings is simply that they express preferences, whereas pickings do not? Actual selection behavior is the result not simply of preferences, that is, dispositions to choose, but also of other factors, including salience. Pickings are selectings explainable by factors such as salience and not by preference, where choosings are those that do express preferences. We can make the distinction, then, without appeal to implicit judgments about reasons and thereby avoid the conclusion that preferences are themselves rationally criticizable.[6]

The problem with this approach is that it is still quite unclear *why* intransitive choices, hence intransitive preferences, are contrary to reason. It may, of course, be replied that either 'preference' or 'rational preference' is simply partially *defined* by the transitivity condition, but that is hardly satisfying. It does not make it at all intelligible why transitivity of preference is a condition of its rationality. The virtue of our account is that it does explain this. We can always simply ask why we should define 'preference' or 'rational preference' by the transitivity condition. A satisfying response must do more than show how transitivity is required for an elegant mathematical treatment.

5. One standard argument for the irrationality of intransitive preferences depends covertly on understanding preferences in this

6. For this objection I am indebted to Jay Rosenberg.

way. Several writers have argued that a person with intransitive preferences can be turned into a "money pump" by a clever manipulator (Davidson, McKinsey, and Suppes 1955, p. 145; Tversky 1969, p. 45). Suppose I prefer A to B, B to C, and C to A, where A, B, and C are mutually exclusive alternatives. Then, it is argued, someone may offer me a series of transactions in which he, in the end, gives up nothing and I give up something I value.

The argument goes as follows. Suppose I now have alternative C. You know that I prefer alternative B to C and am willing to pay some amount (say five dollars) to have it (thus giving up C). I do so. Now, knowing that I prefer A to B, you make the same offer with respect to A. I agree. Finally, knowing that I prefer C to A, you make the same offer with respect to C. The upshot is that I give up an amount of money to be in the same position in which I began. Nor is there any reason why the process should end here.

In precisely what does the irrationality consist? The mere fact that a person can be brought to engage in a series of transactions in which he loses money does not by itself prove irrationality. It may be that he does not think there is any reason to have money or that he thinks there is more reason to give it away than to keep it. We can best understand the series of actions as irrational if we suppose two things. First, we must suppose that the person judges that it is better, other things equal, to have money than not to have it. That is, he must regard the fact that a transaction threatens a loss of money as a reason not to undertake it. Second, we must suppose that his preferences represent his judgment of which act would be best, all things considered.

These assumptions enable us to see the action as self-defeating. In the succession of three acts, each chosen because it promotes a state of affairs that I judge better, all things considered, I end up promoting a state of affairs that I judge to be worse, all things considered, than when I began. The person with intransitive preferences can, through no sort of ignorance or untoward consequence independent of his own action, promote a state of affairs that he judges to be worse, all things considered, by taking actions that promote states he judges to be better.

It might be objected at this point that the money pump problem can be used to display the irrationality of intransitive preferences without assuming that preferences are tied to judgments about reasons for choices. Why not identify preference with a primitive attitude of positive evaluation, one neither based on nor critizable by reasons? An agent with intransitive preferences would simply value A over B, B over C, and C over A. If he then chose A over B plus a small bonus, then C over A plus a small bonus, and so on, he would become a money pump. He would, by choosing acts he valued more, end up in a state of affairs he valued less. We can see the irrationality of intransitive preferences, therefore, without supposing preferences to be tied to judgments about reasons for choices.

The irrationality, however, consists not simply in the intransitive valuings. As long as these are primitive attitudes, why is there anything irrational about that? It consists, rather, in intransitive choices *based on* the intransitive valuings. What is irrational is to choose A *for the reason* that A is valued more than B, B for the reason that B is valued more than C, and so on. So if intransitive preferences are themselves irrational, they must be identified not with primitive valuings but with dispositions to make choices for certain reasons and, consequently, to judgments regarding the support of reasons for choices.

6. Preferences are tied to judgments about the support of reasons. The ruling model here seems to be that how choiceworthy an alternative is, the weight of the reasons that support it, is independent of other alternatives with which it is compared in the choice situation. Deciding which alternative to choose is plainly comparative, but it is to be understood itself in terms of comparing the alternatives with respect to their supporting reasons. It would seem to follow that the weight of the reasons supporting any alternative cannot be comparative. This picture portrays the choiceworthiness of an alternative, the weight of supporting reasons, as something that can be measured with a utility function. It requires, therefore, that judgments about which of two alternatives is better, all things considered, be transitive.

It is possible to object that this picture is based on an illusion. It supposes that comparisons between alternatives are carried out by comparing the weight of supporting reasons for each alternative and that the weight of reasons is judged independently of comparisons. But that, it might be argued, is to put the cart before the horse. We do not compare alternatives by access to some prior measure of the weight of reasons. The only measure we have of that is one that can itself be constructed out of comparisons: from our judgments of which alternatives are better than others, all things considered. According to this view, we cannot merely infer the transitivity of 'is better than, all things considered' from the fact that the weight of reasons is itself linear, representable by a utility function. Rather the issue is *whether* the comparative relation is transitive *so that* the weight of reasons can be represented by a utility function.

This is a serious issue. Consider the following example posed by Tversky (1969, p. 32). Suppose that we are choosing between candidates for a particular position. Two factors are judged to be reasons for choosing a candidate: intelligence and years of experience. There are three candidates; their intelligence and experience are represented in the table. The figures in the "intelligence" columns represent scores on an aptitude test whose margin of error is $2e$. Suppose we think that intelligence ought to be the ruling consideration, but where there is a difference of only e on the test score we treat the applicants as of equal intelligence and look to differences in experience to decide. So, if there is a difference in intelligence of greater than e we take the differential as controlling. This way of comparing the alternatives leaves us with an intransitive set. X is better than Y because their intelligence difference is negligible and X is more experienced. Y is better than Z for the same reason, but Z is better than X because the intelligence difference between these two is not negligible and Z has the superior

	Intelligence	Experience
X	$2e$	6 years
Y	$3e$	4 years
Z	$4e$	2 years

intelligence. It is difficult to see what is unreasonable about these comparisons. Indeed they might even result from a reasonable strategy.

Perhaps, however, the intransitivity comes from the fact that one of the desiderata is a test score that is valid only within a couple of points. If somehow we could measure intelligence more accurately, then the intransitivity would disappear. Admittedly, that would be true for this case, since we are taking any real difference in intelligence to be a ruling consideration. But we could still construct a plausible case by supposing intelligence to be important but not always overriding. A difference in intelligence greater than a predetermined amount would outweigh experience, otherwise experience would rule.

If we focus only on pairwise comparisons it seems that we could come very reasonably to make comparative judgments that are intransitive. There is still the money pump problem to contend with. In reply to that it might be argued that after the first two or so offers, a rational decision maker would realize that a simple pairwise consideration of his choices is much too shortsighted. From the behavior of his clever manipulator, it is evident that he is in effect being given a choice among *three* alternatives, *none* of which is better supported than the other two. Therefore, there is no reason to select one over the rest.[7]

Alternatively, this kind of argument might be taken as showing that it is rational to *introduce* a transitivity into judgments that would otherwise form intransitive cycles by considering the alternatives to be equally well-supported. It is rational because otherwise one will be likely to forgo the promotion of other states that there is reason to promote or will even promote states that there is reason to avoid by moving from one to another alternative within such an intransitive cycle when one really has, or will have, a choice among a wider range of alternatives in that cycle none of which is better than all the rest. So Aristotle wrote in *De Anima:* "for whether this or that shall be enacted is already a task requiring

---

7. This point is made by Thomas Schwartz (1972, p. 107). He argues against the transitivity requirement.

Desire and Reasons

calculation; and there must be a single standard to measure by, for that is pursued which is *greater*. It follows that what acts in this way must be able to make a unity out of several images" (434a7–10; 1968, p. 600). There can be such a "single standard" of value only if 'is better supported than' is transitive. The rational agent, in this view, must "make a unity out of several images" by rendering his comparative judgments so that such a unifying standard can be constructed. Transitivity is required for a unified and coherent conception of reason that can provide a consistent basis for action.

7. Regardless of how the issue of transitivity is resolved, it is by regarding preference as criticizable in the light of judgments about which alternative is better, in the sense of being supported by weightier reasons, that we can best understand the requirement that preferences be transitive. To prefer one alternative to another is to judge it better in some crucial respect.[8] If reason requires that preferences be transitive it is because we choose according to reason only if we prefer, hence choose, alternatives that we judge to be better, *all things considered*, and because we cannot coherently judge that, all things considered, A is better than B, B better than C, and C better than A.[9]

Since preferences are tied to judgments regarding the strength of reasons for preferring or choosing one alternative rather than another, they are appropriately criticized by assessing whether there are, as the agent judges, reasons, or sufficiently weighty reasons, for them. Most likely, such reasons will include those that refer to the agent's own tastes, desires, and interests, but there is certainly no reason to suppose in advance that they will be limited to these. Far from requiring the DBR Thesis, formal decision theories, with

8. Wright (1963a, pp. 13–17) makes this point. Ward Edwards also brings out the role of evaluative judgment in preference when he writes, "The fundamental content of the notion of maximization is that economic man always chooses the best alternative from among those open to him, as he sees it" (1954, p. 382).
9. Gary Watson (1975) points out the difference between motivational strength of desire and the agent's judgment of value. He suggests that preference is related to the latter rather than to the former.

their requirement that preferences be transitive, appear to point in a very different direction.

To put an even finer point on it we may say that the position that practical reason requires *only* coherence of preference is inherently unstable. It appears that preferences can only be coherent or incoherent if they are themselves criticizable in terms of reasons.

CHAPTER 7

Retrospective and a Framework for Reasons

1. In the preceding chapters we have considered four different formulations of the thesis that reasons to act must be based on the agent's desires and four different kinds of argument that might be given for that position. In order to collect these formulations in one place, let us list the four versions of the DBR Thesis we have . considered.

   I. A reason for a person to act just is a desire of that person.
  II. Reasons for a person to act are such explicitly desire-referring facts as 'that this action will enable me to satisfy one of my desires'.
 III. Reasons for a person to act are facts that though not themselves necessarily desire-referring, evidence the act to promote something that the agent in fact desires.
 IV. Reasons for a person to act are facts an awareness of which would lead the agent to desire to perform the act.

  None of the arguments considered establishes any one of these propositions.
   i. From the fact that any intentional act can be explained as the

result of the agent's desire, nothing follows that would similarly delimit the class of agents' reasons and accordingly the
class of reasons for them to act.

ii. From the fact that maintaining the coherence of intentions
and beliefs is a demand of reason, nothing follows about
whether considerations regarding one's desires or their objects
are the only reasons for an agent to act.

iii. From the fact that reasons for acting must be considerations
capable of motivating an agent, and thus internal in some
sense, nothing follows about whether they must either be
related to one's actual desires or even to desires one would
have on simply being aware of their objects.

iv. Finally, from the fact that the formal theories of decision
under risk and under certainty are valid, nothing follows
about whether all reasons must be based on the agent's preferences or desires.

Indeed, not only do these arguments not establish that considerations regarding one's desires are the only reasons to act. As far as
we can yet see, they do not *establish* that considerations relating to
our desires are even *among* the reasons for a person to act. Considerations of coherence, like the hypothetical imperative and formal
theories of decision, are matters of *relative rationality*. The most
they can tell us is what course of action is rational *relative to*
certain beliefs, intentions, and preferences. But these latter may
either have or lack the support of reasons. Without any assumptions about the support of reasons for our beliefs, intentions, and
preferences, we can conclude absolutely nothing from theories of
relative rationality about reasons to act. Thus neither argument ii
nor argument iv can establish any conclusion about reasons.

Argument i is impotent in this regard also. From the fact that no
action occurs without desire, nothing directly follows about any
relation between reasons and desires, for it may be the case, as the
externalist argues, that both the existence of a reason and the
agent's judgment that something is a reason are motivationally
inert. It is true that the agent cannot act on his judgment without

Desire and Reasons

some desire, but that desire may simply be the desire to act for
reasons and not any more specific desire that is involved either in
something's being, or being judged to be, a reason.

While that possibility is consistent with argument i, it is not
consistent with the more profound connection between reasons
and motivation claimed by Humean internalism. If we suppose
that considerations we recognize as reasons are incapable of moving us at all, then it becomes a mystery what it is for something to
be a reason to act and what it is for us to recognize it as such.
Unless we suppose that a fact's being a reason has something to do
with its capacity to motivate, perhaps under some kind of ideal
consideration of it, there seems no alternative to supposing that it
consists in some kind of nonnatural property. And even if we are
willing to accept that, the resulting picture of rational motivation
is an alien and unsatisfying one. It fails to make the desire to act for
reasons intelligible as one that is central to us and not simply a
superadded fascination with a nonnatural metaphysical category.

This good sense of Humean internalism, as we shall see in the
next chapter, forms the basis for a constructive case that considerations, awareness of which lead us to favor an act, are indeed
reasons to perform it. Nonetheless, that result does not follow
directly, for all that internalism claims is that it is a necessary
condition of being a reason that it be capable of moving, not that it
is a sufficient one.

2. Reasons to act are considerations that support rational choice
and recommend or justify action. They have, then, a *normative
aspect*. They ground judgments about what it would be best to do
or what an agent ought (rationally) to do, all things considered.

In accepting an internalist account of reasons, we accept that
they also have a *motivational aspect*. Reasons are considerations
about an act awareness of which can motivate, or lead an agent to
favor, an action.

We may combine these two aspects and give a general internalist account of reasons to act:

p is a reason for S to do A if, and only if, *p* is a fact about A awareness of which by S, under conditions of *rational consideration*, would lead S to prefer his doing A to his not doing A, other thing equal.

The motivational aspect of reasons to act is clear on this account: a fact can only be a reason for someone to act if consideration of it, under certain conditions, would motivate him. But simply being moved by a consideration is not the same thing as judging it to be a reason. Even more clearly, the degree of motivation that a consideration provides is not identical with its weight as a reason. Reasons also have a normative aspect; they are grounds for a person's judgment of what it would be best to do, all things considered, or of what he ought (rationally) to do. [1] The way in which this normative aspect is brought into an internalist account of reasons is through the idea that what establishes some fact as a reason (and its weight) for someone to act is his rational consideration of it resulting in some motivation to prefer the act. The normativity of reasons, according to an internalist account, arises from an ideal of rational consideration and not through the externalist idea that there are simply some facts that have the intrinsic property of being action-guiding and some that do not.

1. Richard Brandt maintains that the normative aspect of rationality can be eliminated by analysis. Following his late colleague Charles Stevenson, he proposes to use the method of "reforming definitions" to replace vague, unclear, and apparently mysterious language with definitions that lack these vices. Significantly, Brandt's own definition of 'rational' "does not import any substantive value judgments." But can we adequately characterize rationality in nonevaluative terms? What permits Brandt, for example, to speak of rational *criticism* when describing the way in which beliefs and desires are modified in the face of information and experience. Can there be criticism where there is not evaluative judgment? Must not the rational critic be capable of judging that beliefs or intentions are better or worse supported by reasons? See Brandt 1979, pp. 10–23, for this view.

Moreover, the reforming definition of 'rational' has the effect of not allowing certain issues even to arise. For example, we cannot sensibly ask whether it is rational for a person to do what is right even though the person does not want to do so on a full "Brandtian" reflection. For a criticism of Brandt's views along these lines, see Nicholas Sturgeon 1982.

3. We shall accept this general internalist account of reasons in what follows. It is important to appreciate that it is not intended as a reductive analysis. Its purpose is simply to highlight both the normative and motivational aspects of reasons.

Aside from the cogency of this internalist account there is an important dialectical reason for accepting it. Those who have rejected the view that self-centered considerations provide the only reasons to act have often been vulnerable to the charge that they can give no intelligible account of rational motivation. They have rightly insisted that it does not follow that some consideration that moved a person was a *reason* for him to have acted. A distinction must be made, they have urged, between *motivating* reasons and *justifying* or *recommending* reasons.

But this account can be only the beginning of illumination and not the end of it. Once the distinction is made, the issue then arises of how people *are* moved to do what there is reason for them to do. If the existence of reason is simply a normative fact about an act, external, as it were, to anything about the person and what he is, then how and why is it that people are moved to do what reason recommends? Simply adding a desire to act for reasons does not make that desire intelligible to us, for what then are reasons? And why is it that we do, or should desire to, act for them?

The real attraction of the DBR Thesis, and more generally of self-centered theories of reasons to act, is that they seem to provide a more or less satisfactory account of these matters. By accepting an internalist account of reasons to act, we gain not only that strength but the dialectical advantage of basing the case for a theory of reasons that is *not* self-centered on a foundation that its likely opponents should be disposed to accept.

Part II

Reason and
Personal Good

CHAPTER 8

Rational Consideration:
An Initial Account

Reasons to act are facts that motivate us to prefer an act when we give consideration to them in a rational way. Rather than approach directly and all at once the question of what rational consideration itself consists, I propose to build up an account indirectly and somewhat dialectically. We shall begin with what is uncontroversial—that rational consideration involves making oneself aware of relevant factors, putting oneself in mind of them in a way that allows one to appreciate their relevance. From this point we shall move to the question of how considerations that move us in conflicting ways can be evaluated, developing out of our initial account an enriched analysis of rational consideration. In Chapter 9 these preliminary accounts will then be linked to the notions of a unified self and of a person's conception of the good life for him. The initial perspective of rational consideration, then, will be the *person's own* point of view, albeit as informed and dispassionate and as having a life that extends through time.

1. We begin very simply. Rational consideration of a fact requires, obviously enough, being aware of it on reflection—thinking about it in connection with the act in question. Let us call the sort of awareness one has when reflecting on or thinking about a

fact in connection with whether to perform a given act *reflective awareness*. Since a reason is a fact that motivates when rationally considered, we may conclude that:

If *p* is a fact about A reflective awareness of which would move S to prefer his doing A (to his not doing A), then *p* is a (presumptive) reason for S to do A.

If reflective awareness of *p* is motivating, therefore, *p* is at least presumptively a reason.

Further reflection, say in the light of other facts, or perhaps from some other point of view from which we might rationally deliberate, may altogether cancel any initial motivation we had to prefer A. So any reason that *p* provides is only presumptive, and defeasible. Not only may a reason be overridden by other, weightier reasons (and still hold its weight as a reason), but further reflection may cancel any motivating power it had and convince us that what we took to be a reason was in fact no reason at all.

For example, when I consider the fact that it will give a child pleasure to have an object, I am moved to give it to him. When I consider the fact that the child's pleasure will itself consist in teasing his sister with the object, the motivation lapses. What seemed a reason for me to give the child the object turned out on further reflection not to be one after all. Its presumption as a reason was defeated by further considerations. That the object will give the child pleasure, I might think, is no reason at all if it is that kind of pleasure.

Nonetheless, if reflective awareness of a fact motivates, that does create the presumption that it is a reason for one to act. And that, at least, is a place to start. Let us call this the *initial account of rational consideration*.

2. Within the class of facts that motivate an agent to prefer some act or state of affairs when reflectively considered, we may distinguish roughly between those that concern properties intrinsic to the preferred act or state and those that concern the act or state's relation to some further preferred state. Whenever something is

preferred purely for its relation to some further state, the latter will itself also be the object of preference. We may distinguish, therefore, between acts or states preferred for their own sakes and those preferred for their relation to further preferred states. [1]

Let us call the former preferences *intrinsic* and label *extrinsic* any preference whose object is preferred for the sake of something else. These categories are not mutually exclusive. For example, as Glaucon remarks in the *Republic*, we value knowledge and understanding both for their own sake and for their consequences. Let us say, then, that a preference is *simply extrinsic* if its object is preferred simply for the sake of something else.

3. Facts that when we are reflectively aware of them move us to have (or maintain) an intrinsic preference for something are presumptive *reasons* to prefer it. Moreover, a reason to prefer some state is, other things equal, a reason to prefer an act that will promote it. Reasons that support intrinsic preferences, therefore, support extrinsic preferences, other things equal, for acts promoting the intrinsically preferred state.

We should note that a preference may be created by reflection on its object's relation to the objects of other preferences and still be intrinsic. It is only simply extrinsic if it is preferred simply on account of properties not intrinsic to it. The standard way in which reflection on other preferences gives rise to a new one may indeed be the generation of an extrinsic preference by the realization that its object causes the object of another preference; but that is by no means the only way.

For example, a preference to ski cross-country may be generated by reflection on it in relation to other preferences. On reflecting on my intrinsic preference for running and canoeing I may realize that I have a general intrinsic preference to move through nature in an autonomous and self-propelled way. I see that it is these

1. The distinction between properties that are internal and those that are external to the object of preference is rough at best. There is an intuitive sense, however, in which if I prefer to play tennis this afternoon, my preference is intrinsic if what attracts me is the thought of hitting the fuzzy object on a beautiful day and extrinsic if I am attracted by the thought of staying in shape.

aspects of running and canoeing that lead me to prefer them. I further see that cross-country skiing also has these properties and form on that account a preference to ski cross-country. But this makes the resulting preference intrinsic rather than extrinsic. The facts about cross-country skiing that motivate my preference for it concern aspects intrinsic to the activity itself.

4. The reasons to prefer an act provided by facts that motivate the preference when they are reflectively considered are not necessarily *universal*. I may be moved to prefer eating a particular ice cream by reflective awareness of the fact of its particular taste. And hence, that fact may be a reason for my preference even if no one shares my taste and, therefore, even if that fact is not a reason for anyone else, much less for everyone else.

In the internalist account, reasons to act are facts that when considered rationally lead an agent to prefer the act. Unless we can assume that everyone will be moved by the same facts to the same preferences on giving those facts rational consideration, there will in general be no warrant to expect reasons to be universal. In particular, there is no reason to expect that the sort of rational consideration involved in simple reflective awareness will lead agents to be moved to the same preferences.

Nonetheless, it is important to appreciate that what makes a fact a reason for a person *is* a universally valid standard, namely, that rational consideration of the fact, in particular, reflective awareness of it, moves the person to prefer the act, other things equal. This universal aspect of reasons, their grounding in principles valid for all rational agents, will be an important element in the argument of Part IV.

5. In Chapter 6 we saw that preferences must themselves be held *rationally* criticizable. Even intrinsic preferences can be based on reasons. If one thing is rationally preferred to another, certain facts about the former, when considered rationally, lead the agent to prefer it. The sort of rational consideration may simply be that involved in reflective awareness. Facts that lead us to an intrinsic

preference when we consider them reflectively provide reasons, at least presumptively, for that preference.

So far our account of rational consideration gives us a way only of certifying the presumptive rationality of facts taken one at a time. What if our consideration of two different facts inclines us in different directions? All we can say on the basis of our account so far is that both facts are at least presumptive reasons: one for a particular preference, the other against it. But how is one to consider which reason is weightier? How are we rationally to adjudicate between conflicting intrinsic preferences, each of which is supported by reasons? And, in general, how are we rationally to *order* our preferences even when they do not directly conflict?

Let us consider a case in which an agent has two conflicting intrinsic preferences that are themselves the result of reflecting on two different facts. Suppose that Otto returns from a Friday night of drinking to deaden the pain of a week's work in the mill and faces himself in the medicine-chest mirror. When he considers how he will feel tomorrow if he does not take Bromo Fizz, he prefers to take it rather than not to. When, however, he considers its taste, which he abhors, he prefers not to take it. The facts, that Bromo Fizz tastes as it does and that if he takes it he will feel better in the morning, provide him with reason not to take and to take Bromo Fizz, respectively. But which reason is weightier? And how is Otto rationally to discover that?

The two intrinsic preferences in question are Otto's preference to avoid tomorrow morning's hangover and his preference to avoid tasting Bromo Fizz. It is important to appreciate that neither we nor Otto can judge which preference he rationally ought to act on simply on the basis of which is *stronger*, when this is determined by which he actually acts on. Rational deliberation is a process of canvassing and weighing reasons with a view to affecting behavior. If the rational solution to a conflict between intrinsic preferences were simply to act on the strongest, then there could be no coherent notion of settling the conflict between them by rational consideration. To know on which preference one had weightier reason to act, one would have to know which was stronger. And to know that, one would have to know on which preference one would act. This would make rational consideration impotent with respect to action. It could only ratify a fait accompli.[2]

In Part I, I suggested that in having a desire or preference we, to some extent, experience the world from the perspective of that desire or preference. We are fastened, to some extent and in a variety of ways, on its object. This way of speaking is metaphorical, but it shows that a preference for something is a *cluster* of dispositional states concerning not merely behavior but also attention and affective response. A person is more apt to notice things relevant to the objects of her preferences, even if she is not looking for them. She is more likely to think and dream about them than about things to which she is indifferent.[3]

An agent with two conflicting preferences has a problem of *integration*. She has contending conative, affective, and attentional perspectives that cannot be integrated in any simple way. Jointly satisfiable preferences do not present this problem of integration, since one can simply form a preference whose object is conjunctive. But the agent with conflicting preferences cannot so simply integrate them. And as they are in conflict so is she. Her attention, thoughts, and dreams draw her in conflicting directions. In order to remove the conflict and integrate herself, she must decide between them. And to do this she must be capable of assuming a perspective distinct from that internal to each individual preference and of getting the object of both in view.

When Otto considers the fact of Bromo Fizz's taste, that moves him to prefer not to drink it. When he considers its medicinal properties, he is moved to prefer to take it. But he cannot do both; he is in conflict. Rationally to adjudicate the conflict he must bring the reasons for his two individual conflicting preferences *together* and reflectively consider them at the same time. This enables him to judge whether, *all things considered*, he prefers to

2. On this point see Foot 1972b, p. 204, and K. Baier 1978c, p. 711.

3. Many philosophers have maintained the view that to want something is to be in a cluster of dispositional states. Their arguments apply, though not with the very same force, for preference. See Brandt and Kim 1963; Hempel 1965, p. 473; H. P. Grice 1974–1975; Churchland 1970; and Goldman 1970, pp. 109–121.

take or not to take the Bromo Fizz. If what makes the facts of Bromo Fizz's taste and medicinal properties reasons not to take and to take it, respectively, is that reflective awareness of each is motivating, then he appropriately judges which reason is weightier by considering them together and seeing what he prefers when he takes both into account. This requires that he adopt a standpoint from which he can consider and assess in a unified way the motivating power of considerations relevant to the objects of both preferences.

6. The essential role of *reflection* in practical rationality is worth pausing over for a moment. It has been seized upon recently by a number of writers attempting to give an adequate account of free action (Frankfurt 1971, Körner 1973, Neely 1974, Schiffer 1976). Writing in the broad compatibilist tradition that takes freedom to consist in action in accordance with desire, they have been stimulated by the objection that there are instances in which we act unfreely though we do what we want. We can be compelled not only by external forces but also, it seems, by our desires themselves.

The strategy taken by these writers has been to show that in the relevant sense a person is not doing what she wants most when she is compelled by a desire. Since the cases typically under discussion are those in which an agent acts contrary to what she judges to be the best reasons for acting, this strategy simultaneously generates an account of what it is for an agent to judge there to be better reasons to satisfy one of two competing desires (or preferences) in terms of what she wants (or prefers), in some sense, to do. It seems relevant to Otto's problem, therefore.

The key to the solution proposed by Harry Frankfurt and Wright Neely is a distinction between first- and second-order desires. Unlike first-order desires, second-order ones are essentially reflective. They are desires that take first-order desires as objects. The desire not to have a particular desire, to have one desire stronger than another, and to act on one desire rather than another are all second-order desires in this sense.

Neely argues that while it is true in cases in which a person acts against his better judgment that he acts on his *strongest* desire, he does not act on the desire to which he gives *highest priority*. Neely says that one desire (that-p) has *higher priority* than another (that-q) for an agent if the agent desires that "if he must choose between satisfying his desire that-p and satisfying his desire that-q, he will satisfy his desire that-p" (1974, p. 44). As an example, suppose that a smoker attempting to quit is compelled to smoke against his better judgment by his desire for a cigarette. Neely's suggestion is that though in one sense the smoker does what he wants most, in a more important sense he does not, because he does not act on the desire that has highest priority for him. This is shown by the fact that reflection on the choice between satisfying his two desires yields the second-order desire that he satisfy his desire to quit. As it happens his desire to smoke is stronger, but he *wants* his desire to stop to be stronger.

This suggests a way of rationally deciding between two intrinsic preferences. When intrinsic preferences conflict, there is reason to act on the one that one would prefer to satisfy if given a choice between them.

Bringing in reflection significantly enriches the model of action on individual desires or preferences. We no longer have the simple vector-sum model of action on the strongest individual preference. Moving to the second-order gives scope to joint consideration and comparison of intrinsic preferences. And this brings with it the possibility of bringing coherence to our preferences through the formation of all-things-considered preferences.

It should be noted in passing, however, that talk of second-order desires and preferences misleadingly encourages the inference that *what* we consider in reflection when we act freely and rationally is simply the fact of our first-order desires and preferences. But first-order preferences are themselves based on reasons to the extent that rational consideration of facts about their *objects* motivates them. What we reflectively consider when we decide in a free and rational way which of two intrinsic desires or preferences to act on is not, therefore, the fact of our desire or preference itself but rather considerations relating to their *objects*.

Reflection, while a necessary component of free and rational choice, is hardly sufficient. If the only requirement for rational choice is that an agent get his first-order preferences (or desires) in view, what reason is there to suppose that the relative strengths of the agent's second-order desires will not simply reflect the relative strengths of his first-order ones? On what basis do we say, for example, that at the moment at which the smoker decides to take the cigarette, he desires that if he must choose between satisfying his desire to stop and satisfying his desire to smoke, that he satisfy his desire to stop? After all, when presented with that choice he in fact satisfies his desire to smoke. That would suggest that, at that moment, he desires to satisfy his desire to smoke rather than his desire to stop. How does mere reflection change the relative strengths of the desires?[4]

Nonetheless, it does seem right to say that in an important sense the smoker who is trying to quit does desire or prefer, if he must choose between satisfying his desire to smoke and his desire to quit, to choose the latter. Why is this? The answer is that while our smoker, at the moment he reaches for the cigarette, plainly more strongly desires to satisfy his desire to smoke than his desire to quit, when he considers the matter in what Gary Watson (1975) has called "a cool and non-self-deceptive moment," he more strongly desires to satisfy the desire to quit than the desire to smoke. Insofar as there is a second-order desire or preference that is generally characteristic of him (though not always in moments of extreme nicotine deprivation), it is this one.

This is the sense in which the smoker acts contrary to the way he really wants or prefers to act. He acts contrary to the way he *would* prefer to act were he to consider *all* relevant information in a *dispassionate* way. Mere reflection, simply getting our individual intrinsic preferences with their objects in view, though it surely has some effect on the strength of desire or preference, may give rise to second-order desires or preferences that substantially reflect the relative (momentary) strengths of first-order ones. So a second-order preference for one of two conflicting first-order preferences is not necessarily rational.

4. This point is made in Grandy and Darwall 1979, p. 194. Watson (1975, pp. 218–219) makes a somewhat similar criticism of Neely and Frankfurt.

7. Let us say, as a start, that when intrinsic preferences conflict, there are weightier reasons, other things equal, to act on the preference that one would prefer acting on were one to give the matter *dispassionate consideration*. But how, exactly, are we to understand this idea? The phrase itself suggests a state in which one is somehow immune to any motivating force provided by the considerations that support the individual preferences themselves. But that cannot be right. If we put so much distance between ourselves and the objects of our intrinsic preferences that what initially attracted us about them no longer does so at all, then we are left with no basis for choice. Dispassionate choice may be cool, but it cannot be completely cold.

It is illuminating to take the model of *adjudication* between the two individual preferences seriously. We may think of Otto's intrinsic preferences not to taste Bromo Fizz and not to suffer through a hangover as making claims on him. His problem is rationally to adjudicate between these claims. Taking note of the two claims together is necessary but not sufficient. We may think of a dispassionate judgment between the two preferences as analogous to the idea of an impartial or unprejudiced judgment between two contending claimants. As Otto reflects on his two preferences he realizes, let us suppose, that he is initially more repelled by the thought of drinking Bromo Fizz, something he would be called upon to do presently, than he is by the now fairly distant thought of what he will feel like the next morning. Indeed, his distaste for Bromo Fizz may incline him not even to think about the next morning. While he might in fact find the thought of the hangover similarly, or even more, distasteful were it similarly impending, the thought of having to face the vile liquid presently drives such considerations from his attention.

Temporal perspective makes Otto initially inclined to favor the claim of his intrinsic preference not to drink Bromo Fizz. This initial favor might be reversed, however, were Otto *vividly to imagine* what it would be like to act on that preference and live through the hangover the next day. As Hume reminds us, "the same good, when near, will cause a violent passion, which, when remote, produces only a calm one" (1739/1967, p. 419).

Rational Consideration: An Initial Account

A dispassionate judgment between two preferences must correct, then, for such accidents of perspective. To allow the one preference to suppress appreciation of the object of the other is to undermine genuine joint consideration of them. One suspects that the participants in Milgram's famous experiments wanted neither to hurt those to whom they thought they were administering shocks nor to disappoint the authoritative experimenter who ordered them to continue. But the fact that the experimenter was present in the room with them, within eye contact, and the shocked victims cried only from the next room, unable to engage the subjects' view, undoubtedly affected which preference was acted on (Milgram 1974, pp. 32–43).

That which is psychologically near to us commands our attention and often leads us to divert our view from other matters that are also of genuine concern. In order rationally to consider facts relevant to alternatives before us, it is necessary to take thought and to *imagine* what we would be doing and its consequences. Otto's present aversion to drinking Bromo Fizz is, after all, not fueled simply by a purely intellectual acceptance of the proposition that it has an awful taste. Rather, it is fraught with vivid expectations of that taste. Since this is what gives the thought so much of its motive force, a rational adjudication between his two preferences must likewise be based on similarly vivid imaginings of the morning after.

Dispassionate judgment between our intrinsic preferences requires that we represent to ourselves in an imaginatively vivid way what we know to be relevant to their objects.[5] Genuine *consideration* is, the *Oxford English Dictionary* reminds us, an *attentive* view or survey.[6] This corrects both for errors of perspective (whether temporal, spatial, or some other sort with psychological relevance) and for errors that arise because of the sheer sweep of a

---

5. Many of the points in my discussion of dispassionate and attentive reflection derive from the work of W. D. Falk and R. B. Brandt; and, of course, from Hume's classic discussion of calm and violent passions in the *Treatise*. See Falk 1975, 1976, and Brandt 1979, pp. 110–129.
  6. *The Oxford Englis Dictionary*, S.V. "consideration."

present desire, whether the blindness of infatuation or of rage. We may say, therefore, that

> *p* is, other things equal, a weightier reason for *S* to prefer *A* than is *q* a reason to prefer *B* if dispassionate consideration of *p and q* would move *S* to prefer *A* over *B*.

8. Dispassionate consideration of what we know to be relevant to the objects of intrinsic preferences cannot, however, be sufficient to adjudicate between them. There may be relevant things that we do not know. Otto's deliberative problem would be much easier, though he would feel no better the next day, were he to know that the only Bromo Fizz in the house is three years old and has lost its medicinal potency as well as its fizz.

Information is relevant to a decision between intrinsic preferences in at least two ways. Most obviously, it is relevant to how alternative actions will affect satisfaction of each of the preferences. Clearly, Otto will want to know precisely how taking the Bromo Fizz will affect his morning after. He will also want to know whether if he takes the contents of the bottle he is in fact taking Bromo Fizz.

Information, appropriately considered, is also relevant to decision between intrinsic preferences in another way. As Richard Brandt has pointed out, desires (and, we may add, preferences) can arise because of accidental associations or stimulus-misgeneralization. Or they may acquire an inordinate force for us because of overreaction to trauma or severe deprivation. Were it the case that a preference would vanish, or its strength be greatly diminished, if a person "repeatedly brought to mind, with full belief and maximal vividness, all the knowable facts that would tend either to weaken or to strengthen the desire or aversion," then it ought to be discounted in an ideally rational decision (Brandt 1972, p. 683; see also Brandt 1969–1970). Suppose, to use one of Brandt's own examples, that a person develops an aversion to a profession and people in it just because his parents expressed contempt for it. Further, suppose that were the person to be acquainted with the profession the aversion would not be sustained. If a preference cannot survive confrontation with accurate representations and experience of its object, there seems to be reason to take it less seriously than if it could, and perhaps to discount it altogether. Though the aversion is directed at an object, it is not the product of any experience or contemplation of what the object is really like. This is the most extreme kind of case. There will, of course, be others in which the person's preference is based on abnormal or fragmentary experience or information and thus is not reflective of his true feelings toward it, or more properly, his feeling toward it as it truly is.

Once we bring in the need to give imaginative attention to information, the range of choice may well extend beyond a comparison of two individual preferences. For as we learn more, and attend to what we learn, we enlarge the area of potential concern. This happens in two ways. Most obviously, we may discover new facts, or rediscover those we already knew, that are relevant to other intrinsic preferences we already have but that we did not think relevant to our present situation. Suppose Otto discovers that Bromo Fizz is a mild carcinogen. His potential taking of the drug is then seen to be relevant to his preference for living a long and happy life in a way that he had not realized.

Another way in which attention to information may enlarge the pool of claimants between which one must adjudicate is by giving rise to *new* intrinsic preferences, like Roberta's preference for helping textile workers after seeing a film about their conditions of life or my preference to try some of my neighbor's apple pie, which I did not know existed until I smelled its aroma.[7]

This is an important point. The point of view from which one rationally adjudicates between two conflicting intrinsic preferences is not internal to either individual preference. It is a reflective standpoint from which one can dispassionately consider facts that support the two preferences. But from this standpoint there is no reason to restrict consideration to facts regarding the objects of the two preferences, for there may be facts regarding other alternatives before one that when dispassionately considered would moti-

7. These examples are discussed in Chapter 3, sec. 2.

vate one to prefer one of them over both of the two conflicting preferences with which one began. What one prefers, all things considered, may be not to act on either of the initial conflicting individual preferences but rather to act on a third that arises in the process of rational consideration of facts related to one's situation. As any negotiator knows, a risk of arbitration is that the arbitrator may act on the basis of considerations that are not in the interest of either contending party.

9. In this chapter we have drawn some initial consequences from the internalist conception of reasons as rationally considered facts that motivate preference. Rational consideration begins with reflective awareness; so a fact is a reason for someone to act if reflective awareness of it moves her to prefer the act, other things equal. It follows from this that agents have, presumptively, reasons to satisfy their intrinsic preferences: those reasons being whatever considerations regarding properties internal to the objects of intrinsic preference motivate the preferences.

To adjudicate rationally between conflicting intrinsic preferences we adopt a standpoint from which we can reflectively and dispassionately consider the reasons for our individual intrinsic preferences, feel the force of these different reasons, and come to an all-things-considered preference. From this standpoint there is no reason to restrict our reflection to considerations that motivate our actual intrinsic preferences. There may be other considerations that would motivate yet other intrinsic preferences were we aware of them in a way that allowed us to feel their force. Since what gives us reason for our actual preferences are the facts that motivate them, and not the simple fact of preference itself, if further facts would motivate yet further preferences were we to consider them, then they give us reasons also.

Rational consideration involves in the limit, then, the ideal of reflection on all relevant considerations. According to our initial account, *relevant* considerations include those that provide an agent some motivation to prefer an act when she reflects on them in an imaginatively vivid way. At this point, however, we have no reason to suppose that rational consideration is limited to this sort of reflective awareness (from the agent's own standpoint), and I shall argue in Parts III and IV that it is not. Nonetheless, we may say on the basis of the argument so far that any consideration that would move an agent to prefer an act were she to "bring it to mind with full belief and maximal vividness" is a reason for her to act.[8] The rational agent, therefore, does not merely find herself with preferences. We have already discussed three ways in which preferences may themselves be based on rational consideration. First, our individual intrinsic preferences are based on reasons if, though not necessarily only if, they would result from a vivid awareness of facts concerning properties intrinsic to their objects. Second, an ordering of two individual intrinsic preferences is based on reason, other things equal, if it would result from a dispassionate weighing of considerations that motivate both individual preferences. Finally, our preferences and their relative ordering are in general based on reason, other things equal, if they would result from a dispassionate reflective awareness of *all* relevant facts (where 'relevance' has the above sense). In each case, the preference is *based on* reasons not necessarily in the sense that it was itself generated by a consideration of reasons but in the sense that reasons exist for it. In the internalist account this means the preference would result from the right sort of consideration of facts that are reasons for it.

We may end this chapter by developing some terminology that will help us in the next. Let us call an individual intrinsic preference *informed* if the agent would have it were he to be reflectively aware, in an imaginatively vivid way, of all facts regarding properties that are internal to the thing preferred.[9] It is informed in the sense that it is based on an informed view of its object. A preference is not informed if it would not be sustained in such a view: if it

8. Hereafter, references to the "initial account" of rational consideration will be to this enriched version.
9. This will usually involve having had relevant experience. For example, for Otto's preference not to suffer the hangover to be informed, he must be able vividly to imagine what it would be like to live through the hangover. This will require either some experience of hangovers or other experience that can be brought to bear to give his imagining sufficient vividness.

is the result of misconception, fragmentary information or experience, or a failure to appreciate certain of its object's crucial aspects.

In addition to the idea of an informed *individual* preference, we may form the idea of the preference *ordering* a person would have, in a given situation, were he to be reflectively aware in an imaginatively vivid way of all facts relevant to his situation in the sense of our initial account. We may call these preferences, the agent's *informed all-things-considered preferences.*

This ordering is often referred to as the agent's *true*, as opposed to his *expressed*, preference ordering. [10] To the extent that an agent expresses other preferences in his actual choices it is because he is either ignorant of or inadequately attentive to information or experience that, were he to consider it closely, would incline him to different choices.

10. See, for example, Harsanyi 1976, p. 32. It is also assumed that a person's true preferences have been fine-tuned for transitivity.

CHAPTER 9

Unified Agency

Theories of practical reason and of ethics that fasten on the satisfaction of preference as itself of value, regardless of whether a preference can be supported by reasons, are open to the challenge that their underlying conception of the person or agent is that of a mere collection of preferences. Rawls's criticism of utilitarianism as an ethical theory is famous in this regard. He argues that utilitarianism disregards the integrity and distinctness of persons and views them simply as occasions where pleasure occurs or preferences are satisfied (1971, pp. 27, 29, 184–190).

The same criticism can be made of theories of rational decision that focus exclusively on maximizing individual preference satisfaction. The argument of Chapter 6 can be viewed as establishing that the notion of preference utilized by formal theories of rational decision requires a richer conception of the rational agent than that of a mere collection of preferences, even of transitive ones. It requires a conception of the agent or person as an integral being who has the capacity to consider whether his preferences can be supported by reasons and to revise them accordingly. The rational person is not constituted by whatever ends or preferences he happens to have at any given moment. Rationality consists, at least partly, in our capacity to make our ends and preferences the object of our rational consideration and to revise them in accordance with reasons we find compelling. This is an important point and one that will be further elaborated and defended in the present chapter. It vindicates Rawls's conception of the rational person as having a fundamental interest in rationally choosing his or her own ends: "free persons conceive of themselves as beings who can revise and alter their final ends and who give first priority to preserving their liberty in these matters" (1974, p. 641).[1] This is a richer conception of the rational person than is orthodox in formal theories of decision. And it plays an important role in Rawls's arguments, both for his theory of justice as fairness and for the rejection of utilitarianism.[2] It is exceedingly important, therefore, that this conception is grounded in a broader theory of practical reasons; one, indeed, that I have argued in Chapter 6 is presupposed by decision theory itself.[3]

In this chapter we shall explore the relation between what we may call the *unity of agency* and our initial account of rational consideration. This unity may be viewed both synchronically and diachronically. At any moment we may consider our situation and preferences and unify and order them in an informed way. But we also perdure as agents; and this raises the question of what attitude a rational agent should take to his future. The chapter will examine the light that our initial account of rational consideration sheds on both synchronic and diachronic unity of agency.

1. This same idea is expressed in Rawls 1975a, p. 553, and 1975b, p. 94. T. M. Scanlon has emphasized this aspect of Rawls's notion of the person (1975, p. 178).

2. Allen Buchanan (1975) points out that inattention to this aspect of the rationality of Rawls's choosers in the original position infects much criticism of Rawls. I discuss this point in connection with the Kantian interpretation of Rawls's theory in Darwall 1980, pp. 323–327.

3. Samuel Scheffler has argued that if Rawls's principles of justice would indeed be chosen from the original position, they could then be defended as hypothetical imperatives binding on agents who prize an ideal of the person as (among other things) a rational chooser of his own ends. The present argument shows that ideal to be not simply optional for rational beings. Resulting imperatives would, therefore, be not hypothetical but categorical, at least insofar as they are conditional simply on having that nonoptional end. See Scheffler 1979, 1982a, and 1982b. For an earlier criticism of Scheffler's view, see Darwall 1982a and 1982b.

1. The relation between what we would prefer an adequate reflection and what we prefer as single, unified agents is an important and profound one. Our different individual intrinsic preferences are simply for their objects, considered as such. Were we but a bundle of such individual preferences we would have no way of coming to and expressing one mind on the question of what to do; for we would have no perspective other than that internal to each individual preference from which to order our different individual preferences, consider how to deal with conflicts between them, and decide what *we* prefer, on the whole, to do. Wright Neely gives a graphic description of this situation using the language of desire: "A man with incompatible desires . . . is less *a single agent.* Rather, he is two (or more) agents competing against each other. From the point of view of one of the agents, the others are external circumstances tending to frustrate the efforts of the one. They represent obstacles to be overcome no less than do purely external factors" (1974, p. 39).[4]

We can consider which of two contending individual intrinsic preferences we prefer to act on only if we can get the objects of both in view and consider them dispassionately. And in general we can decide what we prefer on the whole only by placing ourselves in a position from which we can consider whatever is relevant to our situation.

2. Some writers, following Sidgwick, have used the idea of a person's informed, all-things-considered preferences to define the notion of *a person's good*, on the whole, or of *a person's conception of the good.* Sidgwick held that "a man's future good on the whole is what he would now desire and seek on the whole if all the consequences of all the different lines of conduct open to him were accurately foreseen and adequately realized in imagination at the present point in time" (1967, pp. 111–112).[5] For example, Rawls (1971, pp. 399–424) takes an approach similar to Sidgwick's that highlights the way in which a rational person's preferences reflect

---

4. For a similar point see Perry 1926, p. 662.
5. See also Wright 1963b, pp. 86–113, and Rawls 1971, pp. 399–424.

not only a deliberate awareness of considerations as they arise in distinct situations but also an awareness of different *kinds of lives* that are available to him.

This latter is an important point. As beings who can reflect on ourselves as perduring through time, we form preferences with much wider scope than those that we are likely to be able to satisfy by specific actions in specific situations. In the limiting case, we may prefer, on the whole, to lead one kind of life rather than another. When such preferences are informed and all-things-considered preferences, they provide a rational framework within which we may pursue our lives in various situations as they arise. They are not, of course, absolute, inflexible, or unrevisable, and they do not always take precedence over what seems preferable in specific situations. They are usually sufficiently vague that significant choice is still left in individual situations, and whatever preferences we have for our lives considered on the whole will themselves likely change (and in a reason-supported way) when we reconsider them in the light of new developments or experience.

Rawls captures the idea of an informed, all-things-considered preference for one life rather than another with the notion of a *rational life plan* (1971, p. 408). A life plan is some more or less determinate notion of what one prefers, on the whole, to do in one's life. Rawls counts a life plan *rational* if it meets two general conditions. First, since a plan will include not simply a preferential ordering of the ends one wants to achieve in life but also some notion of how those ends are to be achieved, it is necessary that the plan relate means to ends in a rational way. This involves satisfying a set of principles of means-end (or relative) rationality; such as, a plan is to be preferred if, other things equal, it achieves more ends, or is more likely to achieve ends, and so forth. But this is not sufficient, Rawls points out, because the ends promoted may not themselves be rational. The second necessary condition of a rational life plan, therefore, is that the plan be one that one would choose "with full awareness of the relevant facts and after a careful consideration of the consequences" (ibid.).[6] In our terms this

---

6. Rawls uses the term 'deliberative rationality' to refer to an all-things-considered reflection. He discusses it more fully on pp. 416–424.

means that a rational life plan is one for which the person would have an informed, all-things-considered preference.

As Rawls points out, it may well not be rational for a person actually to reflect and deliberate to the point of discovering the plan that is most rational for him. Thinking about our lives, reconsidering our plans in the light of new experience and information, and seeking out more and more information and experience on which to base our plans, are all activities that themselves take time, energy, and attention. How much of our lives we have reason to devote to these activities cannot solely depend on whether the plan that results accords with our informed, all-things-considered preferences. It must depend on how much of our lives we would prefer to give over to such activities when we adequately consider both the results and what is involved in the activities themselves (together with what is forgone). There may, on the whole, be reasons for us to do things differently in our lives even if there is not, on the whole, reason for us to discover what those reasons are. Often we have reasons to leave well enough alone.

Rawls identifies the plan of life that is most rational for a person (in the sense of our initial account) with what he variously calls *the person's good* or *a rational conception of the person's good*. Now, our ordinary meaning of 'a person's own good' is perhaps related to what benefits the person *himself* in a way that makes the phrase to some degree inappropriate to express the notion that Rawls has in mind. Probably better would be *a rational conception of the good life for that person*. Or, most simply, *the good*, or *best, life for that person*. While it does sound distinctly odd to say that a person embarked on a life of self-sacrifice and devotion to others is pursuing his own good, there is nothing at all misleading in saying that he is pursuing his conception of the best life for him if that life is the result of his own informed, free choice.

Once we talk about something's being part of the good or best life for a person, however, we make a claim that must itself be supported by reasons and, more important for our present situation, that may be refuted by citing the existence of overriding reasons against a person's leading a given life. While on the basis of the argument so far we may say that something is part of the best life for a person, *other things equal,* if it is part of a life for which he would have an informed, all-things-considered preference, we cannot make that claim in an *unqualified* way. For that would assume that our initial account of rational consideration is itself complete.

3. The ideas of a rational life plan and of a person's conception of the best life for her presuppose a conception of ourselves as having an existence extending through time. And that commits us to the view that acts judged equally good from the standpoint of their contribution to the best life for one are supported by equally weighty reasons for acting, regardless of their relative position in time. In particular, if one has a choice between an act that can satisfy some current preference and an act that must be performed presently to achieve some future good, then if dispassionate consideration would leave one indifferent between the two goods, the choice of either act appears equally well supported by reasons.

According to the crudest versions of the DBR Thesis, one can have a reason to do only those things for which one presently has some desire. So if a present act guarantees a future benefit (in the sense of satisfying a *future* desire) equal to some presently achievable benefit, that does not necessarily show that there is an equal reason to perform it. Indeed, there will be no reason at all to perform it unless there is some present desire to have the future benefit. Of course, generally we do care about what will happen to us in the future, though often we may not care directly about the specific things about which we will come to care. Still, in these versions of the DBR Thesis, our concerns about the present will generally provide us with weightier reasons than will our concerns about the future, since they are usually more "violent" in the Humean sense.

Nagel (1970, p. 57) gives an argument that seeks to show that if present desires provide reasons of a certain weight, then comparable future desires that one will but does not presently have must provide reasons of comparable weight, other things equal, to take present action that will enable them to be satisfied. Of course, other things are almost never exactly equal. Present action to satisfy present desire may be more assured of success than present action to satisfy future desire. And we are usually more certain that we have present desires than that we will have future desires. But if other things are equal, Nagel argues, the fact that one desire is in the present and the other will be in the future can make no difference in the weight of the reasons they provide.

The main argument Nagel develops is isomorphic to one he advances later in his book to show that reasons not only extend their rational influence across time, for a particular person, but also span the gap between persons. This latter argument attempts to show that if some fact is a reason for one person to do something, then it must at the same time be a reason for anyone to promote the person's doing it. We shall consider this version of the argument in some detail in Part III when we consider the relation between reasons and what a person would informedly prefer when he adopts an impersonal standpoint. I shall show that version of the argument to be invalid. It will follow, therefore, that the analogous argument for the conclusion that temporal difference cannot affect rational weight also fails. Still, Nagel is right to suppose that it is irrational to give greater weight to the present simply because it is present. And it is especially clear that whether a present act will satisfy a present desire or enable satisfaction of a future desire cannot itself mark the difference between whether or not there exists reason to perform it.

In our initial account, the reasons that there are for agents to act are not given by the fact of desire or preference itself but by facts that motivate preference when dispassionately considered.[7] So, in general, the lack of a present desire or preference for something does not by itself show that there is no present reason to promote it. Whether there is a present reason depends on whether one *would* have a present preference were one to consider it fully, dispassionately, and in an imaginatively vivid way. In cases of pressing present concerns that obscure our view of future goods, present preference is no guide to what course is supported by reasons.

7. It should be noted that sometimes we may prefer an alternative because we have a relevant desire. Gary Watson (1975) points out that some of our preferences, for example, for sexual experience, are to engage in certain activities when certain desires are present.

According to our initial account, to discover reasons for present acts, other things equal, we consider all (including future-regarding) facts relevant to our situation in a way that corrects for the increased salience of what is temporally proximate. Whatever considerations incline us to prefer some present act, whether they are themselves future regarding or not, are reasons for the present act.

By the same token, however, it is not necessarily the case, as Nagel holds, that a fact that *will be* a reason of a certain weight for a person to perform a certain act at some later time must also presently be a reason of the very same weight for the person to do what will promote his later action (ignoring the costs of the means, including opportunity costs). According to our initial account, whether something will be a reason for someone at a point in time, depends on whether the person would *at that time* be motivated to prefer an act were he reflectively to consider it in an imaginatively vivid way. And it may simply be the case that a consideration that would motivate a person on reflection at some time would not at some other time, *even if* the person were to give it the same careful imaginative consideration informed by no further experience.

It is irrational for the person to give any preference to the present over the future in rational consideration. So he gives the same consideration to future-regarding facts as he does to present-regarding ones, exercising even greater care to represent future matters vividly to himself so that he is not carried away by present concerns. But whether something is a (present) reason for him depends on whether rational consideration of it would (at present) give him any motivation to prefer it. And rational consideration of a fact may move him at some point but not at another.[8]

4. Earlier we saw how, when a person's individual preferences conflict, she can nonetheless come to one mind in rationally settling that conflict by assuming a standpoint from which she can dispassionately consider on which to act. She comes to a unified

8. Bernard Williams (1976, p. 209) criticizes Nagel's view that the rational standpoint toward one's life is atemporal. The rational place to view one's life, Williams argues, is from a place within it—"from now."

sense of what she prefers on the whole. A rational life plan, then, will seek to mitigate such conflicts and achieve coherence among our various pursuits. Directly conflicting intrinsic preferences are only one source of incoherence, however. Intransitive cycles of preference are another. We may have preferences for A over B, for B over C, but for C over A. Moreover, it seems that if we simply consider these options two at a time, the respective preferences may be *considered* ones with respect to all facts about the two options. But even if each of these preferences could be individually rational, they cannot be tolerated in a rational, all-things-considered ordering of preferences, since a series of actions on such preferences can be self-defeating (the money pump problem).[9]

Finally, individual preferences may cohere not simply in the sense that potential conflicts within them are resolvable, nor in the sense that they are transitive, but in the more positive sense that they fit together, complement, or mutually support each other. This can happen in a number of ways. Something can be preferred both for its own sake and for the sake of its enabling the satisfaction of some other preference. One works not just for a wage, but also, one hopes, because aspects of one's work are intrinsically desirable and promoting of other ends that one intrinsically prefers.

Also, two intrinsic preferences may support each other if what one finds intrinsically desirable about both are the same or similar aspects. One obvious case of this is when one thing is intrinsically preferred because it has properties that specify more general aspects that one finds intrinsically desirable. An example would be specific individual preferences for distance running and for cross-country skiing, both of which specify and support a preference for moving through nature in an autonomous and self-propelled way. The more specific and more general preferences support each other in the sense that finding the more specific activities intrinsically desirable supports one's sense that the general sort of activity is, and conversely.

In Chapter 6, I argued that it is because preferences are criticiza-

9. See Chapter 6, sec. 5.

ble in the light of judgments about the *reasons* for them, that intransitive cycles of preference are contrary to reason. Put most generally, rational preference can be measured by a utility function only if we suppose it accountable to an underlying linear standard. What provides this standard is the idea of the *weight* of reasons for a preference, all things considered, since without this standard we can make no clear sense of the irrationality of intransitive preferences. We must conceive of preferences as supportable by reasons.

It is, again, the fact that preferences are themselves supportable by reasons that explains the other ways in which they can support or conflict with each other. To see why this is so, let us consider more familiar cases in which *beliefs* conflict or cohere because of their basis in reasons.

The most obvious way in which two beliefs may conflict is if they are directly inconsistent, but this is not the only way. If one believes *p* and has *q* as one's reason for believing *p*, and if *q* equally supports a belief that *r*, but one believes that not-*r*, then one's beliefs are in conflict. The conflict does not consist in a strict incompatibility of beliefs. Rather, it comes about because of the way in which one's beliefs are, and are not, supported.

Beliefs may cohere because of their basis in reasons. If one believes that *p*, and has *q* as one's reason, and if *q* equally supports *r*, and one also believes *r*, then one's beliefs that *p* and that *r* are mutually supporting.

Because preferences call for support by reasons, they may conflict and cohere in these same ways. If one prefers A for the reason that *p*, and *p* is also true of B, but one prefers not-B, then one's preferences for A and for not-B are, other things equal, in tension. They do not conflict in the sense that it is impossible to satisfy both. Rather they are prima facie in *systemic* conflict. They cannot be brought simply into a coherent conception of the good life, since what grounds, in one's view, the goodness of the one tells against the goodness of the other.

Likewise, preferences may cohere if the same reasons support them. Such preferences are mutually supporting in the sense that what, in one's view, grounds the goodness of the one also grounds the goodness of the other. So if the one is good, then so is the other, other things equal.

What enables us to unify our preferences into some kind of coherent system is, then, their basis in reasons. It is illuminating to consider in this connection Kant's remarks about the unity of experience: "If each representation were completely foreign to every other, standing apart in isolation, no such thing as knowledge would ever arise. For knowledge is (essentially) a whole in which representations stand compared and connected" (1781/ 1964, p. 130 [A 97]).[10] Knowledge and rational belief require input, experiences, that can be "compared and connected." We can unify our experiences only if individual experiences can either conflict with or confirm each other. Otherwise, each stands "apart in isolation" and no coherent sense can be made of them.

The analogous point holds true in the practical realm. If our preferences were not themselves criticizable and supportable by reasons, then each would be "completely foreign to every other." Their only conflict could be a tug of war, pulling the agent (which agent?) in different directions, with no possible basis for coming to an all-things-considered preference between them.

Unified rational agency, a kind of "transcendental unity of practical apperception," is possible, therefore, only because preferences are themselves criticizable in terms of reasons.[11] It requires the capacity to adopt a reflective standpoint from which we can consider what reasons there are to prefer one act over another, and from which *we* form an all-things-considered preference. This includes, in our initial account, the capacity to reflect dispassionately and to be motivated by our awareness of different considerations. On this basis we are able to draw a distinction between informed preferences and those that are not, between all-things-

---

10. For references to *The Critique of Pure Reason*, A refers to the 1781 edition and B to the 1787 edition.
11. This unity is more fundamental and a prerequisite for the unity of the self that emerges from the self's own unifying activity in articulating and expressing a unified and coherent conception of the good. Analogously, on the theoretical side, the transcendental unity of apperception is a prerequisite for the construction of a fully coherent conception of the world.

considered preferences and preferences that give way in the face of an imaginative review of information and experience. The correspondence between this idea and the conclusion of Kant's transcendental deduction that experience must purport to be of objects and incorporate within it a distinction between the way things are and the way things merely appear is not mere coincidence. Without the objective purport of experience and the synthesis of experience in accordance with rules that makes it possible, Kant held, "I should have as many-colored and diverse a self as I have representations of which I am conscious to myself" (1787/1964, p. 154 [B 134]). Analogously, if we did not take preferences to be criticizable in terms of reasons, we would have no way of forming all-things-considered preferences, and we would have "as many-coloured and diverse a self" as we have different individual preferences.

5.   Beginning with a basic internalist framework, we have in this part followed out the implications of our initial account of rational consideration. Our first conclusion was that facts that motivate an agent to prefer an act when he is reflectively aware of them are reasons for him to act. From that point we have moved, through various way stations, to the conclusion that facts relating to what is the best life for a person, other things equal, are reasons for him.

To this juncture no challenge has yet arisen to a fundamentally self-centered view of practical reason. While the considerations that our initial account certifies as reasons need not be restricted to self-*regarding* ones, that account appears to make the standpoint of rational consideration the *agent's* own. According to it, we cannot judge whether a fact is a reason for someone to act unless we are somehow able to assume *his* point of view and see whether *he* would be motivated by reflective awareness of it.

In the next two parts, we shall consider challenges to the view that rational consideration is wholly self-centered. The most basic challenge is Thomas Nagel's view, considered in the next chapter, that the *only* reasons for agents to act are those that can motivate them from an *impersonal*, rather than their own personal, standpoint. I shall argue against this view but use some of its resources to construct a notion of intersubjective value that, I shall argue, is our own. We implicitly take intersubjective values to give us (*and others*) reasons, I shall maintain, when we adopt certain extremely familiar attitudes toward ourselves and others. The standpoint from which we are moved by considerations of intersubjective value is not our own personal one but an intersubjective standpoint with which we identify.

But even if we do in fact identify with intersubjective standpoints, and implicitly hold others to doing so when we do, could not a person reject all such standpoints and still not act contrary to reason? That is, could not a person rest with our initial account of rational consideration as defined by his own standpoint, as such? I shall argue in Part IV that this is impossible. The normativity of reasons requires the perspective of *a rational agent as such* as the standpoint from which all reasons, including those grounded in what motivates an agent from his own point of view, are ultimately assessed.

Part III

Reason and
Intersubjective Good

CHAPTER 10

Nagelian Objectivity

Our initial account of rational consideration appears to make the agent's own standpoint the appropriate perspective from which to assess what reasons there are for an agent to act. We see a fact to be a reason for a person when we see that *she* would be moved by reflective awareness of it to prefer an act. To this extent, then, our initial account is a self-centered one.

In Part III we shall begin to consider how this initial account might be extended in a way that makes the perspective of rational consideration neither solely nor even primarily the agent's own particular point of view. Our starting point will be to consider what is perhaps the strongest view possible regarding the extension of rational influence across persons. According to this position no consideration can possibly be a reason for one person to act unless it bears on the issue of what others (indeed *all* others) have reason to do.

1. Two kinds of practical relevance need to be distinguished here. Sometimes it is said that no fact can be a reason for someone unless that same fact would be a reason for anyone to act similarly in relevantly similar circumstances. We may call this the *thesis of universality*. If it is correct, a potential relevance of any reason

consists in its being the case that the same fact must also bear on what it would be rational for others to do in relevantly similar situations. But even if all reasons for acting are universal in the sense that they bear on what others should do in the same *kind* of situation, the existence of a reason for one person to act may not bear at all on what others have reason to do with respect to *that person's* situation. Thus, even if the fact that it will contribute to the best life for me is a reason for me to act only if *any* agent has reason to do what will contribute to the best life for him, nothing follows about whether one agent has any reason to do what will contribute to the best life for another.

Some philosophers, however, have urged that reasons for acting transfer their rational influence across persons, so that if a reason exists for one person to do something, then it also exists, at least prima facie, for others to enable him to do it or at any rate not to interfere with his doing it. [1] In this view no reason for acting can be irreducibly self-regarding.

After Thomas Nagel, let us call any consideration *subjective* if its expression contains a "free agent variable," a phrase whose reference is given by the agent for whom it is supposed to be reason. Thus, 'that something is in *his* interest' is a subjective consideration if we read 'his' as a variable to be instantiated by the person for whom it is a consideration. If, however, we mean 'his interest' simply to have the force of *a person's interest* or to refer to a particular person's interest, thinking that there is something about his interests in particular that gives anyone a reason to promote them, then the consideration is not subjective. Any consideration that is not subjective in this sense, Nagel calls *objective* (1970, p. 90).

We may call, then, the position that there are no subjective reasons the *thesis of objectivity*; that any reason for a person to act must be, or be based on, an objective consideration. [2] According to

1. In addition to Nagel's *The Possibility of Altruism* (1970), in which the author defends the position that will be considered in this chapter, see Gewirth 1971. Since this earlier article, Gewirth has slightly changed his view; see Gewirth 1978.
2. Thus Nagel: "the only acceptable reasons are objective ones" (1970, p. 96). In the preface to the second edition, however, Nagel concedes that this strong a thesis cannot be demonstrated, and he no longer accepts it.

this thesis the fact that it will satisfy his intrinsic preference is a reason for a person to act only if its subjectivity is superficial. A person's intrinsic preferences give him reason to act not because they are *his* (where *he* is whatever person is in question) but because, perhaps, they are *a person's* preferences.

If both the thesis of universality and the thesis of objectivity are true, then something can be a reason for one person to do something only if it is at least prima facie a reason for anyone to bring about that person's doing it. Notice that both theses are required to obtain this result. Even if all reasons for acting are objective, a reason for one person to do something will not always give others reason to aid him unless universality holds. Universality guarantees that if a reason exists for a person, it is to do a *kind* of thing *everyone* has reason to do. Objectivity guarantees that the kind of thing is not instantiated differently for different persons and thus that the present action is an instance of something they also have reason to promote.

To this point we have seen no reason to accept either the thesis of universality or that of objectivity. Indeed, the argument of Part II that agents are given reason to act by facts about the *objects* of their intrinsic preferences entails that reasons for acting need not be universal. If I want the Pirates to win the pennant, then there are facts related to their chances that give me reason to act but not anyone not likeminded. And while it is true that according to the argument these facts are only reasons for me to act because I have the appropriate preference, it is false that the only ultimate reason for me to act is the fact that it will satisfy my preference, a (subjective) reason that anyone has. It is false because it implies that people are rationally moved only by the fact that they prefer, rather than, as the argument of Part II contends, by facts regarding the objects of their preferences.

In this chapter we shall consider Thomas Nagel's argument for the view that something can be a reason for one person to act only if it is also a reason for others to enable her to so act. Because it is addressed solely to the thesis of objectivity, even if the argument succeeds in its own terms this further conclusion will follow only if universality also holds. Let us, however, grant this latter assumption arguendo.

2. *The Possibility of Altruism* is a misleading title for Nagel's book, for what he tries to demonstrate is not just that acting for the sake of others *can* be in accordance with reason, if, for example, one intrinsically prefers their welfare, but that considerations regarding the good of others *must* be reasons for *any* person to act. What moves Nagel's thought in the direction of what might be called the rational necessity of altruism is the thesis of objectivity. According to it, *no* reasons for acting are ultimately subjective. If reasons exist at all, they do so only for the promotion of states of affairs describable without free agent variables. Assuming universality, if a reason exists for one person to promote a given state of affairs, it likewise exists for any person. Since we all think that facts about our own preferences and interests give us reason to act, Nagel argues, the objectivity thesis forces us to suppose that what really gives us reason is not that the interests are *ours* but that they are the interests of a person, or of a sentient being, or that they are just interests, or some such. Whichever of these we choose, we are forced to conclude that the interests of others also give us reasons to act on their behalf, whether we want to or not.

Nagel's argument marshals several profound themes—the relation between justification and motivation, the relation between conceptions of ourselves and others and the expression of these conceptions in acknowledging different sorts of reasons, and the practical consequences of rejecting solipsism. It is a very difficult argument, and few have attempted to come to terms with it in print. Nonetheless, one is apt to feel, as Nicholas Sturgeon has remarked, that it "would come startlingly close to succeeding, if only one could put the pieces together" (1974, p. 375).[3]

3. Put most generally, Nagel argues that the person who acknowledges subjective considerations as reasons for acting is committed to a kind of solipsism. He must hold true certain judgments about himself that he in principle cannot hold true of others or, indeed, of himself when he considers himself from an impersonal

---

3. This essay of Sturgeon's is a substantial exception to the general lack of careful criticism of Nagel's position.

standpoint: as one person among others equally real.[4] Since Nagel believes that the person who acknowledges subjective reasons cannot make the same *practical* judgments of himself that he can of others, or even of himself impersonally viewed, Nagel dubs this position *practical solipsism*. Surely he is right to suppose that this would be a high price to pay for holding on to the thesis that some reasons for acting are subjective.

Before we consider the argument in detail we would do well to develop Nagel's precise distinction between objective and subjective reasons. Nagel treats all reasons for acting as identifiable with

a predicate R such that for all persons *p* and events A, if R is true of A, then *p* has prima facie reason to promote A. [1970, p. 47][5]

Apart from assuming universality this does not diverge too sharply from the approach that we have taken. In our terms a reason is not to be identified with the predicate 'R' (or with the property it expresses) but the (believed to be) fact that R is true of A.

Although Nagel's approach commits him to the universality thesis, our provisional acceptance of it poses no particular problem, for universality cuts across the subjective-objective distinction. Even if a reason is universal, Nagel terms it *subjective* if its "defining predicate R contains a free occurrence of the variable *p*" (1970, p. 90). Thus, if there is some linguistic item in the expression of the reason that functions as a variable referring to the person for whom the fact is a reason, then it is a *subjective* reason. Otherwise, it is an objective reason.

By this test the consideration that an act would promote something *one* intrinsically prefers or something that is part of the best

4. Sturgeon argues that this is not strictly solipsistic, since Nagel believes that the person who acknowledges subjective reasons must also believe that we cannot hold true of others what they can hold true of themselves. We are all in the same boat. Sturgeon is doubtless right about this, but I cannot see that much hangs on it. Is it not bad enough to suppose that the person who acknowledges subjective reasons cannot make the same judgments of himself from personal and impersonal standpoints?

5. Nagel treats reasons for acting in terms of the general notion of reasons "for promoting an end."

life for *one* is subjective. But it is important to appreciate that the class of facts that would be subjective reasons, were they reasons at all, is by no means limited to those relating to self-benefit. The following would also be classified as subjective: that A would harm *one*, that A would benefit *one's* friend, and that A would benefit some person other than *oneself*. All of these considerations are subjective if there is no way of eliminating the "free agent variable" within each substitution for *R*.

Because an objective reason contains no free occurrence of an agent variable, it follows from the universality thesis that if there is an objective reason for someone to do A, then there exists a reason for everyone to enable him to do A. The universality thesis guarantees that if a person has a reason to do something then everyone has reason to do the same kind of thing in relevantly similar circumstances. And if the reason is objective, it is guaranteed that the kind of thing is not something like 'satisfy the agent's interest' that is instantiated differently by different individuals. If one person has an objective reason to do A, then anyone has the same reason to promote *the very same* state of affairs that he does, which includes enabling him to do A.[6]

Reasons that are merely subjective must be rejected, Nagel thinks, because a person who acknowledges them cannot hold true the same judgments made about *him*self (as such) that others can hold true of him or even that he can hold true of himself when he considers himself impersonally. This means a split in perspective, depending on whether he is considering himself *as himself* or not, such that he cannot make judgments with the same content about himself from these two perspectives. Nagel terms the two relevant perspectives or standpoints the *personal standpoint* and *impersonal standpoint*, respectively. A person takes the impersonal standpoint when he abstracts from any information about himself *as himself* and views the world from the personal standpoint when what is

6. It is significant in this regard that Nagel quotes approvingly from Moore's discussion of the incoherence of egoism (in 1962, p. 99). Moore argued that considerations regarding one's own good could give reason to act only if it is good absolutely that one should have one's good; i.e., there must exist reason for anyone to enable one to have one's good. See Nagel 1970, p. 86.

viewed is informed by his awareness of its relation to himself as such.

Surely Nagel is right to regard the incapacity to make the same judgments of oneself from personal and impersonal standpoints as a very considerable cost. The simple knowledge of who we are should not affect our capacity to hold true judgments *about* who we are. When Sylvia judges that *she* is a resident of Cincinnati, what she holds true about herself could equally well be held true, we think, from an impersonal standpoint were she to judge (disregarding that *she* is Sylvia) that Sylvia is a resident of Cincinnati. Otherwise there is no common world judged of from the two different standpoints; not only does perspective skew our view of an objective world in a way that must be tempered by other views but it brings a completely *different* world into view—one that cannot be integrated with what is judged from the other standpoint.

The person who acknowledges subjective reasons gives, Nagel believes, a special primacy to himself as such in practical judgments that is tantamount to accepting a kind of solipsism. If we reject solipsism we think that the content of any first-person judgment ('I have property X') can be rendered by an impersonal judgment ('S has property X') together with the "basic personal statement" ('I am S'). We think that the property does not change when it is ascribed from the personal or impersonal standpoint. If it does, then we must hold that certain properties apply to one only because one is oneself (where that refers to something uncapturable from the impersonal standpoint). And that is solipsistic.

The same considerations require that what is held true of someone be expressible by first-person and second-person judgments within the personal standpoint. When I judge of myself that I have property X and you (attempt to, at any rate) judge of me that I have property X, which you express by saying, "*You* have property X," then we both hold the same thing to be true of me. Otherwise, we must think that the perspective from which properties are ascribed itself affects which properties can be ascribed. And that, Nagel contends, is a kind of solipsism.

The next major step in the argument is to transpose these points to the practical realm and to note there the essential link between practical judgment and motivation. As a self-described internalist, Nagel believes that there is a close relation between judging there to be reasons to do something and being moved to do it. Time and again his reader is reminded that reasons to act are reasons to *act* and not simply to believe that one should (1970, p. 64, for example). Nagel's general account of reasons is not itself internalist. His internalism is expressed, rather, in the contention that personal practical judgments ('I have reason to do A') have *motivational content*. In accepting the judgment that one has reason to do something, one is ordinarily moved to do it. Though not always, normally the person who accepts that there is reason for her to do A is given some desire to do A. And on many occasions when a person does accept the judgment that she has reason to do A and does it, her doing A may simply be explained by her acceptance of the practical judgment without reference to any further desire. This is the fundamental idea of internalism: judging some consideration to be a reason for one to act is itself ordinarily motivating. Action for reasons is often motivated simply by the recognition of reasons themselves and not (not always anyway) by a superadded desire to act for reasons. It is therefore part of the *content* of the personal practical judgment, Nagel says, that the judge (the agent) is ordinarily moved. He refers to this as the *motivational content* of the personal practical judgment.

Since motivational content is part of the personal practical judgment, if one is to be able to hold true the *same* practical judgment of oneself from an impersonal standpoint, the impersonal practical judgment about the person who one in fact is must also have motivational content. This means, Nagel claims, that if we are to be able to make the same practical judgments about ourselves from personal and impersonal standpoints, then accepting an impersonal practical judgment ('S has reason to do A') must routinely move one to *want* S to do A and to do whatever would lead to S's doing A. Likewise, if we are to be able to hold true practical judgments about others in the same sense that they hold them of themselves, then the judgment 'You have reason to do A' must have motivational content also. The judgment must be such that on accepting it one is moved to want the other to do A and to do what would lead the other so to act.

The problem with subjective reasons is that on their basis it is impossible to make impersonal or second-person practical judgments with motivational content. If I judge that S has subjective reason to do A, then nothing follows about what I have reason to do at all. Therefore, accepting the judgment that he has subjective reason so to act carries with it no intrinsic motivation for me to aid his acting or to want him to act. I may, of course, want him to do what there is reason for him to do, but the point is that it is not part of the content of my judgment that he has reason to act that my accepting it gives me any motivation at all. If, however, I judge that S has *objective* reason to do A, then, since it follows that everyone has reason to promote S's doing A, it follows that I have reason to promote S's doing A. Because this latter judgment has motivational content, in accepting the impersonal judgment I am committed to accepting something that also has motivational content. Its motivational content is perhaps somewhat less direct than that of the personal practical judgment, since I must make the appropriate inference, but the inference is routine enough that we can suppose it regularly to be made by those who acknowledge objective reasons.

Acknowledging objective reasons, therefore, is necessary to holding true the same practical judgments of oneself from the personal and impersonal standpoints, and of others, those that they hold true of themselves. So if we are to deny solipsism in its practical form, the reasons for acting that we acknowledge must be thought to be objective.

4. The basic flaw in Nagel's argument is that it trades on an ambiguity in the idea that personal practical judgment has motivational content. To see how this is so let us consider an alternative suggestion regarding the motivational content of the practical judgment. Suppose we were to say that there is a sense in which a person who recognizes irreducibly subjective reasons can make impersonal practical judgments with motivational content; name-

ly, when he judges that S has reason to do A he judges that acceptance of the judgment by S, knowing himself to be S, will ordinarily give S some motivation to do A.[7] What is judged to be true of S, then, is not simply that his doing A falls into some category that may make no difference in his conduct at all. Rather, one expresses a conviction about the connection between reasons and motivation by saying that were S to make the same judgment and to realize that he is S, then he would normally be moved to do A. And, we might say, this is the same sort of content that one expresses *about* oneself when one judges that *one* has reason to do A: acceptance of the judgment about oneself (trivially, knowing oneself to be oneself) ordinarily moves one to do A. The common motivational content of personal and impersonal practical judgments according to this suggestion, then, is this: acceptance of the judgment by its subject, knowing himself to be its subject, is ordinarily motivating.

It turns out now, however, that the person who makes subjective practical judgments makes the very same judgment of himself from the personal and impersonal standpoints. In each case the motivational content of his judgment that M has reason to do A (where M ranges over *both* personal and impersonal substituends) is that acceptance of the judgment by the person referred to by 'M', knowing himself to be that person, is normally explanatory of his having some motivation to do A. Of course, it will only be in those cases where a person can make a first-person practical judgment that she will actually be given motivation to do A. But whether the person is actually given motivation does not change the judgment she makes, in the sense of *what* she judges of herself: the practical scene judged to exist. Whether she is given motivation is, if she recognizes subjective reasons, rather an expression of the perspective from which her judgment is made.

Nagel considers something like this proposal but rejects it:

7. Sturgeon (1974, p. 380) makes a similar proposal, though he leaves out the crucial phrase "knowing himself to be such." Notice, by the way, that simply saying that the personal practical *judgment* (i.e., what is judged) has the property that anyone who accepts *it* will be given motivation amounts to begging the question. On this point see Darwall 1974.

It is futile to argue that an impersonal judgment can contain the appropriate *attitudes* in hypothetical form. The suggestion would be that my application of a subjective principle to a particular person (impersonally specified) includes the provision that *if* I am that person, then I should act in the way prescribed (*with all the motivational content that judgment implies*). But such an account fails to preserve the impersonal view, for the motivational content of the general subjective principle has now become simply: 'For each person, if I am that person, then I should act as the principle prescribes for him.' But that is nothing more than the personal maxim that *I* should do as the principle says. *Since no impersonal attitudes to one's action can derive from such a maxim*, nothing has been done towards meeting the congruency condition. [Nagel 1970, pp. 117–118; emphasis added except for "if" and "I"]

What this passage makes clear is that, as Nagel is thinking of it, the motivational content of the personal practical judgment cannot simply be some fact about how one *would* be moved were one to make the judgment, rather it is *the motivation or attitude itself*. The reason why the person who acknowledges subjective reasons cannot make impersonal practical judgments of himself "with all the motivational content" of his personal judgments is that the content of his impersonal judgments does not include the motivation or attitude itself. And this makes our suggestion an inappropriate rendering of the motivational content of practical judgments (personal or impersonal). As Nagel puts it at one point: "The difficulty is, however, that an individual's impersonally derived attitude toward his own acts in consequence of a universal subjective principle can be no different from his attitude toward any other person's acts" (1970, p. 117).

But now, if motivational content has to do with actual motivation or attitude, in what sense does the personal practical judgment have motivational content? Is it part of *what one judges*? Or is it, rather, part of one's *judging*: namely, the attitude that one normally has when one judges that there is reason for one to do A? Nagel's argument requires that it be part of *what* one judges, part of its content. This is what must change with one's perspective if one cannot hold true the very same things *about* oneself. But what reason do we have to believe that the attitude is itself part of *what one judges* to be true when one accepts the personal practical judgment rather than the attitude one normally has toward an act on *judging* there to be reason to perform it?

It might be argued that an internalist cannot make such a marked distinction between *what* an agent judges in judging there to be reason for him to act and the attitudes that are part of his *judging*. And there is a sense in which this is correct. For an internalist, I have argued, something's being a reason for someone to act consists in its being the case that the person is given some motivation to prefer the act upon rationally considering the fact. This means that the acid test of whether a fact *is* a reason for a person is for the person rationally to consider the fact for himself and to notice whether he is motivated to prefer the act. We judge *for ourselves* whether a fact is a reason for us by actually going through the process of rational consideration and noticing whether we are in fact moved to prefer the act. So, *in the process of rational consideration itself*, we judge whether something is a reason by how we are motivated, by our attitude. The presence of the appropriate attitude appears to be itself part of what we judge to be the case when, within rational deliberation, we judge something to be a reason, or reason enough, for us to act.

Still, even if it is true that the presence of attitude is part of what we judge about ourselves when we *establish for ourselves by our own rational consideration* that something is a reason for us to act, it does not follow that part of what we hold true when we hold that we have reason to do A is that we are in fact moved. For an internalist the content of the judgment that there is reason for one to do A is simply that *were* one rationally to consider facts relevant to doing A, then one *would* be moved to prefer doing A. One may hold the conditional to be true and utterly lack any motivation to do A. This may happen whenever one's reasons for believing that there is reason for one to do A do not arise from a contemporaneous rational consideration of the reasons for doing A, If, for example, one simply remembers having gone through the process or has other reasons for thinking that were one to go through the process one would be appropriately impressed. *What* one judges, then, in judging for oneself that there is reason for one to do something, is the truth of the conditional by a crucial experiment in one's own case.

Nagel's argument commits, therefore, a fallacy of ambiguity. The sense in which the actual motivational attitude is part of the personal practical judgment is as part of the judging (when one makes the judgment for oneself). But the sort of content relevant to the charge that the person who recognizes subjective reasons cannot make judgments with the same content from personal and impersonal standpoints is *what* one judges or holds true. And in this sense, motivation *itself* is not part of the content of the practical judgment. *That* sort of motivational content of the practical judgment can be adequately expressed by the suggested hypothetical: the subject of the judgment, knowing himself to be such, will routinely be moved in accepting the judgment. Moreover, this content can be quite adequately expressed by someone who recognizes subjective reasons.

CHAPTER 11

Objective Reasons and
Intersubjective Value

Nagel's notion of an objective reason for acting combines two elements that may profitably be distinguished. One element is that of *impersonality*: an objective reason is one that rationally motivates a person from an impersonal standpoint. The person who acknowledges an objective reason recognizes the relevance of a consideration that makes no essential reference to himself *as such*. Consequently, it is one whose truth he can judge and be moved by from an impersonal standpoint.

Since an objective reason makes no essential reference to the agent, it might seem to follow that if there is an objective reason for some particular person to do something, then there is an objective reason for everyone to promote his doing it. And this, of course, Nagel believes. In point of fact, however, this follows only if one accepts Nagel's view that all reasons for acting are *universal*: that a fact, pA, is a reason for S to do A if, and only if, $(A)(X)$ (if pA, then X has reason to do A). If, however, we accept, as we have throughout this study, that a reason for someone to do something is a fact about an act rational consideration of which would motivate the person to do it, other things equal, then there is no a priori reason to accept the universality of all reasons. Different agents may be motivated differently by their rational consideration of the same

Objective Reasons and Intersubjective Value

facts. When we bracket the issue of universality, consequently, we see that the judgment that there is an objective reason for S to do A does not necessarily commit us to the judgment that there is a reason (even prima facie) for everyone to promote S's doing A. Distinguishing these two elements liberates our thought. Adherence to the universality thesis requires Nagel to demonstrate the rational necessity of altruism in order to show its rational possibility, for universality requires that if an objective consideration is a reason for someone, then it is a reason for everyone. If, however, we do not suppose a priori that all reasons for acting are universal, it becomes a live possibility that altruism is rationally possible without being rationally necessary, that an objective consideration may be a reason for some person to act without its being a reason for everyone.

1.   In Part II we concluded that facts that lead an agent to prefer an act when reflectively considered are reasons to perform it. Now it seems plain that often our preferences are or can be motivated by considerations that make no essential reference to ourselves as such, and therefore, that there are objective reasons for us to act.

To be sure, sometimes the objectivity of our reasons is but a surface one—analysis makes plain their deeper subjectivity. For instance, by considering the fact that it is likely to rain today I may be motivated to prefer to take an umbrella. The consideration, 'that it is likely to rain', makes no obvious reference to myself and seems, therefore, to be objective. However, it may be perfectly clear that what really motivates me to prefer to take an umbrella is the subjective consideration that unless I take an umbrella *I* am likely to get wet. One way to think of it is this: the *informed intrinsic preference* establishing the existence of prima facie reason to take an umbrella is the preference that *I* not get wet (or, perhaps, run the risk of getting wet). And the considerations that motivate that preference are subjective: for example, *my* getting wet will feel like X, Y, and so on.

Whenever we are motivated by our reflective awareness of facts to prefer some act, there will be an associated intrinsic preference. Whether the reasons established by our being moved to prefer acts on reflection are ultimately objective or subjective depends on what considerations motivate the associated intrinsic preferences. Sometimes, as in the umbrella case, what motivates the intrinsic preference is a subjective consideration. In that case it is a fact about how *one* will feel. In other instances, however, the considerations that motivate an intrinsic preference appear irreducibly objective. Devoted friends, for example, have considered intrinsic preferences for each other's flourishing that are not motivated by considerations relating entirely to themselves as such. To care deeply about others is to be motivated to at least some extent by the thought of their welfare considered quite independently of their relation to one.[1] To the extent that our intrinsic preferences are motivated by considerations making no reference to ourselves as such, we have objective reasons for acting. Indeed, to the extent that there exist objective considerations that *would* motivate intrinsic preferences *were* we to be vividly aware of them, there are objective reasons for us. It does not, of course, follow that these objective reasons are universal, and consequently, it does not follow that anyone else has a reason to promote what one has objective reason to do.

2.   If objective considerations motivate us to have a particular intrinsic preference, then there is an important sense in which that preference is impersonal.[2] It is a preference we have when we view the world from an impersonal standpoint, abstracting from our place in it. Intrinsic preferences motivated by subjective considerations are, by contrast, personal. Their objects are states of affairs from which one cannot, as such, be eliminated. Since these two notions will play a crucial role in the rest of Part III, let us define them more explicitly.

1. Though perhaps only partly. Friends, as Lawrence Blum points out, are also concerned that *they* benefit each other (as an expression of their friendship). Still, he says, a concern for their weal simpliciter is part of friendship. See Blum 1981, pp. 43–44, 67–81.
2. Nagel himself makes a distinction between personal and impersonal desires: "Why can there not be desires which are completely impersonal in the sense that their objects and their grounds are formulated in completely impersonal terms" (1970, p. 121).

An intrinsic preference is *impersonal* if its object can be expressed without free agent variables. Impersonal intrinsic preferences are motivated by objective considerations.

An intrinsic preference is *personal* if its object can be expressed only with a free agent variable. Personal intrinsic preferences are motivated by subjective considerations.

Personal preferences can only be for states of affairs viewed from a personal standpoint. They get no grip on the world seen from an impersonal perspective. What is preferred is something considered in relation to oneself. Impersonal preferences, on the other hand, are for states of affairs viewed independently of their relation to one—from an impersonal standpoint.

One may wonder how any preference can arise within an impersonal standpoint at all if that standpoint is confused with a passionless, or purely intellectual, perspective. There is no reason for such confusion, however. The only thing lacking in the impersonal standpoint is certain information: who one is and how what one considers relates to one. Desires, cares, values, and preferences that can be formulated impersonally remain intact. What distinguishes impersonal from personal preferences are their respective objects and the sorts of considerations that can motivate them. A preference is no less a person's preference for being impersonal.

Many of our intrinsic preferences appear to be impersonal in the sense indicated. A preference for the happiness of a particular person, or persons in general, would be impersonal. Even if our wishes for a particular person arise out of our individual relationship to that person, we do not ordinarily simply prefer her flourishing as an instance of the general personal preference that *our* friends flourish. While we might not have done so without the development of friendship, nonetheless, what we come to prefer intrinsically is *that she flourish*. And this makes the preference impersonal.

Altruistic preferences may be either personal or impersonal depending on how they are understood. A preference that *others* flourish is personal, since we cannot impersonally judge the otherness of persons. A preference that people, or that Tom, flourish, however, is impersonal.

Impersonal preferences are by no means limited to altruistic ones. General malevolence, or the specific preference that Harry suffer, is every bit as impersonal (in the sense with which we are concerned) as benevolence, whether general or particular. Nor need such preferences be limited to those concerned with benefit or harm. The intrinsic preferences that an elegant proof of a mathematical theorem be found, that the historical roots of a people be recaptured, or that the Pirates win the pennant are each impersonal.

3. The question of which, if any, impersonal preferences we have, or would have if adequately informed, and therefore which, if any, objective reasons there are for us to act, appears at this point to be unavoidably empirical. However, there would appear to be little doubt on the evidence available that objective reasons do arise for human beings in this way.[3] Bishop Butler put the point most forcefully when he urged that the presence in us of impersonal preferences for the welfare of others is "as strongly and plainly proved . . . as it could possibly be proved, supposing there was this affection in our nature" (1950, p. 23n).

While we may perhaps conceive of rational agents who can take no intrinsic interest in anything impersonally describable, it seems undeniable that we are given to such attitudes. The admiration one feels for a work of art is not directed at the experience of one's viewing it per se but at the work of art and its existence itself. The quiet solicitude felt for a mountain meadow, though involved in one's pleasure in being there, is directed toward the meadow itself. We are moved to care about it because we have experienced it, but that makes the caring no less impersonal.

4. Objective considerations move us, if they move us at all, from an impersonal standpoint. It is an important consequence of this

3. On the evidence for the existence of benevolent desires in humans, see Brandt 1976.

that the *sort* of reflective awareness necessary to establish whether an objective consideration is a reason according to our initial account is awareness of it from an impersonal perspective. In that account, something is a presumptive reason to act if full and dispassionate reflective awareness of it motivates a preference for action, other things equal. But as long as an agent considers matters from his own personal standpoint he cannot give any consideration to objective considerations in themselves. For example, a person who derives pleasure from making others suffer cannot really be said to have even considered the fact of their suffering *itself* if he only considers, gleefully, that they will be suffering at *his* hand. To consider the fact that they will suffer, itself, he must avert his eye from himself, and from them viewed in relation to himself, and consider them and their suffering independently. And this can be done only from an impersonal standpoint. To consider objective considerations rationally, then, one must adopt an impersonal standpoint.

The initial account of rational consideration in Part II seemed, at first, to be a self-centered one. And indeed it *is* the case that we cannot tell, in its terms, whether a fact is a reason for someone to act unless we can tell how *he* would be motivated on making himself vividly aware of it. Nonetheless, it is important to appreciate that even according to our initial account we cannot assess whether facts are reasons simply in terms of how a person would be motivated when he considers them from his own *personal* standpoint. Whether a person would be motivated by his vivid awareness of an objective consideration turns on how he would be motivated from an impersonal standpoint. As long as he considers matters with an eye to their relation to him he cannot be vividly aware of objective considerations themselves.

Still, why should a person even take into account facts that must be considered from an impersonal standpoint? The answer to this question is simply that there is no more reason to take into account facts that can be assessed only from a personal standpoint than there is to take into account facts that must be considered impersonally. An internalist theory of reasons is *agent centered* to the degree that the test of a fact's being a reason is how the agent would be motivated were he rationally to consider it. But such a theory is by no means necessarily *self-regarding*. Neither subjective nor objective considerations have any a priori primacy as reasons. For any consideration, then, it is true that if an agent would be motivated to prefer an act were he to be vividly aware of it on reflection, then it is a reason for him to act. For subjective considerations this can be established only by how an agent would be motivated from the personal standpoint. For objective considerations the impersonal standpoint is required. On the basis of our initial account, therefore, we may conclude that any consideration that would motivate an agent to prefer an act when the act is attentively considered from an impersonal standpoint is an objective reason for that agent.

5.   While this conclusion is significant, it is a modest one. All that we have established is that if the stated conditions are met, then objective considerations are *among* the reasons for a person to act. This refutes one version of rational egoism—the view that subjective considerations are the only reasons to act. Or, more precisely, it shows it to rest on the extremely unsure foundation of psychological egoism—the view that people can be motivated only by subjective considerations of their own interest.

We have not, however, attempted to establish, as Nagel did, that the *only* reasons to act are objective; nor could we. Moreover, as far as our initial account goes, a person *may* rationally choose personal rather than impersonal preferences if that is what he would be inclined to do on considering all, including personal, information. That is, his informed, all-things-considered preference orderings may systematically rank personal preferences over impersonal ones even if considering matters from an impersonal perspective does motivate him, other things equal, to have preferences. So as far as our initial account goes, subjective reasons may generally be *weightier* reasons than objective ones. They are weightier, other things equal, if the agent would be moved by them *more* when he considers both. There is, actually, a puzzle about how a person can bring both subjective and objective considerations together in forming an all-things-considered preference, for that appears to require a person simultaneously to see things both from personal and impersonal standpoints.[4]

6. So far the case against exclusively self-regarding theories of reasons may seem to amount to a superficial victory at best. We have shown that considerations other than self-regarding ones are among the reasons that there are for agents (like us) to act, but no more than that.

In fact, however, some objective considerations have a much greater weight as reasons than our initial account indicates. In what remains of Part III, I shall argue that only a conception of value based on objective considerations is sufficiently rich to fund a number of deeply rooted evaluative attitudes that we take toward ourselves and others. In Part IV, I shall argue that objective considerations of morally right conduct generally override subjective reasons when they conflict.

To begin the first line of thought we must introduce the notion of an *impersonally basable* preference. We recall that a preference may be impersonal even though the explanation of why one has the preference may include a history of *personal* experience, beliefs, and so on, relating to the object of the preference. Earlier we considered the example of friendship. Friends come to value the welfare of each other for its own sake. But often this results from a history of interactions in which each views matters from the personal standpoint. The other-regarding acts of friends are not simply perceived by each as acts that benefit someone or other. Rather the friend who is benefited sees the friendly act as directed toward *him*, and this inspires reciprocal friendly feelings. It is quite possible, therefore, for preferences that end up being impersonal to be

---

4. This sort of dissociation is different from the sort that Nagel argues accompanies the recognition of irreducibly subjective reasons. That dissociation is supposed to consist in the impossibility of integrating judgments about subjective reasons from the personal and impersonal standpoints. The sort of dissociation threatened here is that involved in being unable to make an all-things-considered judgment that incorporates both subjective and objective reasons. It is a considerable strength of the position offered in this book that it affords a standpoint to integrate these two perspectives (see Chapter 15, sec. 8).

the result of a history of beliefs and experience from a personal standpoint.

The notion of an impersonally basable preference contrasts with this. It is the idea of an impersonal preference that does not depend in any way on seeing things from a personal standpoint. Let us say that:

> If S would prefer that *p* be the case, were he to consider in an imaginatively vivid way all and only objective considerations relevant to *p*'s being the case, then a preference that *p* is *impersonally basable* for S.

As with our earlier accounts in Part II, a fact is relevant if imaginatively vivid consideration of it (in this instance from an impersonal standpoint) would affect S's preferences with regard to *p*, other things equal.[5]

For example, let us suppose that Hume is right in thinking that "there is no human . . . whose happiness or misery does not affect us, when brought near to us, and represented in lively colours." If so, then, a preference for human happiness and against human suffering is, other things equal, impersonally basable for us even if we happen to lack it. What makes it impersonally basable is

5. The notion of impersonally basable preference combines those of informedness and impersonality of preference. There are, however, two different ways in which these notions can be combined, and it is crucial to keep them distinct. A preference may be *informed* in our earlier sense of being one that one would have were one to be aware in a vivid way of all relevant (*including* personal) information and still be impersonal. It is impersonal if its *object* is irreducibly impersonal and if one is motivated to have it, other things equal, by consideration of (only) objective considerations. The notion of an impersonally basable preference combines informedness and impersonality in a different way. One way to think of it is that the informedness of impersonally basable preferences consists in their being preferences that one would have on considering everything relevant, *subject to the constraints of the impersonal standpoint.* A preference may be impersonally basable for a person, then, even if it is not an informed impersonal preference for that person. It may be that were S to consider everything relevant to *p* from an impersonal standpoint, he would prefer that *p* be the case even though he would not prefer that *p* be the case were he to consider *p*'s relation to *himself* (personal information) as well. He might prefer *p* when he considers it impersonally and disprefer it, for example, when he sees how it affects *his* interests.

that it can be motivated entirely from an impersonal standpoint, given suitable attention to the facts of human happiness and suffering themselves, considered quite independently of the person's relation to us.[6]

7. We are willing to regard some of our impersonal preferences as idiosyncratic, but with others, we are loath to suppose that a conflicting attitude could be impersonally basable for someone. We take the value of these states to be independent of *our own* preferences as such, and see such preferences as *appropriate* to that value rather than its source. Moreover, these preferences are apt to be of special importance to us. As I shall argue in the next chapter, our sense of our own worth and of the meaningfulness of our lives derives from them.

Consider the way in which we regard many of the things we think most important in our lives: the welfare of loved ones, work we find meaningful, efforts toward political and social goals we embrace, and the enjoyment of nature and the fruits of our common culture. We rarely suppose the value of these things to be dependent on our own *individual* tastes as such. In valuing them as we do, we do not think them good simply because *we*, as individuals, happen to prefer them. Rather, as I shall argue in the next chapter, it is only by virtue of taking their value and importance to be independent of our own individual responses to them that we can take them to endow our lives and selves with meaning and worth.

We have, it appears, a conception of value that is not relativized to ourselves as individuals. When we hold something to have this sort of value we suppose its worth to be independent of our own individual preference (whether actual, informed, or impersonal) *as such*. When we think, for example, that the elimination of racism has value in this sense, we suppose its worth not to be a

6. Consider, in this connection, a remark of W. D. Falk's: "And, maybe, that some ultimate choices are more proper for a human being than others is also something that one just has to see for himself. Supposing that one said: 'You may not feel this now, but if you thought, you would not have it in your heart to stand by while others suffer'" (1956, p. 126).

matter of idiosyncratic taste or feeling. Milton Friedman's description of a racist as one who simply has a "'taste' . . . that one does not share" (1962, p. 110), jars us by trivializing both the depth and the nature of our feeling. But does this imply that in thinking these values to transcend our individual preferences as such we are committed to a nonnaturalist metaphysics of value? Even if some nonsubjective notion of value is necessary to do justice to what we think and feel, can that notion be made intelligible only in such terms? Or at all?

That we can frame such a conception of value without nonnaturalism is apparent when we realize that taking such values to be independent of our own individual preferences does not mean that their value is independent of the responses of *any* valuing subject. The sort of value we take things to have when we assess them in the above way is perhaps best termed *intersubjective value*. It is intersubjective in two senses. First, the perspective from which such assessments of value are made is intersubjective in that it is available to all within a relevant group of valuing beings (whether members of a particular culture or the human race). Judgments of intersubjective value are not made from a personal standpoint. To ascribe this sort of value to something is to suppose that it rests on features that can be apprehended and appreciated from a perspective common to a community of valuing beings: an intersubjective standpoint. Such a perspective may not be *purely* impersonal, since it does not abstract from the information that one is a member of the relevant valuing community; but because many of our most important intersubjective values are held relative to very wide communities, such as the community of man, this difference tends in practice not to be too important. Second, intersubjective values rest on an *intersubjective agreement* in preference when the object is fully and appreciatively considered from the intersubjective standpoint. To suppose that something is valuable and important in this sense is to suppose that *anyone* within the community capable of appreciating those aspects in which its value consists would be moved to the appropriate impersonal preference by considering them.

Let us say, therefore, that something has *intersubjective value*

Objective Reasons and Intersubjective Value

(relative to a community of valuing beings S) if a preference for it is impersonally basable for *any* member of S. This means that if something has intersubjective value, any lack of preference (within the relevant group) toward that thing must be explainable either by failure to consider impersonally everything relevant or by failure or incapacity to appreciate what is apprehended. In supposing, for example, that the elimination of racism has intersubjective value, we suppose that racists do not simply differ with us in taste but that they are *blinded* to the impersonally apprehensible evils of racism, either by a refusal to consider them impersonally or by an incapacity to appreciate what they apprehend. If, we think, the blinders of privilege, self-interest, and ignorance were to be stripped away in a situation that allowed full impersonal attention, they too would share our impersonal preference.

8. This rough characterization of intersubjective value shares several important aspects with Hume's account of virtue sketched in the *Inquiry*. "When," Hume writes,

> a man denominates another his *enemy*, his *rival*, his *antagonist*, his *adversary*, he is understood to speak the language of self-love and to express sentiments peculiar to himself and arising from his particular circumstances and situation. But when he bestows on any man the epithets of *vicious* or *odious* or *depraved*, he then speaks another language and expresses sentiments in which he expects all his audience are to concur with him. He must here, therefore, depart from his private and particular situation and must choose a point of view common to him with others: he must move some universal principle of the human frame and touch a string to which all mankind have an accord and symphony. [1751/1957, p. 93][7]

7. One prominent exception is that Hume's account is given explicitly in terms of sentiment. Also, I have characterized the intersubjective value of states of affairs, whereas Hume is concerned to give an account of the sort of (intersubjective) value that a *quality of mind* has when we consider it a virtue. This raises the question, which we must consider in the next chapter, of the relation between the value of a human trait and the value of a state of affairs in which it is exemplified. Nonetheless, these two accounts square in basing the relevant intersubjective value judgments, of states of affairs and human characteristics respectively, on the universality of impersonally basable response.

141

Hume stressed the connection between judgments of value and expressions of sentiment and attitude. While he is ordinarily understood either as an emotivist or a subjectivist, and there are certainly passages that encourage that reading, his account of personal merit in the *Inquiry* makes it plain that such judgments are *appropriate* only when the attitude of favor or disfavor meets three conditions.[8] First, the attitude must be an impersonal one. Our attitude can appropriately be expressed only by the "language" of virtue when it is from an impersonal intersubjective standpoint. Otherwise we should use the "language of self-love" (expressions proper to the personal standpoint) to express ourselves. Second, our attitude must be *impersonally based*. It is not enough that we simply view the object of assessment impersonally. Rather we must consider whatever is relevant and impersonally apprehensible about it. This involves not just putting oneself in mind of things but also doing whatever is necessary to appreciate them: "But in order to pave the way for such a sentiment and give a proper discernment of its object, it is often necessary, we find, that much reasoning should precede, that nice distinctions be made, just conclusions drawn, distant comparisons formed, complicated relations examined, and general facts fixed and ascertained" (Hume 1751/1957, p. 6). Finally, we rightly express our attitude with the language of virtue only if it is indeed one with which all other human beings would concur were their attitudes also impersonally based.

Each of these conditions moves Humean judgments of virtue and, in the view I am suggesting, judgments of intersubjective value generally, farther away from personal preferences. At each stage greater and greater personality is abstracted. By assuming the impersonal standpoint we exclude all information about ourselves as such and consider the object of evaluation exclusive of our relation to it. By making our attitudes impersonally based we abstract whatever attitudes toward the object result from a history of awareness from our own personal standpoint and make ourselves aware, with developed powers of appreciation, of whatever is

8. David Falk's essays on Hume (1975 and 1976) are especially helpful on these points.

impersonally apprehensible about it. Finally, by abstracting those of our impersonally based preferences that conflict with the impersonally based preferences of others of our community, we exclude what is idiosyncratic to us. This treble abstraction leaves us with a filtrate of shared communal attitudes that forms the basis for a notion of intersubjective value.

9. The concept of *appreciation* occurs essentially in this rough characterization of intersubjective value. A particular person's failure to have an impersonal preference, say, for the fostering of a particular sort of artistic expression, will not count against its intersubjective value if the person is incapable of appreciating those aspects that motivate the impersonal preferences of others. But how exactly are we to mark the distinction between a simple difference of taste between persons and a difference in their capacity to appreciate? Or between a change in taste and its development?

We do think the capacity to appreciate some things depends on mature sensibility or developed taste, while with other things we think there to be no failure of appreciation in those who find them not to their taste. Sometimes we can give some account of what developed sensibility consists of, where "nice distinctions" can be made and "distant comparisons formed." But in other cases it is difficult to see how the development of powers of appreciation is to be distinguished from a simple change of taste. How, for example, does the acquiring of a taste for beer differ from a change in taste due to the continued drinking of it?

These are questions to which any complete theory of intersubjective value must give answers. And they are difficult questions. On the one hand we want to avoid the implausible Moorean view that developed powers of appreciation are powers of metaphysical insight. On the other hand, making the existence of intersubjective value relative to shared impersonally based response threatens us with the possibility that there is no philosophically defensible distinction between simple change and the education of sensibility and attitude. We may be vulnerable to the charge of legislating that those who do not share our predominant impersonally based attitudes simply fail to appreciate them.

My task in this book is not, however, to develop a detailed

account of intersubjective value. Rather, I have given this rough sketch in order to make four points. First, whether or not a concept of intersubjective value can be articulated in a complete and coherent way, it is a well-entrenched part of the way we see things. For better or worse some concept of intersubjective value is our own.

Second, by making judgments of intersubjective value we commit ourselves to judgments about *shared objective reasons* for acting. If *p* is a state of affairs that has intersubjective value for community *S*, then it follows that a preference that *p* is impersonally basable for any member of *S*. And this means that any member of *S*, were she to be aware, in a vivid and appreciative way, of objective considerations relevant to *p*, would be motivated, other things equal, to prefer *p*. If something has intersubjective value relative to a community therefore, there are objective reasons for *any* member of the community to promote it.

Third, while it is perhaps conceivable that rational action requires no notion of intersubjective value, many of the ways in which we regard ourselves are tied to it. As I shall argue in the next chapter, it is only if we have such a notion that we are able to value and esteem ourselves and others and to find significance in our lives. Exhibiting these connections will show the centrality of a conception of intersubjective value to us and to any rational being whose self-reflection extends to self-evaluation and self-concern.

Finally, although judgments of intersubjective value entail the existence of shared objective reasons for any member of a given community, they carry no implication about the existence of objective reasons for all rational beings, whatever their more specific nature.[9] We are told, for example, that Vulcans are not capable of the same emotional attachments that we are.[10] Consequently, there may be no reason to think that states of affairs involving the flourishing of such relationships will be an object of their impersonally based preference, and, therefore, have intersubjective value for them, even if, as it is plausible to think, they have intersub-

9. This is, however, an implication of Nagel's notion of objective value (which is the correlate of his idea of objective [universal] reason).
10. As on *Star Trek*.

144

Objective Reasons and Intersubjective Value

jective value for human beings. While there is reason for us to promote a world in which people can give expression to, and receive confirmation of, their most personal feelings in relationships of shared intimacy with others, this need not be the case for Vulcans.

We began this chapter by distinguishing two different features of Nagelian objective reasons: their impersonality and their universality. If we consider objective reasons as those whose truth can be impersonally assessed, and thus, those that rationally motivate a person from the impersonal standpoint, then objective reasons are as various as there are states of affairs for which agents would have informed impersonal preferences. While objective, however, such reasons need not be universal and may be quite idiosyncratic.

To approach Nagel's notion of a reason that is both objective and universal we have found it necessary to move from the idea of impersonally motivated preferences to that of impersonally basable preferences that would be universally shared (by members of a community). This, I have suggested, is the substance of our notion of intersubjective value. In taking there to be such values, and their existence to give us reasons to act, we commit ourselves to the belief that they exist as reasons for others of our community to act also.

CHAPTER 12

The Pervasiveness of
Intersubjective Valuation

Traditionally, two formidable obstacles have been thought to stand in the way of the view that there exist values that generate objective reasons for any person to act. And, not surprisingly, these same obstacles have figured prominently among the arguments given for versions of the DBR Thesis. To suppose that intersubjective values exist, providing reasons for agents to act even when they lack associated desires, raises these serious questions. First, what is the metaphysical category of such values (and their associated reasons)? Second, how is it that awareness of objective value can *motivate* a person?

In theories of value such as Moore's, both of these problems arise with a vengeance. In his view we are forced to accept two mysteries: we must both acknowledge the metaphysical category of the nonnatural and marvel at the miracle of rational motivation. Occam's razor warns us against the first, but the second is no less serious. Moore's view provides no integrated account of the process that leads a rational person from awareness that a state of affairs has objective value to a desire to promote it. In every case an unexplained desire to realize Moorean intrinsic goodness must be hypothesized to explain whatever motivation arises.

In the view that I have proposed of intersubjective value, neither

146

of these barriers remains. We can frame a conception that requires no nonnatural metaphysical entities and that explains how our awareness of it naturally gives rise to motivation. Intersubjective value turns out to be a complicated fact about the world: its being the case that every member of a community would prefer a state of affairs, other things equal, were his or her attitude impersonally basable. Further, since recognition and appreciation of intersubjective value *for oneself* consists in preference, this explains why our awareness of intersubjective value ordinarily is connected to motivation to promote it. When we come to appreciate something's intersubjective value for ourselves, it becomes itself an object of our own impersonal preference. We do not simply prefer intersubjectively valuable states of affairs in the abstract. While we may well have that preference also, it need not be hypothesized in each case in order to explain action taken to realize intersubjective values. The general preference is integrated with the impersonal preferences for particular states of affairs in which the recognition of their intersubjective value consists.

Intersubjective values are not relative to individual preferences per se, but they do have a more widely based relativity. One conception of intersubjective value relativizes it to the impersonally basable responses of human beings generally. It entails the existence of objective reasons for all human beings, but not necessarily for *other* rational beings. What is intersubjectively valuable for us may not be so for them, and consequently there may be no reason for them to promote it.

Nevertheless, in taking such values to generate reasons for us we commit ourselves to the *essential rationality of motivation from the impersonal standpoint*. Even if a being is unmoved by what has intersubjective value for us, if there are other considerations that would motivate him were he to consider them from an impersonal standpoint, these considerations are objective reasons for him to act.

Still, we have no a priori demonstration that objective reasons would arise in this way for *all* agents. It might be thought, therefore, that our attachment to a concept of intersubjective value is simply a curious fact about us. Could there not be rational agents who were neither subject to motivation from an impersonal standpoint nor disposed to embrace intersubjective values? In this chapter I shall seek to show that a concept of intersubjective value is not simply a projection of the human condition. Having such a notion is intimately tied to the capacities both to view one's life as meaningful and to bear attitudes toward oneself that seem central to any being whom we would recognize as self-reflectively rational: self-respect, self-esteem, and self-concern.[1] A conception of shared objective reasons for acting based on intersubjective values is not simply a human fetish: something we can easily imagine rational agents without. Because of its connection to other aspects central to our picture of rational agency it cannot be simply localized and excised. Tear it away and you tear away much that is at the heart of anything we could imagine to be rational.

1.   The connection between a conception of intersubjective value and the capacity to have *respect* for oneself is perhaps the most obvious and least likely to give pause. Two different, though related, attitudes are referred to as respect, and both may be borne to oneself.[2]

One sort of respect consists, most generally, in a disposition to give appropriate *recognition* to something by conducting oneself toward it in ways one believes respectful of what it is. Respect, in this sense, is something one can give or fail to give. And one gives it by taking appropriate account of the object of respect and by acting appropriately toward it. We are said to *have* such respect for something when we so act out of a sense of respect. The person who goes through the motions without this sense may be respectful but has no respect. What he lacks is an internalized conception of the importance or value of respectful conduct. The person who

1. My reason for focusing on these attitudes as they are borne to oneself, as opposed to others, is dialectical. Those who deny the existence of objective reasons are more likely to include within their picture of the rational agent a desire to view *oneself* in these ways. I do not mean to suggest that there is any primacy to these attitudes as self-borne. Quite the contrary.
2. This difference is discussed in detail in Darwall 1977–1978.

The Pervasiveness of Intersubjective Valuation

has *recognition respect* for something has a view both about which features of the thing warrant respect and about the appropriate conduct toward it.[3]

Recognition respect involves a notion of intersubjective value. A person who has respect for, say, another's right to privacy is inclined to give the notion what he deems appropriate weight in deciding whether to intrude on the other's personal affairs. He will be inclined to disprefer some acts and prefer others because of the way in which he believes the right to privacy bears on them. But his preferences here are not primarily about his own conduct. Insofar as he prefers *his* doing something because it is what proper respect for privacy requires, he equally prefers anyone's so acting. Recognition respect, then, involves impersonal preference: a preference that *people* conduct themselves in certain ways toward the respected object. Moreover, recognition respect involves the judgment that something is *worthy* of respect, that is, worthy of anyone's respect.[4] This means that the person who has respect for something believes that his impersonal preference for certain treatment of it is not idiosyncratic but is, rather, an attitude that is impersonally basable for anyone (in the community). And this amounts to the judgment that people's acting in the appropriate way has *intersubjective value*—that there is a shared objective reason for anyone so to act.[5]

Before we consider what it would be to have recognition respect for oneself we should notice how it contrasts with the other attitude we also refer to as respect. We may call this second attitude *appraisal respect*, since it consists in the (usually emotionally toned) positive appraisal of a person. Only persons, more precisely, beings who can have a *character*, can be objects of appraisal re-

3. For the general point that approval of something is implicitly regarded to be based on properties of the object of approval, see Pitcher 1958.
4. Of anyone, that is, within the relevant community of valuing beings.
5. Recall that the reason for anyone to promote the intersubjectively valuable state of affairs is only prima facie. One may, for example, hold self-respect to include the intersubjectively valuable state of affairs of being self-reliant. This generates a prima facie reason for anyone to enable others to be self-reliant. But that reason may be overridden, indeed systematically so, by considerations related to one's own self-reliant conduct.

spect. Unlike recognition respect, it is not something that we give or fail to give. It is rather an attitude of positive appraisal that we may express or show with our behavior but that demands no particular behavior from us. To have appraisal respect is not necessarily to have a view about how it is appropriately expressed.

The difference between recognition and appraisal respect may be illustrated by the difference in these attitudes as they are borne toward persons considered as such. In the familiar Kantian view, all persons are, by virtue of their rational capacity, entitled to respect. This is consistent with its also being the case that in another sense some persons are more or less *deserving* of respect as persons. No inconsistency arises, since different sorts of respect are involved. Any person can claim title to recognition respect; a person may or may not deserve appraisal respect.

Our respect on the whole for someone is an appraisal of the person's whole character; in addition, we may speak of having respect for people in particular roles. The grounds for these more specific assessments often include skills that are not simply traits of character. Thus the respect that one social worker has for another *as a social worker* may be based on her ability to use her experience and skills to the benefit of her clients. Even here, however, it is significantly skills and their use, and not simply talent, that we respect, for both of these involve traits of character.

Appraisal respect requires a conception of intersubjective value. Like recognition respect, appraisals of a person's respect-worthiness are both made from an impersonal, intersubjective standpoint and implicitly assumed not to be based on idiosyncratic preference. They involve, therefore, a valuation of the person that is intersubjective, both in the sense that it is taken to be impersonally basable and in the sense that we believe that it would be shared by others were their attitudes also so based.

Such an intersubjective valuation of a person's character, however, is not identical with holding any particular *state of affairs* to have intersubjective value. The judgment that someone is to be respected for her fair and sensitive dealings with others, for example, is not *identical* with the judgment that a state of affairs in which she expresses these traits has intersubjective value. So it might be objected that in one's taking as a *reason* for action the fact that such action is something to be respected in persons, a person does not commit herself to the proposition that anybody's so acting is an intersubjectively valuable state of affairs that there is a reason for anyone (including her) to promote. There is a logical gap between the thought that there is reason for me to be courageous, because that is to be respected in anyone, and the thought that there is reason for anyone to promote states of affairs in which people are courageous. This gap is closed, however, by the account I have proposed of intersubjective value. In that view, the state of affairs of somebody's acting courageously has intersubjective value just in case any human being would prefer it, other things equal, were his attitude impersonally basable. *If we consider both in an informed way from an impersonal standpoint*, it seems inconceivable that we should have a favorable attitude toward a particular trait of character (and consequently toward persons on account of their having and exercising it) and not, *other things equal*, toward the state of affairs of its being exercised in situations that call for it. Any consideration that motivates one preference would motivate the other, other things equal.

Both recognition and appraisal respect (and their contraries) are tied to a conception of intersubjective value. This general truth finds special application in the capacity to bear these attitudes toward oneself. Of the two, appraisal respect is perhaps the simplest to extend to the self, since, like any being with a character, one may be appraised for respect by oneself. But what about recognition self-respect? As an attitude, recognition respect for any individual thing requires some view about its general character that warrants respect and about the sort of respect warranted. This means that the capacity to have recognition respect for ourselves requires some view of our nature in virtue of which we hold certain treatment of ourselves by ourselves to be warranted. At the least this will require a view about the intersubjective value of (and hence, shared objective reasons to promote) states of affairs in which any beings with that nature treat themselves in certain ways.

2.   It is unsurprising that the capacity to bear one's own respect involves a conception of value as creating objective reasons for any member of one's general community. Respect, is, after all, an

attitude closely associated with the moral. Appraisal respect may be considered an assessment of aspects of a person relevant to moral praise and blame. And attempts to systematize our notions of moral right and wrong often take as a fundamental organizing idea some specific interpretation of the recognition respect that, it is held, is appropriate to all creatures of a certain sort. Since it is essential to our notion of morality that the validity of moral judgment is independent of personal preference and interest as such, it is not at all surprising that someone who has internalized a notion of respect would be committed to the view that there are intersubjectively valuable states of affairs that any person has reason to promote.

Just for this reason, however, we may think it not at all difficult to imagine a rational agent without such notions and without, consequently, the capacity or desire to bear his own respect. If ethics is, as many have urged, distinct from reason, why should we suppose that any rational agent must confront his own respect or lack of it? All that has been shown is that *if* he does, he must acknowledge objective reasons valid for all persons. But that does not mean *that* he must, and hence, that, for any rational agent, some objective reasons must exist.

Moreover, even if an agent does not care to bear his own respect, this does not mean that he cannot engage in any sort of self-appraisal. The attitude we call self-esteem is by no means limited to the assessment of moral character; there seem to be no logical limits at all to the kinds of things a person can hold to warrant self-esteem. So could we not perfectly well imagine a rational being who had the capacity and desire to bear his own esteem but who lacked any conception at all of intersubjective value?

We group together a variety of attitudes toward ourselves under the heading of self-esteem and do not usually well distinguish them.[6] Indeed, in some cases we have no proper word for them, though description makes their content clear. Most usually, what we have in mind is some kind of positive *evaluative judgment* of

---

6. One, a sense of the worth of our very existence and flourishing, I shall discuss below in sec. 5.

ourselves. Here, however, the relevant evaluation *is* intersubjective. We can make the kind of *appraisal* of ourselves that comprises self-esteem only by taking an impersonal, intersubjective standpoint and assessing ourselves from it. Although self-appraisal is by no means limited to human qualities that we take to have moral relevance, it is tied to a notion of qualities estimable in people more generally. If I am disposed to think well of myself on account of some feature, this commits me to thinking it a feature positively relevant in appraising people in some more general reference group with which I identify. The real vanity of a person whose self-esteem rests on fatuous grounds is his presumption that those grounds are genuinely admirable.

Evaluative self-esteem ordinarily involves an appraisal of oneself within the set of individuals with whom one fundamentally *identifies*, most broadly, perhaps, within the human species.[7] To have this sort of self-esteem requires, therefore, some notion of qualities that are admirable or estimable in any human being.[8]

A positive appraisal of oneself is thus implicitly a judgment that certain qualities are estimable in any member of one's community.[9] These appraisals share the two essential general features of intersubjective value judgments: they are assumed to be impersonally basable and to coincide with the impersonally basable preferences of others. While the object of self-esteem plainly is the self, it is so in an impersonal way. The moment we become conscious that we esteem ourselves for certain qualities that we do not admire in others, something must give way.

We may, of course, have subjective reasons for desiring or

7. I am indebted to Hudson 1977, which treats the role of identification in self-respect.
8. This point is eloquently made in Lovejoy 1961, pp. 102–105. This book, which deserves to be much better known, traces the role of *approbativeness*, the desire that others (and one) have a good opinion of one, in eighteenth-century Western thought.
9. Seeming counterexamples can be accommodated when we consider a more fundamental basis for esteem. Thus Sarah may esteem herself for her capacity to run a marathon though she does not think that the casual jogger need be able to run so far to warrant similar self-esteem. But at a more fundamental level what she esteems is her accomplishment given certain physical equipment, conditions, etc., and this commits her to similar judgments about similar others.

encouraging certain qualities in ourselves that we would not esteem in others. Someone may think, for example, that he should encourage a callousness to the fate of others in himself, since it will better enable him to advance his own interests at their expense; but that does not mean that he thinks better *of* himself for having that quality. A positive judgment of oneself commits one to an impersonal valuing of certain qualities in others also.

That self-esteem has these implications may seem questionable when we consider its intimate tie to the distinctly powerful personal emotion of *pride*. Pride is not at all plausibly regarded as simply a special instance, in our own case, of a more general impersonal attitude of esteem for certain qualities in persons generally. Although it is perhaps not the very same thing as the sort of self-esteem now under consideration, pride is related to it. Annette Baier has recently pointed out (following Hume's famous discussion) that the object of pride is never simply oneself but always some particular thing related to oneself (1978, p. 36). While self-esteem is usually grounded in our perceptions of certain features in us, its object is the self as a whole: *I* am estimable, *I* am no good. Of course we know that people's assessments of their own worth are notoriously variable and subject to the rising and sinking fortunes of the moment. [10] But that does not mean that self-esteem does not have the self as a whole as object; it simply means that our appraisals and, more important, the feelings that both arise from and influence them are rarely subject to careful, all-things-considered judgments. The very reason that failures of the moment can be so devastating is that they loom large in our (momentary) assessment of our *whole* worth.

Pride, however, is always taken in something or other in particular. We have the self in view, but it is always considered in some aspect. We are proud of this, take pride in that. Still, there exists this important connection between self-esteem and pride: whatever qualities ground our self-esteem are qualities of which we are proud.

Donald Davidson (1978, p. 748), in an approving discussion of

---

10. On this point see Gergen 1971, p. 37.

Hume's account, believes him to regard pride as simply the specification in our own case of a more general attitude of approval. For example, a pride in one's fine house, Davidson contends, is both caused by and grounded in a general attitude of esteem for the owners of fine houses. Baier argues, however, that this is almost certainly mistaken as an account of Hume's view. Hume believed pride to be caused by a separate pleasure taken in the specific thing in which pride is taken. Moreover, Davidson's account does not ring true. It does not capture the special ardor of pride, the jealous solicitude for those things in which *we* take pride. Were pride as Davidson imagines, the proud person would have no more special feeling for those things in which he takes pride than he would for those of which he judges others to be justifiably proud.

If pride is not itself a specific instance of a more general esteem, then perhaps there is no connection between, on the one hand, the capacity to feel pride and self-esteem and, on the other, a conception of qualities that are intersubjectively estimable: estimable in anyone by anyone. Even Hume's view, however, maintains this connection. He speaks, significantly, of the "shining qualities" of the causes of pride and vanity (1739/1967, p. 304). The metaphor is apt. For, as Baier remarks (1978, p. 38), when we feel pride we shine "in the reflected glory" of that of which we are proud. And we suppose its reflection to be intersubjectively available—to be perceptible to others if they will but consider what we are proud of in an impersonal and open way. Further, qualities that shine in and for us will likewise shine in others for us. We may likely not notice them with the ardor that marks our own pride, but we are committed to viewing them as qualities worthy of note. Perhaps ironically, then, the capacity to feel pride, and the sort of self-esteem grounded in qualities of which one is proud, does require a conception of qualities that are generally estimable.

As we noted before with appraisal self-respect, there is still a gap between the judgment that a particular quality is to be admired in human beings and the judgment that it is a good thing (intersubjectively valuable) that human beings exhibit that quality. But once again this gap is closed by the suggested account of intersubjective value. If our self-esteem is grounded in the thought that a given property, *P*, is our own, then we are committed to the view that *P* is to be esteemed in members of a more general community with which we identify. And such a property is thus genuinely estimable just in case it is a property to which any member would respond with favor, other things equal, were his or her attitude toward it impersonally basable. Similarly, the state of affairs consisting in *P*'s being true of a person has intersubjective value just in case a preference for it, other things equal, is impersonally basable for any member. From the impersonal standpoint there could be no reason for one to favor a particular property or any member who has that property and not to favor, other things equal, the state of affairs of a member's having it. Therefore, such a property is only genuinely estimable if the state of affairs of a person's having it (and exercising it when appropriate) has intersubjective value. Judgments of the intersubjectively estimable, implied by estimates of self-worth, themselves imply judgments of the intersubjective value, other things equal, of the existence of the intersubjectively estimable.

3. Sometimes what we have in mind by self-esteem is nothing so formal and inherently systematic as a judgment or appraisal of one's own value but simply some kind of favorable attitude to oneself: liking oneself or being the object of one's own pleasure. Since we may so respond to ourselves, or to something in us, without having any view about our value as being grounded in that quality, no question need arise of a consistent extension of our view to the similar value of others who share that quality. While this is undoubtedly true, the capacity to bear such attitudes toward aspects of oneself requires the capacity to respond to similar aspects in others and, therefore, to be motivated from the impersonal standpoint. No question of consistency may arise, but one will be capable of liking, and taking pleasure in the awareness of, certain qualities in oneself only if one is also disposed to respond to their presence in others. The sheer idea of oneself gives one nothing to respond to. If one likes oneself it will be because there are things about or in oneself to which one responds favorably, the awareness of which provides one with pleasure. One's liking of various things

about one cannot be constructed out of a basic liking for oneself (though we may be disposed to find things *about* ourselves to like), for there is nothing in the simple idea of oneself to be liked or not liked. Rather, such a liking for oneself can be constructed only out of responses to qualities one takes to be one's own. Plainly these are qualities that others may have as well, and since it is our responses to the qualities themselves that are basic, the qualities will tend to be an object of favor whether perceived in oneself or in others.[11]

Following Hume we may distinguish two different ways in which a favorable attitude toward oneself or others can arise. Hume characterizes virtue in the *Inquiry* as "whatever mental action or quality gives to a spectator the pleasing sentiment of approbation" (1751/1957, p. 107). But not all desirable qualities of a person give rise to favor in the same way. A relevant distinction marked by Hume is that between qualities that we find "immediately agreeable" and those that we favor because of their "usefulness" (1751/1957, secs. 6 and 7).

The importance of this distinction for our purposes is that the only possible way in which an attitude to oneself might bear the imprint of the personal standpoint would be if it were an attitude to oneself, or to qualities in one, *as related to oneself*—for example, as being useful to oneself. If we are capable of direct or intrinsic response to certain qualities in us, to finding such qualities immediately agreeable, then our response to ourselves is an impersonal one. It is essentially informed neither by our beliefs that such qualities are in ourselves nor by the belief that they are useful *to* ourselves.[12] Indeed, since it is informed by no beliefs about our own position relative to the person having the requisite quality at all, we will only have that response to the quality in ourselves if we

---

11. This is not, of course, to say that one *will* always respond equally to these qualities in oneself and others. For one thing, we typically have a particular interest in esteem for ourselves that we do not always have for others. But this does not gainsay the point that the likings or evaluations out of which this esteem is itself constructed in a response to the qualities themselves, which presupposes a capacity to respond to them *whether* in ourselves or others.

12. By this statement I do not mean that one could not in addition be pleased that the qualities are one's own.

are disposed to find it "immediately agreeable" in persons generally.

To make this contrast clear, consider the difference between taking direct pleasure in the thought of one's own wit and liking it purely for its consequences, say, that it enables one to satisfy other desires.[13] It is only in the latter event that response is informed by the personal standpoint. If one is disposed to like oneself because one is witty, it can only be because of a general tendency to respond favorably to wit. As with pride, this does not mean that liking one's own wit is simply an instance of liking wit generally. We may be more likely to attend to, and be jealous of, qualities that we like in ourselves when they are considered in connection *to us*. Nonetheless, we must be capable of responding to them in others if *they* are to strike us when we consider them our own.

Interestingly enough, the implicit impersonality of a like or dislike for ourselves does not always characterize our responses to others. Often these responses are very much influenced by personal considerations. We come to be favorably or unfavorably disposed toward people not just because we like or dislike something in them (viewed impersonally, as in admiration) but often because we see their acts to express certain attitudes *toward us*. For example, we may respond not simply to our apprehension that someone is a friendly person but to her friendliness to us. If we come to discover that a smile, gesture, or benefaction was not in fact intended for us, we may cancel our favor even though we still have an awareness of the very same qualities in the person.

Conversely, being hurt by another will often elicit an unfavorable attitude toward a person that is by no means impersonal. Our good feelings for another may survive our impersonal awareness of injuries rendered by him to others only to be undermined by a personal injury from him.

Although these responses of favor and disfavor to others are plainly personal, they appear to have no analogues in attitudes that

13. Note that there is a difference between taking pleasure in the thought that one is witty (a reflective pleasure) and enjoying being witty, just as there is a difference between enjoying the feeling of potency and having one's self-esteem enhanced by the thought of one's own potency.

we may bear toward ourselves. We can neither please nor hurt ourselves in the way that others can by directing our own good or ill will toward ourselves. If we could, we would be capable of having with ourselves the sort of relationships, with all the complicated levels of mutual response, that we can with others.[14] But we cannot. We can neither be laid low by our own cutting remarks about ourselves nor be buoyed by the thought that at least we care for ourselves. Such responses are essentially interactive; they are reciprocals for attitudes that others are perceived to bear toward us. Biological persons are capable of them only by splitting into multiple psychological selves.

Some evidence might seem to suggest, however, that we can bear such interactively responsive attitudes toward ourselves. For example, the realization that we have acted in a way that is manifestly self-frustrating may engender anger with ourselves. But there is an illuminating difference between this situation and one in which anger is elicited in one person toward another. Our anger toward ourselves does not arise, because one sees that action as *self-directed*: an attempt by oneself to sabotage one's aims. Of course, we may come to believe that our so acting is due to deeply seated self-destructive motives. But that discovery is not an occasion for anger at ourselves so much as sadness or depression (or possibly relief). When we have discovered ourselves to be "our own worst enemy" it is impossible to gain the satisfaction of victory over that enemy by unleashing our anger on it. Any such infliction of pain is an infliction on ourselves.

Thus, though some of our responses to others bear very clearly the imprint of the personal standpoint, this cannot completely be the case with our attitude toward ourselves. Our liking or not liking ourselves is not simply the result of our awareness of our own self-directed actions. A being's response of intrinsic favor or disfavor to himself is a response to himself from an impersonal standpoint. Consequently, any being capable of such an attitude must be susceptible to motivation by objective considerations.

14. On the role of mutually reflective attitudes in relationships, see Nagel 1979, pp. 39–52.

4. There are many distinguishable attitudes included within the idea of self-love or self-concern, some of which, it is evident, are irreducibly and wholly personal. It is difficult to imagine a better example of a personal attitude than self-love understood as the desire to promote one's own happiness, welfare, or interest. There is, however, a sort of self-concern that consists in the capacity to respond spontaneously to the apprehension of one's condition—to be moved to sorrow (and to action)) on realizing that things are not going well for one or to happiness or joy on realizing that one is flourishing. This sort of spontaneous self-concern does involve an impersonal response; it requires the capacity to be moved by *plights* in general—the capacity to *care*. The clearest instances of this sort of attitude are, of course, with respect to others. Consider the difference between a trustee who is simply charged with promoting the welfare of another and a person who genuinely cares about the other. Though both are in a certain sense concerned with the other's welfare, only the latter will be moved spontaneously to sorrow or joy by his apprehension of the condition of the other considered in itself.[15]

The sort of heartfelt concern that one person can have for another can also be had for oneself. One can be moved spontaneously to feel sorrow or joy for oneself and moved to do things for one's own sake in the same way that a person who genuinely cares for another can act for his sake.[16] The crucial point is that one's heart can be open to oneself only if one has a heart to open, if one has the capacity to respond with sorrow, joy, and spontaneous concern. And this is a capacity to be moved by an impersonal view of a creature's condition. To feel sorrow for oneself is to be moved by one's pitiable condition, but one can do this only if one can respond with pity to what one (impersonally) deems pitiable. To be moved to feel happy for oneself is, likewise, to be moved by one's happy condition. But one can do that only if one can respond with joy to what one (impersonally) deems joyful.

The main character in Sartre's short story, "The Wall," facing

15. See Blum's discussion of this point (1981, pp. 146–151).
16. The last section can be illuminated by noting that one cannot do these things as an *expression* of concern for oneself. That would require some sort of interactive relationship with oneself.

his own impending execution while locked in a cell with his other doomed colleagues, describes his condition: "I felt inhuman: I could pity neither the others nor myself" (1975, p. 294). Pity, whether for oneself or others, is felt from an intersubjective standpoint—in this instance from a human standpoint, the narrator seems to say. We express our common humanity with others when we feel such emotions, because in order to feel them we must occupy a place they can share. Only I can desire my own happiness simply because it is mine, because only I can take my own personal standpoint and have desires from it. But not only I can care about myself in the sense of being able to respond to and be concerned about my plight as such. Indeed, because such responses are from an intersubjective standpoint, I can have them only if I can similarly respond to similar plights of others. This particular sort of self-concern, therefore, involves a susceptibility to motivation by objective considerations of welfare or harm.

5.   In having the capacity to be moved to joy or sorrow by the apprehension of our condition and, in the same spirit, to desire our welfare, we come to a sense of the intersubjective *importance* or *value* of our flourishing. We see that we and our welfare *matter* in a way that transcends the mere fact that *we*, both individually and personally, prefer our own welfare. Our response to our condition is an impersonal one that we can both experience others sharing and imagine yet others sharing were they to consider our condition with an open heart. We suppose, that is, that our existence and flourishing have an *intersubjective value* that gives anyone *capable* of recognizing that value through his own sympathetic response an objective reason to promote it.

Our sense of the intersubjective value of our existence and flourishing, then, is intimately bound up with the impersonal response to ourselves that we experience in caring for ourselves and that we experience from others who care about us.[17] But if this

17. This statement misleadingly suggests that we come to a sense that others would care about us by realizing that our caring for ourselves is impersonally based. The truth is, of course, quite the reverse. We initially come to care about ourselves by identification with significant others who care about us. See Mead 1934.

is what supports our view of the value of our own existence and welfare then we must also so view the existence and welfare of any being to whom we would respond similarly were we to consider them with an open heart.

This is the good sense of Hume's view of the centrality of *sympathy* in ethics. Our capacity for sympathy, both with others and with ourselves, underwrites our conviction that the flourishing of any creature with whom we are capable of sympathy has a value and importance that gives any of us an objective reason to promote it. Moreover, we can see also how an ethic based on sympathy will be fundamentally teleological. The conviction to which our capacity for sympathy brings us is that the flourishing of creatures has value *independently of how it is brought about.* The reasons for people to promote creature flourishing consist in the intersubjective value of that state of affairs. Regardless of how it occurs, it is prima facie good that creatures flourish and bad that they suffer. And the value of acts that promote the former and prevent the latter derive from the value of the resulting states of affairs.

Because we are capable of caring about ourselves and others in this way, we come to a sense of the reasons for not harming them that spring not simply from any independent conviction regarding the wrongfulness of the *act* of harming them but from the sense that their harm is itself a bad thing, whether or not it is brought about by an act. It is important to stress that this way of regarding ourselves and others is tied to our nature as *emotional* beings. Take away that aspect of ourselves and though we would perhaps recognize the remainder as a rational agent, we would have removed this basis for seeing our welfare and existence as having intersubjective value. So we would have taken away the teleological ethic internal to caring—our conviction that at least part of the value of beneficent conduct derives from the intersubjective value of creature flourishing itself.

As important as this conviction is to us, I shall suggest that there is another basis for a conception of intersubjectively valuable conduct that is neither teleological nor limited to rational creatures who share our capacity for sympathy. In Chapter 15, I shall argue that it is compellingly rational for *any* rational agent to act on

principles on which it would be chosen from an impartial standpoint that every agent act. In particular, I shall argue that these
principles include deontological principles of the right to guide
conduct in conditions of possible cooperation and conflict. This
ethic is different from that based on our capacity for sympathy, but
it is by no means incompatible with it. Indeed, I think the view
that ultimately emerges of teleological and deontological *aspects* of
our conception of ethics, having their different sources in different
aspects of us, is most adequate to the complicated truth.

6. There has been, as the reader will have noticed, a pattern to
the reflections in the chapter to this point. In each case, I have
linked the capacity to have a particular sort of attitude toward
ourselves to a capacity similarly to respond to others. There is a
general explanation for these links. In each instance the response
to ourselves is occasioned by our awareness of something in us or
about us that is the *basis* for the attitude. If we have appraisal
respect for ourselves it is because we take ourselves to have
qualities that we would respect in anyone. If we feel sorry or happy
for ourselves it is because of a broader capacity to be moved by the
conditions of beings more generally. If we like or esteem ourselves
it is, again, in virtue of liking or esteeming certain things in us to
which we would similarly respond in others.

In each case the relevant attitude cannot be based solely on the
bare idea of ourselves. That gives us nothing to respond to. Nor
can our attitudes toward ourselves arise, as do some of our personal
attitudes toward others, as reciprocals for attitudes directed toward
us. We can only bear these attitudes toward ourselves because of
their basis in impersonal responses that we can have to persons and
their qualities generally. It is this aspect of these attitudes, self-
borne, that commits us to, or puts us into a position to elaborate, a
conception of intersubjective value, of states of affairs that would
be the object of anyone's favor were his attitude fully impersonally
based. For any being to bear these various evaluative attitudes
toward himself and to regard the values on which they are based as
reasons to act, he must acknowledge the intersubjectivity both of
those values and, consequently, of associated objective reasons.

7. The final aspect of ourselves that I shall seek to relate to a conception of intersubjective value is our desire to see our lives as *meaningful*. This is more properly an attitude toward our lives than it is toward ourselves, but it is extremely difficult to separate the two. The person who thinks her life meaningless is apt to feel empty and diminished herself as well. Conversely, the sense that our lives have meaning enhances our sense of our own worth.

It is no coincidence that the things for which we care are also said to have meaning for us. We consider something that we seriously care about to place constraints on our lives. We may not feel these *as* constraints if there is nothing conflicted or halfhearted about our concern, but we nonetheless suppose that things that genuinely matter and give our lives meaning have a kind of importance that does not simply derive from our own individual and personal preferences for them. In caring deeply about her craft, for example, a craftsperson is disposed to take pains with it. In her view, the craft warrants care and not just in the sense that it cannot be successfully executed without watchful attention. A game such as pick up sticks may require care in that sense. The sense in which she believes her craft to warrant care is rather that the activity, its products, and the tradition she carries on are things of genuine worth and importance; they matter. The way in which she believes they matter is not simply that they matter *to her*—though, of course, they do. She believes their worth to transcend her own preferences as such. Their worth is, she believes, intersubjectively available. Others can recognize it and affirm it. It matters not simply to her, in the way that objects of either idiosyncratic or personal preference do. It is, she believes, something others would also favor were they to view it impersonally and understand it as she does. In short, she sees its value to be intersubjective and not simply to derive from her own individual preference as such.

Something can give meaning to our lives only if we believe it to have intersubjective value. The reason for this is simple. Values that give our lives meaning both inspire and root our lives. They give our spirits the very air they need to breathe. They give us a rootedness: a place to stand, to defend, and to hold precious. But the value of what both enlivens and supports us cannot itself be based on our own individual responses as such. Since we could derive neither breath nor support from them unless we perceived them to be of value, we cannot see their own value as emanating simply from us. The moment we are aware that something has value only *for us* we cannot draw the craftsperson's distinction between the way she regards pick up sticks (which she may intrinsically like) and the way she regards her craft. The difference is not that one is liked more than the other but that one is taken to be more important or serious, a more meaningful enterprise. That which endows our life with meaning must be something whose value we regard as self-transcendent.

In general, what is required in order to see one's life as meaningful is to see it as a worthwhile kind of life for a person, a human being, or, at any rate, for a being of *some* sort (impersonally described) with whom we identify. Any attitude that endows something with value sufficient to support our sense of meaningfulness and importance, then, must be an *impersonal* one. Further, in taking something to be a worthwhile activity for any person to engage in we suppose it to be such that any person, were he capable of appreciating it, and were he to comprehend whatever there is to appreciate about it from an impersonal standpoint, would favor it. That is, we suppose the values that endow our lives with meaning to be intersubjective.

It is easy to be somewhat misled here. We certainly do not think that to find one's life meaningful because it embodies a particular value one must regard the importance of that value *to one* to be a reflection of its intersubjective importance, of the importance it should have to anyone. The person who devotes himself to his children gives them an importance in his life that he need not think children should have for everyone. Nor as they acquire more and more importance to him need his view about the intersubjective importance of childrearing change. The point, rather, is that in order for him to see his own childrearing as a meaningful activity at all he must regard childrearing as intersubjectively valuable: one that is at least prima facie worthwhile for anyone to engage in. But there are, of course, many other activities that are similarly worthwhile. There are a great variety of worthwhile lives, and to live one sort in a way adequate to the care that one thinks it warrants, one must make commitments that rule out others. The importance that the particular intersubjective values we choose to embody come to have *to us* is a product of our own individual situation, commitments, and even preferences. It does not reflect a view of their intersubjective importance, nor is the pursuit of what one holds to have intersubjective worth sufficient to endow one's live with meaning. There may be many lives that one thinks intersubjectively worthy but that one would not find fulfilling.

8. I shall close this chapter by briefly considering the relation between intersubjective value and the good of *community*. This is an important topic, one whose surface we shall be able only to scratch.

Intersubjective value and community are interpenetrating notions. We have defined the former by its relation to the latter, and certainly community cannot itself be adequately understood independently of the idea of shared intersubjective values. In saying, therefore, that the attitudes discussed in this chapter require a conception of intersubjective value, we should add that they require a conception of community—of individuals with whom one *identifies* in taking the intersubjective standpoint implicit in intersubjective valuation. This is a pregnant and suggestive idea. It means that when we pursue ends on account of their intersubjective value, when we derive a sense of the significance of our lives because of them, or when we allow our sympathies to be engaged, we implicitly identify with others and affirm community with them. Part of the good of community, then, is simply a shared sense of the importance of what the community finds intersubjectively valuable. But this is by no means all. A community's sharing certain values begets a sense of the importance of sharing the community's sense of values; that is, giving and receiving *expressions* of that shared sense.

What might be called the *expressive* aspect of conduct, as it relates to the common acceptance of values, is a much-neglected topic. By evidently and openly prizing intersubjective values held in common with others, we not only foster the values themselves but also express our identification with others and affirm the importance of their lives, insofar as they manifest those values. By responding to others with concern for their plight, we bestow upon them the benefits of our expressed concern, our expressed sense of their intersubjective importance and, consequently, of our identification with them. [18]

Consider the difference in the way those who pursue a common end regard colleagues, who share their sense of the end's importance, as opposed to others, who pursue the end purely for ulterior purposes. Those who defend their homeland out of loyalty and a commitment to its survival, for example, are apt to regard their comrades differently from mercenaries fighting for the same end. Only the pursuits of the former express community with them.

These remarks are only the beginning of an account of the goods of community and interpersonal relationship. It is significant, however, that the proposed account of intersubjective value enables us to make this beginning.

Our attachment to a notion of intersubjective value is not a simply localizable or insular aspect of ourselves. It and the underlying capacity to be motivated impersonally pervade a whole panoply of ways in which we are given to regarding ourselves, our lives, and each other. It is not surprising that any being who is profoundly social and inclined to partake of community will embrace an intersubjective notion of value. What is surprising, though, is that this notion, or the capacity to respond impersonally that funds it, is also necessary for a variety of attitudes that seem on their face to be personal: self-esteem, self-respect, self-concern, and the desire to find one's life meaningful. In each case the personality of the attitude is superficial. A being is capable of any of them only if it is susceptible to impersonal motivation by objective considerations. And some require a conception of intersubjective value that generates shared objective reasons. For any being capable of any of these attitudes, therefore, there will be objective reasons to act.

---

18. Particularly interesting in this regard is Adam Smith's description of the "commerce" in communal and friendly feelings: "These affections, that harmony, this commerce, are felt not only by the tender and the delicate, but by the rudest vulgar of mankind, to be of more importance to happiness than all the little services which could be expected to flow from them" (quoted in Wills 1978, p. 193). See also Blum 1981, pp. 140–151.

Part IV

Reason and Right

CHAPTER 13

The Hobbesian Approach

We may view Part III as having established three significant propositions. First, objective reasons exist for any being who is capable of being motivated from an impersonal standpoint. Second, we possess a concept of intersubjective value a rough account of which shows there to be objective reason for any member of a community to promote what has intersubjective value. And third, any being who can bear his own respect, esteem, or spontaneous concern, or see his life as significant, must also be capable of impersonal motivation. For any such being, therefore, there will be objective reasons to act.

However significant these attitudes are to us, though, there is still the possibility that they have nothing to do with rationality per se. Could not perfectly rational beings exist without them and without, therefore, the concept of intersubjective value they involve? In short, could there not be beings for whom there are no objective reasons to act at all even though, we may imagine, they are often in a position to benefit others or not to harm them, states we believe there is objective reason to promote?

It is a conceit, surely, to think that whatever we take to endow our lives with meaning, or to have intersubjective value for all human beings, would or should be so regarded by any rational agent. Moreover, within human societies a number of distinct communities may exist with quite different and to some degree conflicting conceptions of intersubjective good. Nonetheless, it is an important aspect of some considerations that we take them to be objective reasons for any rational agent.

In particular, we have a conception of *morality* or *right conduct* whose most fundamental requirements and recommendations are thought to provide reasons for any agent who is capable of rational action and who exists in the company of others. Morality, so conceived, is distinguished from the particular mores or conventions of actual societies or their subgroups. It is thought, rather, to be a set of requirements and recommendations, whether substantive or procedural, that at some level of generality apply to all beings with the capacity to recognize and regulate their behavior by them.

Even if we may not expect any rational creature to share the sense of intersubjective value of our specific community or to have the capacity for sympathy requisite for him to view our welfare *itself* as having intersubjective value, we may well expect him to recognize the validity of *certain* moral requirements regarding interactions with us. We may think, for example, that he would have reason to recognize a requirement of fairness or a prohibition against wanton cruelty, even if we must lack his sympathy. In thinking this, we must consequently also think that the validity of such moral requirements cannot solely be based on the intersubjective value of states of affairs we bring about by moral action. We are committed to a conception of the moral value of *conduct* that is sui generis and not simply derivative from the nonmoral intersubjective value of states of affairs. [1]

These different elements are characteristic of a Kantian view of morality. Moral requirements are, in Kant's terms, *categorical*. They provide reasons for any being to whom they apply, and the most general and basic ones apply to all rational beings. [2] Their

1. That the *concept* of moral value or rightness is not simply derivative from other concepts of value, subjective or intersubjective, is consistent with the thesis that what it is right to do is to promote such values.
2. Although at times he gives a contrary indication, Kant's most fundamental theses about morality do not require that all categorical imperatives apply to all

universal application is assured by their basis in our rational nature. Neither our capacity for sympathy nor a conception of the intersubjective value of creature flourishing to which it gives rise is sufficient by itself to form the notion of morally right and wrong action. That requires, he believed, the idea of a *law* under which we stand solely by virtue of being able to conceive it. But it is precisely this, Kant argued, that constitutes properly rational action: "Only a rational being has the capacity of acting according to the conception of laws" (1785/1959, p. 29; Ak. p. 412).[3] Even though the moral law directs us to consider the welfare of others, the sense that it is *right* to do so, and *wrong* not to, is not simply derivative from our thinking that it is a good thing that people flourish. Indeed, we may think acts to be morally required even if we think that they bring into existence no state of affairs that would be good, however brought about.

While other elements of Kant's theory of morals, for example, his absolutism, perhaps reflect rather poorly any very widely shared view about morality, his insistence that moral requirements are categorical expresses our common sense about an important part of ethics. Consider, for example, the requirement of fairness or reciprocity implicit in the "natural law" formulation of the categorical imperative: "Act as though the maxim of your action were by your will to become a universal law of nature" (Kant 1785/1959, p. 39; Ak. p. 421).[4] It is notorious that teleological theories of ethics, such as Hume's, that seek to base all of ethics on our capacity for sympathy (and hence on our capacity to recognize the intersubjective value of creature flourishing itself), have difficulty with the ideas of justice and fairness. As we ordinarily conceive it, the reasons that exist for doing what is just, in a particular case at any rate, do not appeal to the value of what the just act will

rational beings. What is central to his view is that any such imperative must be grounded in a principle that does apply to all rational beings: the categorical imperative (in its various formulations). On this point see Buchanan 1977.

3. Compare here Butler's criticism of Shaftesbury that benevolence can only be the sum of virtue if "it is not spoken of as a blind propension, but as a principle in reasonable creatures, and so to be directed by their reason" (1950, p. 77).

4. Colin Strang (1960–1961) maintains that the force of generalization arguments is their appeal to fairness.

bring about considered in abstraction from how it is brought about. They appeal, rather, to a notion of right conduct that includes the requirement of fairness itself. The reason to act fairly, we believe, is simply that fairness requires it. This explains why we view fairness as something that morality demands of any being capable of regulating his conduct by the principles of fairness, whether or not he can sympathize with our flourishing itself. Only if the reasons to be fair were derivative from values that require sympathy to be recognized would the bindingness of this part of ethics be thus restricted.

Kant termed "material" any "practical principles which presuppose an object (material) of the faculty of desire as the determining ground of the will" (1788/1956, p. 19; Ak. p. 21). And as a psychological hedonist he was led to think that "all material practical principles are, as such, of one and the same kind and belong under the general principle of self-love or one's own happiness" (ibid., p. 20; Ak. p. 22). This way of conceiving the matter, however, obscures more than it enlightens, for there is, as we have seen, a very real difference between reasons to act that are based on our own personal preferences as such and those that constitute an intersubjective conception of value. Nonetheless, Kant's complaint against both sorts of value as a basis for morality was really the same. Whether something is the object of a personal preference or the object of an informed impersonal preference common to a valuing community, "we cannot know, *a priori*, of the idea of any object, whatever the nature of this idea, whether it will be associated with pleasure or displeasure or will be merely indifferent" (ibid.). The most basic moral requirements cannot be applicable to any beings capable of moral agency if they derive from nonmoral value, since *both* subjective and intersubjective nonmoral values derive from the informed *responses* of beings, and no such responses are, of necessity, common to all rational agents.[5] The sui generis character of moral requirements, then, goes hand in hand with their validity for all rational beings.

    5. Kant himself appears to have been committed, however, to the position that there are preferences which rational beings can be assumed to have, whatever their specific ends. That is, he seems to have been committed to something like a

The Hobbesian Approach

Many of us share the Kantian conception of at least a part of morality as embodying requirements and recommendations for action which, at their most basic and general level, are common to any being who is capable of recognizing and regulating his life by them. Many, though assuredly not all, see these considerations as *reasons* for us to act: reasons whose existence depends simply on the validity of the moral considerations themselves. The deep attraction of this view is shown by the fact that a perennial and seriously defended position in moral philosophy is that it is impossible even to raise the question whether there is reason to be moral.[6]

Moreover, morality is thought to generate reasons *superior* and more weighty than reasons of other sorts. It claims by its very nature final jurisdiction for itself, and its requirements must override all others when they conflict.[7] So important is this feature of our notion of morality that there has always been some tendency, both in moral philosophical and lay thought, simply to identify (a person's) morality with whatever considerations are (thought by him to be) most weighty.[8]

But how is the claim to be sustained that morality provides all agents with the weightiest reasons for acting? Considerations internal to morality itself cannot do so. In taking up what has been called the "moral point of view" we may judge that it is right for all agents to be fair—that the moral requirement of fairness *applies* to them. But as Philippa Foot (1972a), among others, has pointed out, that does not guarantee that there is a *reason* for any agent to be fair, much less that there is a reason that overrides nonmoral ones. If we take up the point of view of etiquette, she argues, we may likewise judge *from that point of view* that its requirements apply to every member of society. And this does not show that everyone has a reason, much less a very weighty one, to be polite.

The assertion that morality provides all agents with reasons for

---

theory of "primary goods" for rational agents considered as such. See Darwall 1980.

6. See, for example, Becker 1973 and Falk 1952, pp. 503–510.
7. See K. Baier 1978b and Taylor 1978, among others.
8. See note 6.

acting is not itself simply a moral one. Were we to understand it in that way it would be no different from the assertion that considerations internal to any point of view are considerations from that point of view: for example, that considerations of etiquette bind from the point of view of etiquette. Rather, it is a view about the *rationality* of moral conduct. It is the claim that there is reason for any agent to act as he would be led to do were he correctly to assess the moral nature of his situation.[9]

1. One very influential and suggestive attempt to sustain this common view derives from Thomas Hobbes's theory of the state. In *Leviathan*, Hobbes showed how the situation of individuals without any common authority sufficiently strong to compel compliance with its directives has the following remarkable quality. If each acts individually to secure his own livelihood and does whatever he wishes in that regard, feeling no constraint on action in his own interest, then each will end up worse off than if all were under a common power sufficient to compel each to obey directives in their common interest, *even when* the obedience of each is contrary to his interest, save for the existence of the sanctioning power. When people are left to their own devices, conflict of interest, indeed the very suspicion of conflict, leads inevitably to a situation where individuals compete against each other to their mutual disadvantage.

In a recent discussion of this point, James Wallace refers to any situation that has the following features as a *Hobbes situation:*

1. Everyone is apt to benefit if all or most people in the situation conform to B, but this benefit is not realized unless most conform.
2. Conforming to B generally involves some sacrifice, so that, other things being equal, it is apt to be maximally advantageous for an individual not to conform when most conform.
3. As a rule, the sacrifice involved for an individual in conforming

9. But see Brock 1977, who denies that there can ever be point-of-view-neutral assessments of reasons for acting.

The Hobbesian Approach

to B is small in comparison with the benefits to him of the conformity of most people to B.

4. It is apt to be maximally disadvantageous to an individual to conform to B when not enough others conform to realize the benefit. [1978, p. 96]

This characterization matches pretty well Hobbes's description of the situation facing individuals in a state of nature. For reasons that we shall explore later, Hobbes thought that there could be general conformity to such a rule or practice only if there were a sanctioning authority sufficient to compel it. And he thought that given the existence of such an authority, it could never benefit a person to violate the rule. He thought, therefore, that condition 2 would never actually be the case. It is sufficient, however, that many people may *believe* that condition 2 is true. Like Hobbes's famous "fool," they may "questioneth, whether injustice, . . . may not sometimes stand with that reason, which dictateth to every man his own good" (1651/1957, p. 95).

If we consider these four conditions in a two-person case (substituting 'all' for 'most'), we can see that they define an ordering of preferences that has come to be well known in the theory of games as Prisoners' Dilemma.[10] Although named for a particular example involving the decisions of two prisoners whether or not to confess to their crime, Prisoners' Dilemma refers to any two-person situation with similarly ordered preferences for outcomes resulting from sets of combined possible acts, one by each agent.

Suppose that two prisoners are under suspicion of a joint crime. They are held in separate cells and are incapable of communicating with one another. The district attorney approaches each with the following proposition. If the prisoner confesses and the other does not, then he will be allowed to turn state's witness and get off with no sentence. If, however, they both confess, then both will be given a sentence commensurate with their crime. Further, even if both do not confess there is still sufficient evidence to convict each

10. Attributed to A. W. Tucker. For a formal treatment see Luce and Raiffa 1957, p. 95.

of a lesser crime with a lesser sentence. And finally, if the prisoner does not confess and the other does, then he will get the book thrown at him, receiving a harsher sentence than if he had been convicted subsequent to a confession. Both prisoners are offered the same proposition, and we assume them both to be interested solely in serving the least number of years in prison. Thus, each has the same ordering of preferences: first choice: I confess, he does not; second choice: we both do not confess; third choice: we both confess; fourth choice: I do not confess, he does.

Let us label the prisoners P_1 and P_2 and their possible acts C and NC.[11] We can then describe the situation with a matrix, as shown in the figure. Each set of two acts, one by P_1 and one by P_2, defines an outcome represented by the box that is the intersection of the column and row representing their respective acts. We represent their respective preferences for each outcome by placing numbers in the box giving the place of that outcome in the prisoner's ordering of outcomes: P_1's preferences are always on the left, P_2's are on the right. For example, the outcome of P_1's confessing (C) and P_2's not confessing (NC) is represented by the box in the northeast corner. By inspecting it we can see that the outcome is P_1's most preferred and P_2's least preferred.

		P_2	
		C	NC
P_1	C	(3, 3)	(1, 4)
	NC	(4, 1)	(2, 2)

Prisoners' Dilemma is a particular example of a Hobbes situation. Performing act NC plays the same role in it as does "conforming to B" in the general description of Hobbes situations. Each prisoner prefers most to C (not conform to B) while the other NCs (conforms to B). Further, each would rather that both NC

---

11. Nothing essential depends on its being the case that the two participants are choosing between the same two acts.

(follow *B*) than that both *C* (not follow *B*). And each prefers both of these to the other Cing (violating *B*) while he NCs (follows *B*).

The virtue of Prisoners' Dilemma is that it brings into stark relief the important feature of all Hobbes situations. If each prisoner is to act to promote his most preferred outcome (serving the shortest sentence), then the act of confession is uniquely recommended. For each knows that the other prisoner must either confess or not. Suppose, for example, that one is P_1. If P_2 confesses, then it will be better to (have) confess(ed) oneself, since that will bring about one's third rather than one's fourth ranked outcome. Similarly, if P_2 does not confess, then it is better to (have) confess(ed), since this brings about one's first rather than one's second ranked outcome. So, whatever P_2 does, it is better to (have) confess(ed). Since what P_2 does is *independent* of what one does, it follows that the strategy of confession is uniquely best from the standpoint of an overriding interest in the shortest sentence.[12]

In the terms of the theory of games, the strategy of confessing is said to *dominate* the strategy of not confessing. But if this decision is a rational one for P_1 it is equally rational for P_2, since their situations are identical. The important truth about Prisoners' Dilemma, as Hobbes perceived about individual action in a state of nature, is that if each pursues the course recommended by his own preference, the outcome is worse for both prisoners (for each their next to worst outcome) than another outcome available to them. If they had both not confessed, then the resulting outcome would have been one both preferred (2, 2) to that which their joint

12. The independence assumption is crucial here. If what the other does is dependent on what one does, then it is simply fallacious to argue that *C* is to be done because the other must do one of the two acts and whatever he does, *C* has the best consequence. To understand this, suppose that one is considering whether to tell someone some unpleasant news that one would prefer he learn elsewhere. The possible outcomes rank as follows: (1) I do not tell him, he finds out; (2) I tell him, he finds out; (3) I do not tell him, he does not find out; (4) I tell him, he does not find out (perhaps because he does not believe me). A similar pattern of reasoning would go in this way. Either he will find out or not. If he does, then it is better that I not have told him. If he does not, then it is better that I not have told him. Therefore, it is better that I not tell him. In such a case, where the likelihood of his finding out is dependent on whether one tells him, this reasoning is absurd. See Lewis 1979.

independent pursuit of preference condemns them (3, 3). If somehow they could have both forsaken the pursuit of their own individual preference, and both refused to confess, each would have
been better off.

2. Kurt Baier (1958) was the first of an ever-increasing number of
philosophers to see in the structure of Hobbes situations a source
for the rational justification morality.[13] Hobbes, of course, had
argued that the only way in which individuals could extricate
themselves from being rationally condemned to a mutually disadvantageous war of all against all is for them to place themselves
under the common authority of a sovereign with the power to
compel obedience. Baier, however, saw the solution to Hobbes
situations not to lie only in the potentially obnoxious, externally
imposed authority of a sovereign but also in the mutual recognition of a kind of *reason* as generally superior to reasons of self-
interest. He proposed that we conceive of morality as comprised of
"rules designed to overrule self-interest whenever it is in the interest of everyone alike that everyone should set aside his interest"
(ibid., p. 314). If we do so, then the sincere joint acknowledgment
that the existence of a moral rule requiring an act is an overriding
reason to perform it will be sufficient for us *both* to see our own
actions on it as rational *and* for us jointly to achieve similarly
optimal outcomes. For example, if both prisoners accepted as
giving them overriding reason not to confess, that a rule requiring
that act in their situation would be in the interest of each, and if
both so acted, then each would be better off than if they had acted
in their own interest.

The sincere acknowledgment that moral requirements provide
overriding *reasons* for acting gives morality an internal authority in
addition to the external authority arising from sanctions, formal
and informal, imposed by others. Even if a Hobbesian sovereign,
or all of us acting as enforcers, were sufficient to compel adherence
to mutually beneficial rules, the price in constant surveillance and

---

13. Since that time this suggestion has been picked up by G. R. Grice (1967)
and Held (1977), among others. Also see Sen 1974 for a similar view.

in fear of harassment or meddling would be excessive. We would all be better off if we could trust each other through our shared sense that moral requirements *are* overriding reasons for acting than we would be if we had to rely only on constant vigilance—our own or the state's—to enforce obedience. We are, of course, but imperfect internalizers of morality, and this is only one reason why we need formal institutions to make precise and to enforce those rules most important to us. But if we had to rely completely on external sanctions, things would be much worse than they are.

Both Hobbes and Baier begin with the assumption that the fact that an act would be in a person's interest is a reason for him to do it. And both believe that were we to recognize only this fact as a reason, or as a generally overriding reason, and to lack a common authority over us, we would be enmeshed in a condition of mutual conflict in the interest of none of us. Surely, Baier argues, the use of reason cannot condemn rational beings to such a fate. And though they can be spared from the worst aspects of the state of nature by a Hobbesian enforcer, that is less in the interest of each than a system of self-regulation consisting in sincerely acknowledging a different and superior sort of *reason*.

In Baier's view, then, a moral requirement to do something consists in its being required by a rule "in the interest of everyone alike."[14] Accepting this theory of morality would enable us to explain the common view of morality, that it both applies to all rational beings who interact with others *and* gives them overriding reasons for acting. Moral right and wrong, in this view, are not simply derivative from intersubjective nonmoral value. The validity of moral requirements for all rational beings is argued without regard to *any* theory of intersubjectively valuable states of affairs whose value is independent of conduct.

This will do as a rough characterization of Baier's position for

14. Space does not allow a consideration of the many questions this account raises: Does Baier intend actual or hypothetical rules? If the latter, what if many conflicting hypothetical rules each have the required property? Why should we judge particular rules as opposed to systems of rules? And how are we to judge whether a rule contributes to the good of everyone alike; i.e., as compared with what?

the moment. Its great attraction is what one might call its apparent hardheadedness. By separating the basis of morality from any condition of the heart such as the capacity for sympathy and placing it in objective conditions of life likely to face any rational being, it assures morality the widest possible application. Moreover, the traditional detractors of morality, the moral skeptic and the egoist, seem confounded by it, since it appears to base morality in what Hobbes called "that reason which dictateth to every man his own good" (1651/1957, p. 95). If this is the only assumption it makes about reasons, and the argument is valid, then how can its conclusion be resisted?

3.   Almost a decade after Baier first expressed these ideas in *The Moral Point of View* (1958), David Gauthier published an article attempting to show that the hardheadedness of Baier's argument was more apparent than real (1967). It is both interesting and important to keep track of the history of this debate, since both philosophers now believe that the existence of Hobbes situations makes it rational to conform to the requirements of morality, suitably understood.

Baier's initial argument was given in the chapter of his book entitled "Why Should We Be Moral?" Gauthier argued, however, that the answer can only show moral requirements to provide reasons for a person to act if the question is simply a "compendious way of asking, for each person, 'Why should I be moral?'" (1967, p. 470). If we understand it to be asking why we should all *collectively* be moral, then answering it can provide us only with a reason to act as a collective agent. And that does not by itself show that there is a reason for each of us, taken individually, to be moral.

Gauthier assumed further that "this question, if asked seriously, demands a *reason* for being moral other than moral reasons themselves" (1967, p. 459, emphasis added). [15] Since Baier's argument appealed to the interest that each person has in the general adherence to moral rules, Gauthier wrote: "Those who would an-

15. As we shall see, Gauthier later revised this view.

swer it, like Baier, endeavor to do so by the introduction of considerations of advantage" (ibid., pp. 460–470). So Gauthier believed that Baier's argument could succeed only if he had shown that each person has a *reason of self-interest* to be moral. But as attention to condition 2 of the description of Hobbes situations will show, it is not in general true that each person's interest is furthered by acting as moral rules require. Each person has an interest in the *general* adherence to moral rules and prefers the situation in which everyone (himself included) obeys them to one in which no one does. But there is another arrangement he prefers even more: one where others generally obey and he does not.

Attention to Hobbes situations, Gauthier argued, can show only that we have an interest in all being moral as opposed to all being immoral. It does not show that each has an interest in *his* being moral. If what each does is independent of what others do, then whether others are moral or not, each gains by being immoral. Of course, if their immoral action makes it more likely that others will be immoral also, then they do not necessarily gain, but then the source of the reason for individuals will not reside simply in the *existence* of moral requirements, but in considerations of their own enlightened interest.[16] Because this is true, no argument from Hobbes situations can show that we have a reason to be moral, or so Gauthier argued.

I shall argue presently that Gauthier mislocated Baier's argument. Nevertheless, the criticism does remove some of its air of hardheadedness. It raises the question of how, if we start simply with the assumption that there is reason for any person to act in his own interest, we can ever get beyond that assumption to the conclusion that moral requirements also provide reasons for acting, indeed overriding ones. Even in Hobbes situations, the view that

16. Along these lines consider the views expressed by such writers as Foot (1969) and Thomas (1980) and, more classically, Reid (1969) and Butler (1950), who argue that interest and morality are congruent at least in the sense that one will be better off in the end if one is the kind of person who takes moral considerations as reasons for acting. See especially Foot 1969, p. 259, and Reid 1969, p. 216. These points are also relevant to Gauthier's question, whether it maximizes expectable utility to choose acts on those grounds. Foot has since disavowed her earlier position (1967, p. 9).

every person has reason to act only in his own interest can be consistently carried through. If we are given only that assumption, the reasonable course for a person to pursue would seem to be to try to get others to act on moral requirements but not himself. It is true that if everyone were to act as the only-assumed reasons direct, then the resulting situation would be worse from everybody's standpoint. But, if *that* fact is to be directly relevant, some other principle or assumption must be invoked about reasons for acting. The only-assumed reasons will continue, even in Hobbes situations, to give individuals coherent direction, and not necessarily to act rightly.

Indeed, had Baier been trying to show that acting morally is always in an agent's interest, he would have been in the difficult position of trying to maintain, with Hobbes, that the fool who thinks it in his interest to be immoral must always be mistaken, without even the Hobbesian system of external sanctions to serve as threat. But this could not have been Baier's position. He explicitly rejected the idea that he was trying to show that morality and self-interest coincide: "If [they did], self-interest and morality could never conflict, but they notoriously do" (1958, p. 310).

What he did say to separate his thesis both from the claim that there are reasons of interest for being moral *and* from the assertion that morality is self-justifying and requires no further argument to show that its requirements provide agents with reasons for acting is, however, somewhat puzzling: "The answer is that we are now looking at the world from the point of view of *anyone*. We are not examining particular alternative courses of action before this or that person; we are examining two alternative worlds, one in which moral reasons are always treated by everyone as superior to reasons of self-interest and one in which the reverse is the practice. And we can see that the first world is the better world, because we can see that the second world would be the sort which Hobbes describes as the state of nature" (K. Baier 1958, p. 310). What is puzzling is that this statement seems to recast the argument so that it stems not at all from reasons of self-interest but rather from moral considerations. After all, the point of view of *anyone* has the same impartiality that Baier ascribes to the moral point of view.[17] So it may seem that Baier was giving a moral argument for respecting moral considerations as reasons.

But this easy explanation is still not right. It overlooks a distinction fundamental to Baier's view that has not always been obvious to his readers: namely, the distinction between substantive theories or views about reasons to act and a more general theory of what makes something a reason to act. This is the distinction marked in the present study between the substantive thesis that some fact or other is a reason for someone to act and our more general internalist account of reasons as facts that rationally motivate. In the quoted passage, Baier brings to bear a fundamental background theory about the *basis* of reasons for acting that is not simply an additional substantive assumption, like the proposition that considerations of self-interest are reasons for a person to act.

Attention to other parts of *The Moral Point of View* reveals that Baier held what might usefully be termed a teleological theory of reasons for acting. Of any consideration, indeed even of the consideration that an act is in one's interest, we can ask the question "Why is that a reason for me to act?" Baier's general theory of how that question is to be answered was to consider what the world would be like if people were generally to regard that fact as a reason for them to act. It was his view that "the reasoning game" itself has a purpose: namely, to maximize our satisfactions and to minimize our frustrations (1958, p. 301). We can test whether or not a fact is a reason by seeing how the world fares if the "reasoning game" is played with that consideration treated as a counter in it.

This teleological background theory of reasons is implicit in his argument that considerations regarding the interests of others are reasons for any agent to act:

It is a prima-facie reason for me to do something not only that *I* would enjoy it if *I* did it, but also that *you* would enjoy it if *I* did it. People generally would fare better if this fact were treated as a pro,

17. See, for example, K. Baier 1958, p. 202.

for if this reason were followed, it would create additional enjoyment all around. [K. Baier 1958, p. 304]

The same kind of argument is used to show that while others' welfare is indeed a reason, it is overridden, other things being equal, by reasons of self-regard: people are generally better off if everyone treats his own interests as overriding those of others, other things equal. Of course, if a moral rule is involved, then other things are not equal, and Baier argued that in this case we are all much better off if we all treat moral requirements as providing reasons that override those of self-interest.

The basic assumption of these various arguments appears to be that the test of whether some consideration is a reason for someone to do something is whether everyone's so regarding it is in everyone's interest. Although understanding Baier's position in this way enables one to avoid Gauthier's objection, it does so at the cost of assuming an extremely controversial theory of what it is for something to be a reason. In this reading the apparent hardheadedness of the attempt to derive the rationality of morality from self-interest gives way to a more fundamental theory of reasons that seems already implicitly moral in that it judges whether something is a reason by assessing the consequences for everyone of everyone's acting on it.

4. Recently, Baier has advanced a view seeking to show that moral considerations are overriding reasons without either arguing that it is in our individual interest to *act* morally or assuming that whether something is a reason for acting is determined by the effects on everyone's life of everyone's acting on it. The clearest and most detailed version of this argument appears in his paper, "Moral Reasons and Reasons to Be Moral" (1978a). [18] Baier there makes a number of assumptions about reasons for acting that when combined with facts about Hobbes situations entail, he believes,

18. I am indebted to Gregory Trianosky-Stillwell for a very helpful discussion of this article.

that moral considerations are overriding reasons. Two assumptions bear the primary burden of the argument.[19] Since one retains the teleological flavor of the theory apparently presupposed in *The Moral Point of View*, let us call it the *teleological* requirement:

> The consequences concerning the satisfactoriness of the lives of those who believe that F is a reason for them to do A are relevant to the soundness of this belief. [1978a, p. 240]

There is a way of reading this assumption that makes it identical with the earlier view: whether some consideration is a reason for someone to act is at least partly determined by the consequences for everyone's life of everyone's so regarding it. It is more likely, however, that Baier intends this reading: whether some consideration is a reason for someone to act is at least partly determined by the consequences for *that person's* life of *his* regarding it as such. Reading the assumption in this *individualistic* way holds out the hope that the rationality of moral considerations emerges from the conjunction of a number of independently compelling assumptions rather than simply being implicit in one of them.

The other important assumption might be called a *compossibility* requirement:

> It must be possible for *everyone* always to be perfectly rational; or, in other words, no practical principles could be sound principles of practical reason which could be such only if they were not universally followed. [1978a, p. 240]

It appears to be Baier's view that when we combine the *teleological* and *compossibility* requirements, an argument for the overriding rationality of moral considerations emerges. Furthermore, neither assumption would seem initially unattractive to a person who held

19. Other assumptions—most important, Baier's assumption iii—seem already to entail the collectivist teleological theory of reasons presupposed in *The Moral Point of View*. I shall not consider them here to see if Baier's conclusion can be obtained from weaker assumptions.

that only subjective considerations (for example, considerations of personal interest) are reasons for acting. Taken by itself, the individualistic teleological requirement seems tailormade for his view. And why would he reject compossibility? While he might perhaps not *want* others to act in a way that he thinks rational, promoting their own interests, he could hardly suppose that it was not possible for them to do so and have their actions still remain rational.

Now the existence of Hobbes situations means that if egoism were a rational principle, then everyone's acting rationally would lead to a worse world for each. And so Baier writes:

> But surely if a group of 'perfectly rational people' (that is, people who are always motivated only by what, according to that theory, are the best reasons) lead a life that is worse than a group of people who are less perfectly rational, then such a theory of reasons cannot be sound. [1978a, p. 244]

Of course, simply to state this is just to reassert the collective teleological view implicit in Baier's earlier argument. His present position seems to be, however, that it *follows* from the conjunction of more meager assumptions—in particular, from the conjunction of the compossibility requirement and the individualistic teleological requirement. But does it?

Compossibility requires that something can be a rational principle only if its being one is not conditional on not everyone's acting on it. For example, if egoism were a rational principle for a person to act on only if not everyone acted on it, then it would violate compossibility. Moreover, the teleological requirement tells us something about the conditions under which a principle is rational for a person to act on: roughly, acting on it must make some positive contribution to the satisfactoriness of that person's life. Taken together these two assumptions entail that if my acting on a principle would contribute to the satisfactoriness of my life only on the condition that others not act on it, then it cannot be a rational principle.

It can be argued, however, that egoism does *not* run afoul of this requirement. For the fact of the matter is that regardless of how others act in Hobbes situations, *an individual's* acting on the egoistic principle will, *ex hypothesi*, make a positive contribution to the satisfactoriness of his life. If others are acting on moral principles, then an individual still does better by acting on the egoistic principle (condition 2). Furthermore, the same is true for every individual. So, as far as both compossibility and the *individualistic* teleological requirements go, egoism could be a rational principle. Whether acting on the egoistic principle positively contributes to an individual's life does not depend on whether others act on it. Acting egoistically still dominates *for an individual* whether others act egoistically or morally.

Now it is of course true that there *is* a sense in which a positive contribution to an individual's life as a result of his acting on the egoistic principle depends on whether others so act. That would be the case if in assessing whether an individual's acting on a principle makes a positive contribution to his life, if everyone acts on it, we regard the latter as *dependent* on the former, and assess the contribution to his life not just of *his* acting on it, but of everyone's doing so. Egoism fares rather badly if to assess the rational credentials of a principle we compare the effects on a person's life of *his and others'* acting on it with those resulting from his and others' acting on some other principle, rather than comparing the results for his life of *his* acting on that principle rather than some other, if others' acts are independent of his. Interpreting the assumptions in this way, however, makes them much more controversial. *Why* should something's being a rational principle for one to act on depend on the consequences of *everyone's* acting on it?

5. Regardless of the success of Baier's argument, he is certainly correct in pointing out the important theoretical difference between an egoistic *policy* of promoting only self-interest and an egoistic *theory* of reasons. By affirming that only considerations of self-interest are *reasons* to act, the rational egoist makes a claim not made by someone who merely acts in his own interest without any such view. Moreover, Baier is right to urge that our assessment of the adequacy of rational egoism, or of any substantive theory of reasons, must ultimately bring to bear some more general theory

of the nature of reasons for acting: of that in virtue of which facts are reasons.

It is often said that it is a mistake to suppose either that more general philosophical theories (of the nature of morality, rationality, mathematics, and so on) can be formulated independently of substantive theory or that the latter is justified solely in terms of the former. Likely, illumination proceeds in both directions. But even those who argue that, for example, we cannot hope to arrive at an adequate normative ethic by proceeding from an independently arrived at initial theory of the nature of morality (á la Kant) admit that our deeply held beliefs about morality itself are importantly relevant to deciding between rival substantive normative conceptions. [20]

So a general theory of reasons for acting must be brought to bear at some point to assess the view that only considerations of self-interest are reasons for acting. Philosophers generally tend to think, however, that all the rational egoist must do to satisfy this requirement is simply to suppose that his view applies *universally:* the crucial difference between rational egoism and the cast of mind of the ordinary egoist being that the former recognizes the similar rationality of others' acting as he does. But as Theodore Benditt has pointed out in criticism of ethical egoism: "universalization by itself, the mere affixing of a universal quantifier in front of a personal policy, imposes no limitation on what that policy can be, and hence, from the point of view of the individual whose policy it is, it makes no difference *what* he thinks he ought to do" (1976, p. 45). Since virtually any policy can be universalized in this weak sense, pointing out the universal character of principles that generate reasons for acting can hardly be sufficient by itself to count as a general theory of reasons for acting. Something more must be brought in if a theory about what it is for something to be a reason to act is to have any relevance at all to adjudicating between competing substantive theories.

20. Rawls's method of *reflective equilibrium* admits of a "wide" interpretation in which not merely considered judgments and principles are brought into equilibrium, but also more fundamental philosophical reflections. See, for example, Rawls 1971, p. 49. See also Daniels 1979.

The Hobbesian Approach

But whether such a theory should be built from Baier's teleological axiom (individualist or collective) is another matter. Any argument or theory must proceed from some assumption or other, but it is surely preferable to proceed from those that are most uncontroversial and central to our notion of a reason for acting. That everyone's acting for reasons must lead to a world in which people generally have more satisfactory lives is not obviously such an assumption. For one thing, it seems to make the rational person's desire to act for reasons *conditional* on his desire that he, or that people generally, flourish. But it is not clear that a fully rational person's desire to act for reasons would be conditional in that way. That there is reason for him to act is necessarily regarded by the rational person as a deliberation stopper. Granted, Baier does not hold that there is a further *reason* for everyone to be rational that consists in the good effects of being so, but it is difficult to see how a rational person could accept such a teleological theory of reasons without making his adherence to reason so conditional. It would seem, therefore, that Kant's objection to any "materialist" theory of the nature of morality, that it depends on the existence of a desire rational creatures may lack, can be made in a related way to Baier's "materialist" theory of reason. For the rational person who accepts his theory must see his desire to act for reasons as not a necessarily justified one but one that is itself grounded in a desire that he, or that people generally, flourish. To put this point in Butlerian terms, Baier's theory removes the intrinsic authority of practical reason (Butler's principle of reflection) and subordinates it either to cool self-love or to benevolence.[21]

21. That there could be an argument for the rationality of moral action based solely on Hobbesian grounds is an illusory hope. Everyone's acting on moral requirements is more in a person's interest than everyone's acting on reasons of self-interest, but this does not by itself show that self-interest dictates following moral requirements. It may be even more in a person's interest that he act wrongly while others do not. But even so, perhaps morality could arise out of a rational *agreement* between individuals. If the existence of Hobbes situations makes it rational for individuals to commit themselves jointly to morality, then this might be a strong argument that acting on that commitment is rational. The claim is not, of course, that morality did arise in this way but that it could.

How are we to understand the question of whether it is rational for each to make a *commitment* to follow moral requirements? Clearly the force of agree-

Reason and Right

6. Gauthier's present position (1975) on the rationality of interest-constraining moral action is itself of considerable interest. Despite his earlier objections to his understanding of Baier's at-

---

ment or commitment is not simply each person's *saying* that he will respect moral requirements, for it is not in anyone's interest that everyone merely declare that they will so act; that may only be a charade. But neither can we invoke a notion of commitment with moral force. That presupposes that individuals already are disposed to respect a moral requirement to keep commitments.

We can still get a purchase on a notion of commitment with which to evaluate the argument if we consider whether it would be rational for one to *decide* with others to follow moral requirements. Such a commitment by an individual, then, would consist in his *setting himself* to follow moral requirements, assuming that, other things equal, what it is rational to decide to do it is rational to do. The question then becomes whether it might be rational for a person to make a decision (with others) to follow moral requirements, even when following them conflicts with self-interest.

The major problem with this approach is that it will be rational for a person *genuinely* to make the commitment only if others do so as well. But in a decision situation between individuals with no independent sense of an overriding reason to keep commitments, who simply announce their decisions to act as generally agreed in the future, what could count as security for the sincerity of those declarations? Or even if their *present* intentions were sincerely represented, what could guarantee that they would not be revised in the future? Mere agreement, as Hobbes insisted, is not sufficient to get individuals, solely concerned with their own interest, out of the state of nature: "If a convenant be made, wherein neither of the parties perform presently, but trust one another; in the condition of mere nature, which is a condition of war of every man against every man, upon any reasonable suspicion it is void: but if there be a common power set over them both, with right and force sufficient to compel performance, it is not void" (1651/1957, p. 89). So, it seems, it could not be rational for individuals acting in their own interest to commit themselves to constrain self-interest by acting on rules that, if generally followed, would achieve better outcomes for all.

This may be a bit hasty, however, for committing oneself to the principles of right conduct may not mean committing oneself to act in certain ways *regardless* of how others act. We may suppose there to be a principle of fairness implicit in at least part of morality that requires that we do our part, that we abide by certain rules *if* others do so as well. Would it not be rational for a self-interested person to commit herself to morality if it includes such a principle?

The question now becomes whether it is rational for a person to make a commitment to perform certain sorts of interest-constraining acts *if* they are also being performed by others. Since here one is rather less concerned that others be willing to perform them regardless of what others do, one will be less concerned to secure their performance by the sanctions of a sovereign. What is to be secure is not that the acts will be performed come what may but that they will be performed by persons if others generally perform them.

Still, even if what one commits oneself to is conditional in this way, no such agreement would be worth anything unless it were a commitment to act in an

The Hobbesian Approach

tempt to deduce it from the existence of Hobbes situations, Gauthier himself advances an argument that is similarly based. This does not mean that Gauthier has abandoned his former ob-

interest-constraining way not simply on the condition that one *believe* that others were likewise willing but unless one had good and sufficient reason to believe that they were not. If mere suspicion were enough to remove commitment, it would be insufficiently strong to generate interest-constraining action. So the issue is whether it would be rational for individuals to commit themselves to act in interest-constraining ways unless they have good reason for supposing that others generally are not so acting.

The security that is required to make the decision rational is that if others do break the agreement, evidence of it will be available. What is needed is another aspect of the Hobbesian sovereign's policing function: surveillance. Without the assurance that such evidence will exist it may not be rational for a self-interested agent to agree to respect morality. In many cases, especially involving small groups, the assurance will of course exist.

There are some important exceptions to this general answer, however. If, for example, an individual's commitment to respect moral requirements were *causally* related to others' so respecting them, then it might well be in a person's interest to commit herself. Or imagine the following situation. Suppose a device exists that is capable of bringing about general respect for moral requirements. It is activated in the following way. Each person pushes a button that represents his (conditional) decision to respect morality. That button is connected to a mechanism that will change *that* person's psyche so that *he* regards moral requirements as providing overriding reasons. However, the connection is broken unless every other person pushes an analogous button that is connected in the same way to a mechanism that will likewise bring about his or her moral action. When, and only when, every person has pushed his or her button does the entire device bring it about that everyone respects morality. Since each person's decision to respect moral requirements (conditional on others' deciding similarly) is causally connected to his own future action, since it does not take effect unless everyone decides similarly, and since a psychological change is effected in each that removes the possibility that others will abandon their decision to act morally, this *Gedanken* experiment represents a situation in which the obstacles to rational agreement on moral action are removed. *If* we could decide mutually through such a device to act morally it would be in each person's interest to do so.

There is another condition that would make it in a person's interest for her to decide to respect moral requirements. If everyone were possessed of *perfect information* about the psychological dispositions of others, then self-interest might well dictate a decision to follow moral requirements, though perhaps only with regard to acts affecting other persons who were also so disposed. If everyone knows of everyone else whether he or she is willing to act morally toward others (if they are likeminded), then it is possible for an individual who respects morality to achieve the benefits of moral community with likeminded others and to escape the losses of sacrificing her interests to others who are not likeminded, while the former is impossible for the thoroughgoing egoist.

Indeed, given perfect information, it may be rational for one person to decide

193

jections. He still believes that except for exceptional circumstances rational egoism can be consistently carried through.[22] And when done so, it does not necessarily counsel acting morally in Hobbes situations.

Gauthier is particularly anxious to reject any argument against the consistency of that view based on the rationality of *agreements* to constrain pursuit of self-interest. The very fact that would make agreed joint action in everyone's interest, that the agreement is interest-constraining, would make it contrary to the interest of individuals to keep the agreement. Consequently, "since it is not rational for each to keep it, it is not rational for each to enter it" (1975, p. 426).

Although identifying rational action with individual utility maximizing is consistent, Gauthier holds it to be ultimately inadequate. And like Baier, Gauthier maintains that its inadequacy can be shown only by appealing to a general theory of practical rationality, constituted by more than a simple universality constraint. Rational egoism, or as he refers to it, unconstrained individual utility maximization, is but one of a great number of competing substantive theories of practical reason and cannot adequately be evaluated in terms of internal consistency alone. Many theories may give coherent guidance. Further philosophical reflection on the nature of practical reason must be brought to bear in deciding between competing substantive theories.

Gauthier believes that unconstrained individual utility maximizing has an initial presumption in its favor, since it is embed-

---

to respect morality *regardless* of how others feel. If everyone else is solely self-interested, then there may simply be no moral requirements to sacrifice one's interests with respect to them. In *those* (known) circumstances there will be no practical difference between a willingness to respect moral requirements and an unconstrained pursuit of self-interest. If, however, there are others who are disposed to respect morality if one is, they will be willing to cooperate to achieve the benefits of joint moral action. Under conditions of perfect information, one can only benefit by a commitment to act morally with respect to likeminded others. Again, this argument likely does not go through in the less than perfect circumstances that are our own.

22. For the exceptions, see Gauthier 1974, in which he argues that in some three-person situations it does not give coherent guidance.

ded in formal decision theory, microeconomics, and in the political ideology of many modern Western states. And although we have seen that, for example, the formal theories of decision under uncertainty and risk do not require a conception of practical rationality restricted to individual utility maximization, our initial account gives it a *presumption* lacking in other theories.[23] This presumption becomes especially clear when we realize that Gauthier is understanding utility as a measure of preferences the agent would have "were he sufficiently informed and reflective" (1975, p. 415). We may take it, then, that Gauthier's agents have the preferences they would have were they rationally to consider all relevant information as per our initial account in Part II.

But none of these considerations especially supports a substantive theory of practical reasons that is *restricted* to individual utility maximizing. Furthermore, Gauthier believes that when we add another important desideratum derived from reflecting on practical reason, we see that we must reject any substantive conception of practical rationality thus restricted.

The fullest expression of reason, whether in theory or practice, is *self-reflective*. We cannot, of course, assess the rationality of a particular belief or act unless we take for granted the rationality of certain standards for evaluating them. But since the rationality of any belief or act is ultimately dependent on the rationality of the standards themselves, a fully rational being will reflect on and critically assess even those standards that he normally takes for granted. Indeed, that is precisely what we do when we attempt to settle a dispute between opposing substantive conceptions of rationality. It is only because we can get our own conceptions of rationality in view, and criticize them, that these disputes can arise.

Gauthier takes the self-reflective activity of submitting even one's conception of rationality to critical assessment to be an integral part of the fullest expression of reason: "A person who is unable to submit his conception of rationality to critical assessment . . . is rational in only a restricted and mechanical sense.

23. See Part II.

He is a conscious agent, but not fully a self-conscious agent, for he lacks the freedom to make, not only his situation, but himself in his situation, his practical object. Although we began by agreeing, with Hume, that reason is the slave of the passions, we must agree, with Kant, that in a deeper sense reason is freedom" (1975, p. 431). It might be objected that the self-reflective aspect of full rationality affords no way to assess substantive conceptions of practical reason, for substantive conceptions provide us with whatever standards for rational choice there are. The question whether we should use a particular standard or other for choosing between alternative acts seems not to be answerable unless we already assume some criteria for selecting between alternative standards.

Still, Gauthier argues, at the least we can raise questions of ultimate justification *self*-referentially. We can ask of a given substantive conception of practical rationality whether it would be rational *according to it* to choose to act on it. This could, of course, be a necessary condition only of an adequate substantive conception. Presumably, any number of conceptions might be *self-supporting* in this way.

Even so, this necessary feature is something that Gauthier contends is *lacking* in the theory that identifies practical rationality with individual utility maximizing. The existence of Hobbes situations makes it contrary to the interest of an individual to choose to operate with that conception, for there is an alternative conception that is more in each person's interest to choose: one requiring that when individuals agree to act jointly to achieve mutually beneficial outcomes (as in Hobbes situations), an individual act as agreed. Gauthier calls this conception *constrained maximization*, since it counsels individual utility maximizing except when such agreements can be made.

In addition, he believes that the choice of this conception will maximize individual utility regardless of what conceptions underlie the choices of other agents. If other agents are unconstrained maximizers, then there will be no mutual agreements and therefore no deviation in the practical effects dictated by the principles of constrained and unconstrained maximization respectively. If, however, there are other constrained maximizers who find themselves in Hobbes situations with the agent, then they will be able rationally to agree, and therefore to act, to achieve the mutually beneficial outcomes that would have been rationally denied to them had they been unconstrained maximizers. Each does better (or at least as well) by choosing to be a *constrained* maximizer, regardless of what conceptions others act on. It follows, therefore, that the choice of unconstrained maximization would not itself maximize an agent's expected utility. In this way the theory lacks its own support.[24]

While Gauthier does not explicitly note it, this argument is sound only if we assume conditions of perfect information about agents' motivations. It depends crucially on others' *knowing* whether or not one is a constrained maximizer and on one's knowing whether or not they are. If one is a constrained maximizer and others do not believe it, then one cannot get the benefits of jointly constrained behavior. Either others will refuse to enter into agreements or, wondering whether one's word can be trusted, will "agree" but not do their share, leaving one in the lurch. If one is an unconstrained maximizer and others believe one to hold a constraining conception, then one may get the benefits not only of their agreed constraint but possibly also of not constraining oneself to boot.

The argument that the theory of practical rationality as unconstrained pursuit of informed individual preference (our initial account) is not self-supporting is, therefore, flawed. Even if it is true that *were* everyone perfectly informed about what theory of practical reasons everyone else acts on it would be more in a person's interest to choose to operate with another theory of practical reasons, that by no means demonstrates that it is not in a person's interest to operate with that theory if there is no such guarantee. As Gauthier has himself effectively pointed out in another context, it may well be more in each person's interest to give the appearance to others of being a constrained maximizer while actually being an unconstrained maximizer (1967, p. 468). To put an even finer

24. See Gauthier 1975, p. 429, for this argument.

point on it, we might say that unconstrained maximization is indeed self-supporting in the conditions *according to that theory an agent should try to create*: namely, circumstances in which others are *not* perfectly informed about one's own principles of action.

It might be said in Gauthier's defense that it is not unusual to assume perfect information in deciding what it is rational for a person to do. But that assumption is ordinarily that the *agent* is perfectly informed. It is not at all clear why, in deciding whether it is rational for an individual to choose to act on a principle, we should consider what it would be rational for him to do in circumstances in which he *and others* are perfectly informed.

7.   We can now collect the insights gleaned from our inquiry into the relevance of Hobbes situations to the thesis of common sense that any rational agent has overriding reason to do as he is morally required. Both Baier and Gauthier ultimately agree that the existence of Hobbes situations cannot by itself show that there is always on balance a reason of self-interest to respect moral requirements. Nor, they agree, is there any reason to think that there are no variants of a view identifying rational action with the pursuit of self-interest or informed individual preferences that give coherent guidance to agents who find themselves in Hobbes situations.

Still, each thinks that the existence of Hobbes situations can be combined with deeply rooted theses about the nature of practical reason to show that these views are inadequate as substantive theories of practical rationality. Moreover, each believes that their respective philosophical views about practical reason support a theory that holds there to be overriding reason to act on the requirements of morality—at least when morality is itself properly understood. For Baier, the necessary additional ingredients are a teleological theory of the nature of practical reasons together with an assumed compossibility of rational action. For Gauthier, it is the idea that since full rationality is marked by self-reflective critical assessment, a necessary condition of the adequacy of any substantive theory of practical reason is that it support itself: that it be rational on that conception to choose to operate with it.

In each case I have suggested some reason to dissent. Nevertheless, the efforts of both philosophers each point in their way to a different strategy for anchoring the validity and overriding weight of moral requirements as reasons. In the next two chapters, I shall pursue a line of thought that borrows elements from both approaches.

My strategy will depart from Baier's in its proposed general theory of practical reasons. In my view, the theory of practical reason is not properly conceived as fundamentally teleological. Rather, most basic to our notion of a reason for acting are two different aspects. Up to this point the primary focus has been on the *motivational* aspect of practical reasons. A reason for someone to act is a fact about the act awareness of which would *motivate* a person when he rationally considers it. There is in addition, however, a *normative* aspect to practical rationality. Reasons for acting are considerations by which an agent *ought* (rationally) to be guided in acting. Indeed this normative aspect is itself concealed in our definition of the motivational feature. A fact is a reason for someone if he would be motivated by it on considering it as he rationally ought.

My argument for the overriding rationality of respecting moral requirements embarks from a consideration of this normative aspect. It might be thought of, therefore, as based on a theory of practical reason that is fundamentally deontological. Its basic proposition is that reasons for agents to act are ultimately derivative from normative principles of rational conduct that apply to all agents.

Like Gauthier, I will give a central place in my argument to the notion that full rationality is critically self-reflective. He derives from that a fairly weak condition of self-support; too weak, I think, to support his claim that constrained maximization is a more adequate theory of rationality than unconstrained maximization. I shall argue that since the most basic notion of practical reason is normative, an ideally rational agent would be disposed to act on whatever principles constitute his conception of rationality *on account of* their being principles on which any agent *ought* rationally to act. The conclusion of this line of thought is that a necessary condition of any fact's being a reason for someone to act is that a principle directing that agent to act on that consideration, other things equal, have the following kind of self-support: were a person to consider matters from a perspective impartial as between agents it would be rational, according to the principle, to choose that all agents act on it.

It should not be entirely unexpected that to take seriously the normative character of practical rationality is to be led to these conclusions. This was Kant's view. He held practical reason to require the recognition of *practical laws:* "principle(s) valid for every rational being, and the principle(s) by which it ought to act" (1785/1959, p. 28n; Ak. p. 421n). And he thought it to follow from this that such principles would be the object of choice of rational agents from a perspective impartial between them in what he called a "realm of ends" (ibid., pp. 51–59; 433–440).

The precise line of reasoning that led Kant from the thesis that principles of practical reason are normative for any rational agent as such to the conclusion that they would be *impartially willed* for all has never been entirely clear to students of his thought. Any reasonable reconstruction of what he had in mind seems to require a difficult metaphysical doctrine of noumenal freedom. The argument I shall propose requires no such doctrine, however. It proceeds simply by taking seriously the idea that principles of practical reason are principles that are normative for us simply because we are rational.

CHAPTER 14

Normative Rationality

To this point we have focused primarily on the motivational aspect of reasons for acting: their capacity to motivate when they are rationally considered. Equally central to our notion of a reason is what I have called its *normative* aspect. Reasons for a person to do something are not simply facts about an action that motivate him to act. Rather, they are considerations that rationally *ought* to have force for a person and that do for a person who considers them as he rationally ought. Without the normative aspect of reasons there would be nothing to distinguish reasons *for* someone *to* do something from reasons *why* he did or will do it, reasons that justify or recommend action from those that explain it.

We can see this by considering Hempel's famous criticism of Dray's view that the explanation of action by reasons is of a special, noncausal sort. Against this, Hempel argued that the existence of reasons *for* an agent *to* act cannot by itself explain action. It cannot because it is a necessary condition of the explanation of any occurrence that it provide grounds for thinking that the occurrence took place. And the fact that there was preponderant reason for an agent to have done something gives us no such ground. It affords "grounds for believing that it would have been *rational for* A *to do* x" but no grounds for believing that A did *in fact* do x" (Hempel

1965, p. 471). 'Rational' here has normative force. The hypothesis that there is preponderant reason for an agent to act in a particular way is relevant not to how he will act but to how he rationally ought.

The normative character of reasons for acting explains the *initial* openness of the question of what facts are reasons for a person to act. With respect to any fact we may at least sensibly raise the question whether it is a reason. That no substantive considerations are analytic of the notion of a reason to act is a special case of the logical gap between 'ought' and 'is'.[1]

In this chapter we shall proceed by developing the idea that reasons have a normative aspect. I must beg the reader's patience here. Some fairly tedious and abstract work must be done to articulate a framework within which to understand the normativity of reasons. Ultimately, however, our labors will bear fruit. They will enable us to construct an argument within that framework in the next chapter that vindicates the commonsense viewpoint that at least some basic moral requirements provide overriding reasons for any rational agent who finds himself in the company of others.

Reflection on the normativity of reasons will enable us to incorporate the insights of both Baier and Gauthier and to understand just how the possibility of Hobbes situations ensures the rationality of moral conduct. The resulting view combines the merits of both philosophers' positions without their respective defects. Baier's argument, though fertile, rests on a questionable "materialist" theory of practical reason. And Gauthier's, though it proceeds from meager formalist assumptions, cannot establish, as he thinks, the rationality of constraining individual utility maximizing. With this chapter's framework in hand, our aim in the next will be to combine, in Onora Nell's phrase, "formality and fertility" (1975, p. 1): to advance an argument proceeding from a formal concep-

---

1. I do not mean anything to hang on the much-maligned analytic-synthetic distinction. We may put this same idea by saying that beliefs about what facts are reasons for us to act are closer to the periphery of our beliefs than are those that relate reason to rational criticism and guidance. For a rejection of the view that reason is irreducibly normative, see Brandt 1979. See also Chapter 7, note 1, above.

tion of practical reason to the conclusion that at least some basic moral considerations are overriding reasons for any agent who exists in the company of others.

1. In order to illuminate the normative aspect of practical reasons we shall need the general notion of a *normative system*, or system of norms. Any normative system is comprised of a number of elements including, most obviously, *norms* themselves. Norms are the standards or principles that those to whom they apply, the *subjects* of the normative system, use to appraise and guide their conduct. This element is crucial. Norms are *guides* that subjects can themselves apply to regulate their own conduct. The principle that 'ought' implies 'can' springs from this guiding aspect of norms. Subjects can be guided by their awareness of a norm to do only what it is possible for them to do.

Normative appraisals may be made of conduct and of subjects. In some normative systems, subject-appraisals are simply summations of conduct-appraisals involving the subject. But this is not always the case. Our *moral* appraisal of a person, for example, includes our assessment not only of the acts that he or she has undertaken but also of their motivation.

Finally, a normative system includes some conception of the particular sorts of behavior that are fit *objects* of normative apprisal. It follows from the guiding aspect of norms that this will generally be restricted to behavior that the subject can regulate by his awareness of the relevant norms.

The elements of a normative system include, in addition to the *norms* themselves, then, some conception of those to whom the norms apply (*subjects*); of the behavior of subjects to which they apply (*objects*); of the appraisals of conduct to which they are relevant (*conduct-appraisals*); and of the appraisals of subjects to which they are relevant (*subject-appraisals*).

The standards of a particular normative system that *must* be met by its subjects may be called a system's normative *requirements*. Typically, normative systems include epithets of negative apprisal for acts falling below some minimal standard. For example, an act may be judged wrong or morally unacceptable, illegal, irrational, or boorish, within the normative systems of morality, law, rationality, and etiquette, respectively.

Some normative systems, such as positive criminal law, seem to have a fairly simple deontic structure. Conduct is either legally required, legally forbidden, or neither required nor forbidden. From the legal point of view an act either must be taken, must not be taken, or may be taken or not as one chooses. Other systems of norms, notably morality, are more complicated. In addition to those morally required, permitted, or forbidden, it may be considered that there are acts that moral considerations *recommend* but whose omission is not so serious as the commission of something they forbid. We are apt to use somewhat weaker normative terms like 'ought' or 'should' in these cases. This complexity is not unique to morality. Etiquette may have its recommendations as well as its requirements. Thus a normative system may include considerations its subjects are recommended to employ in guiding their behavior even when they are not strictly speaking required by it to do so.

2.   That our notion of practical rationality is normative, referring implicitly to a system of norms, is perhaps best shown by the fact that our word 'rational' may be applied to each of the elements in the general description of normative systems.

Rationality as a property of subjects. When we say that humans are rational creatures we refer to the *capacity* of humans beings for rational action; that is, for action that would be *appraised* as rational. Implicit in our reference to these appraisals is the idea of standards that underlie and justify them: the norms to which rational creatures as such are subject. In identifying ourselves as rational creatures in this sense we implicitly refer to our status as subject to rational norms. We suppose ourselves capable of making rational appraisals and of guiding our behavior by them.

Rationality as a property of objects. Of course, not all of our behavior is appropriately so appraised. Our movements while we are asleep are not. Indeed, much of what we do in our waking hours, absentmindedly running a hand through our hair or glancing in the direction of a brightly colored object, is not fit for rational appraisal. What we do suppose appropriately appraised is conduct that we take to be rational in the minimal sense that the agent had reasons for acting as he did and acted for those reasons. As Hempel has remarked, when we characterize behavior as rational in this sense we do not critically appraise it but "put forward an empirical hypothesis . . . to the effect that the action was done for certain reasons, that it can be *explained* as having been motivated by them" (1965, p. 463).

We should note parenthetically, however, that while our taking someone to have had her reasons for acting is not itself an appraisal of her act's rationality, it does locate the act within the agent's own positive rational appraisal. What distinguishes the agent's reasons, within the omnibus set of reasons that explain the act in any way at all, is that they are considerations she took to be reasons *for* her so *to* have acted: considerations that, in her view, were grounds for a positive rational appraisal of the act.

It is easy to overstate this point, however. We often act contrary to what, even in our own view, there were the weightiest reasons for us to do. This would perhaps be unproblematic, though still disconcerting, if every case of such contrarational action could be explained as the result of compulsion, ignorance, or loss of control. That would show only that our rational capacities are circumscribed. The most troublesome cases of weak will, however, are, as J. L. Austin observed, not those in which a person gives in to an overpowering temptation that leaves him incapable of choice but those in which a person acts deliberately, as in Austin's famous example of reaching ever so gracefully for an extra portion of bombe at High Table (1961, p. 146n). These cases are troublesome precisely because the person seems to act rationally, to act for what he takes to be a reason, even though in his view the act is less well supported by reasons than some alternative. Such situations seem to introduce an absurdity into the very idea of acting for a reason.

This is not the place to attempt to say anything definitive about the notoriously intractable philosophical problem of weakness of will. I am inclined to think, however, that some illumination can be gained quickly by distinguishing between a person's performing an act *because he thinks that p,* where he *also* thinks that *p* is a reason for him so to act but this second judgment plays no role in his decision to act, and a person's performing the act *because he thinks that there is reason to,* namely *p.* In the troublesome cases the former condition but not the latter obtains. The gourmand could not, for example, have taken the bombe *because* he thought doing so best supported by reasons and also that it was not. He takes it not because, in his view, its enjoyment will provide him with *a,* or with *the best,* reason for so acting, but because it will provide him its particularly delectable taste. What is before his mind and makes him, at the moment anyway, insufficiently attentive to the further, more abstract question of reasons for and against taking the bombe is the specific character of his anticipated pleasure. Indeed, we imagine that he knows that whatever reason that provides weighs in rather poorly against competing considerations.[2] What he could not, however, do, according to our internalist account, is to *judge for himself,* via his own preponderant motivation on rationally considering whether to do something, that the reasons conclusively support action (now) and fail to act, without some sort of incapacitation.

Unless, however, a person is in general disposed to consider the more abstract question of how different particular considerations stack up *as* reasons for or against action, nothing is illuminated by trying to explain any of his behavior as undertaken *for reasons.* He would, of course, have beliefs and desires, and his acts could be explained as expressing these, but nothing would be added by saying that he had *reasons* for his actions. That would imply some disposition to pose to himself, with a mind to acting on his answers

2. The contrast here is between the particular considerations that are reasons and their weight *as reasons.* In order to assess the weight of a reason, we must abstract somewhat from its particularity and consider it along with other reasons. The metaphor of weight and balance is suggestive. To consider different particular reasons we must induce a common measure to compare their various weights. Again, to quote Aristotle, "for whether this or that shall be enacted is already a task requiring calculation; and there must be a single standard to measure by, for that is pursued which is greater. It follows that what acts in this way must be able to make a unity of several images" (Aristotle 1968, p. 600).

to them, questions about what reasons there are for acting and their relative weights.

Rationality as a property of conduct, positively appraised. We have distinguished two different sorts of appraisals of the rationality of conduct, each of which makes implicit reference to rational norms. One sort is an appraisal of the rationality of conduct relative to the agent's ends and beliefs assumed as fixed. This sort of appraisal is of a piece with the appraisal of a belief's *consistency* with a person's other beliefs. The norms of practical rationality that inform it include the hypothetical imperative, the principles of means-end rationality of the sort proposed by Rawls, and the principles of the formal theories of decision making under uncertainty and under risk.[3] All of these principles are norms of *relative* rationality in that they articulate what an agent ought (rationally) to do *relative* to assuming his commitment to pursue certain ends as given.[4]

However, as I have argued, appraisals of the relative rationality of action cannot exhaust our rational assessment of it; for there is the further question of whether there are *reasons* for the act, for the preferences, ends, or beliefs relative to which it is judged rational. Like all normative appraisals, the appraisal of an act as supported by reasons makes implicit reference to norms. This may seem to require that all reasons for acting be universal, grounded in reason-specifying principles on which all agents ought (rationally) to act. Since the universality of reasons is a thesis we have rejected, it might appear that we should be equally skeptical about the depen-

3. Recall that it is only if preferences are criticizable by reasons that the requirement that preferences be transitive is intelligible (see Chapter 6). For Rawls's principles see Rawls 1971, pp. 411–416.

4. It is important to appreciate that hypothetical imperatives are not simply statements of natural necessity, that something must be done if something else is to be accomplished. Rather, they involve a norm of rational conduct binding on rational agents: if one wills an end, then one must will the necessary means. The necessity is a rational one incumbent on agents. It is not simply that it must be the case that if the agent accomplishes the end, then he wills the means. It is the agent who must will the means (or give up the end). It is *he* who will otherwise be inconsistent. On this point see Sidgwick 1967, p. 37.

dence of reasons for acting on norms that apply to all rational agents.

At the very minimum, however, the normative aspect of reasons for acting requires this much: all agents ought (rationally) to act as there is, all things considered, reason for them to act. From this it does not follow that the particular considerations that are reasons for a given person to act must also be reasons for others similarly circumstanced or that their being reasons must be grounded in universal *reason-specifying* principles.

Still, there can be no explanation of *why* a person ought rationally to act on reasons unless something's being a reason relates it to a norm of rationality that applies to all agents. We shall see below how, even if we deny the universality of reasons, we are committed to thinking that if some fact is a reason for someone to act, it is by virtue of the person's acting on it being recommended as a consequence of a principle on which all agents ought rationally to act.

Rationality as a property of subjects, positively appraised. Finally, we apply the epithet 'rational' to persons not simply to mark them out from other creatures as having rational capacities and as being, on that account, subjects of the system of rational norms but also to appraise them with respect to their rationality. Used in this way, 'rational' contrasts with 'irrational' and 'unreasonable' rather than with 'arational'.

3. If we think of rationality in the most general way, therefore, it involves a normative system. Regardless of what the specific norms are for appraising and guiding action as rational, they have a *minimal normative content*: they are principles or standards that are normative for all agents with rational capacity. This content is purely normative, since the capacity to be rational must itself be understood in terms of a capacity to guide behavior in accordance with the relevant norms. In claiming that some particular principle has the status of a principle of rationality, we claim that it is a principle that is normative for all rational agents: one they ought rationally to follow.

This account of rationality as a system of norms enables us to understand the rational 'ought' and 'must' on the model of their similar use in other normative systems. [5] In general, what a person *must* do from the point of view of a particular system of norms is what the norms of that system *require* him to do. And what, from that same standpoint, a person *ought* to do is what is *recommended* by the system's norms.

The precise deontic contours of practical rationality can be sketched only when we have an adequate substantive theory of practical reasons and certainly not in advance. Still, the very idea that reason could *require* a course of action, in the same sense that either law or morality might, may seem foreign. There is nothing to play the role of *sanction* to give rational norms the bindingness that the very idea of a legal or moral requirement may seem to involve.

It is a mistake, however, to think that the notion of what *must* be done or of what a norm *requires* necessarily implies the threat of sanction. Even if systems of positive morality normally have their own sanctions, external and internal, there seems nothing in the simple idea that a course of action morally must be taken, entailing that it must *on pain of* sanction. To say that it must be taken may simply mean that it would be wrong not to take it.

It is instructive in this connection to recall that we also use the strongest modal term 'must' when referring implicitly to a system of *theoretical* principles, where there is no notion of sanction at all. For example, we may suppose that something *must* be wrong with the car's battery if that is the only remaining possibility that is consistent with (and hence *required* by) our theory of auto mechanics. As Roger Wertheimer (1972) has argued, the most perspicuous account of modals like 'must' and 'ought' is that they are univocal in these different contexts, referring implicitly to a system of *principles*, whether one by which we try to *understand* occurrences or one by which we try to *appraise* them. That we have no clear notion of rational sanction, then, does not itself serve to show that there can be no requirements of rationality.

---

5. For a general account of 'ought' and 'must', the general outlines of which I accept, see Wertheimer 1972.

4. Two theses, first, that reasons have a normative aspect, and second, that the normative appraisal of acts as rational presupposes norms applying to all rational agents, together entail that if some fact is a reason for someone to act, then his or her acting on it is recommended as a consequence of a principle on which all agents ought rationally to act. The normative aspect of reasons consists in their being guides to what we ought rationally to do. And our judgment that some act ought rationally to be taken presupposes a general norm of rationality.

As I noted earlier, this may seem to conflict with our denial of the universality of reasons. How can something's being a reason for a person require that his acting on that consideration be recommended by a universal principle of practical reason if reasons are not universal? The answer is simply that while according to our internalist account a fact's being a reason is not grounded in universal *reason-specifying* principles, it is still anchored in a universal principle: namely, for any agent, if he would be motivated to prefer an act by his rational consideration of a fact about it, then that fact is a reason for him to act. Moreover, when we assert that a particular process of consideration is a *rational* one, we are committed to the minimal normative content of all normative rationality claims. We affirm that the procedure determines for any person which acts are supported by reasons; consequently, we are committed to the judgment that any person ought (rationally) to act as he would be motivated to were he to consider matters in that way. Even in our account, therefore, something is a reason only if it is grounded in a principle on which all agents ought rationally to act.

5. Because rational appraisals are based on norms applying to all rational agents, they are fundamentally *impersonal* and purport to have intersubjective validity. When we appraise an act as rational, even if it is our own act, we consider it from an impersonal standpoint—from the intersubjective standpoint available to subjects of the system of rational norms. Thus, when one judges that something is a reason for someone to act, even if that person is oneself, one makes a judgment that is impersonal and purports to be intersubjectively valid.

To be sure, whether a *subjective* consideration is a reason for someone can be judged, according to our initial account of rational consideration, only by whether she would be moved by that fact were she to make herself vividly aware of it. And that turns on whether she would be moved by it from her own personal standpoint (since that is the only standpoint from which one can be aware of the truth of a subjective consideration). But the deeper principle that makes that fact a *reason* for her, in our initial account, is that anyone ought (rationally) to act, other things equal, as he or she would be motivated to act on making himself or herself vividly aware of relevant facts. And she, and we, can affirm *that principle* as a rational principle only from the impersonal, intersubjective standpoint of a subject of rational norms—a member of the community of rational beings.

Again, this does not require that all reasons be either universal or objective. The motivation that establishes some fact to be a reason may be idiosyncratic or personal or both. But the general account in terms of which we judge whether a fact is a reason does imply a principle on which all agents ought rationally to act. To judge reasons on its basis, therefore, is to be committed to its being a normative principle for rational agents considered as such.

6.   Let us term the system of rational norms the *RNS*, short for *rational normative system*. While norms of the RNS apply to all rational agents, it may not be the case that all agents see themselves as subject to them. If, however, an agent makes use of concepts that implicitly refer to the RNS, such as reason for acting, the rational 'ought', and so on, he commits himself to the idea of the RNS and to his status as a subject of it. Let us call an agent who recognizes himself as a subject of the RNS, a *self-identified subject*.

Normative self-identification admits in general of a distinction between that which H. L. A. Hart calls *internal* and that which is merely *external* (1961, pp. 55–57). It is possible for a person to acknowledge that certain norms apply to him, that he is subject to them, without this recognition's making any direct difference to his behavior, motivation, attitudes, or feelings. Such a person's self-identification as subject to norms is purely *external*.

Consider as an example the way someone who cares nothing for etiquette would view the application of its norms to herself. She might well understand the *idea* of etiquette as comprised of norms for polite behavior that apply generally in society and therefore to herself as well as others. And indeed, she might be quite competent at making appraisals of herself within that system of norms, knowing when, from the point of view of etiquette, she is acting as she ought and when not. But since we imagine her not to care about these matters, we suppose that she is never disposed to perform acts simply because they are required by etiquette. She is inclined neither to reproach herself or others nor to resolve to act differently in the future when her acts violate its norms.

All of this will be different if a person's self-identification as subject to norms is not simply external but *internal*. When we speak of a person internalizing norms we refer to the way in which a person's sense of himself as subject to norms *informs* his motivation, feelings, and attitudes toward himself. The person for whom the norms of etiquette bind internally is disposed to act—more important, to *choose* to act—on its norms, to some degree at any rate, just because they do apply to him.[6] Moreover, his appraisals of himself and his conduct in the light of the norms inform his attitudes and feelings about himself. He is disposed to approval or disapproval, self-reproach or self-satisfaction, partly on the basis of his normative appraisal of himself.[7]

Like any normative system, the RNS can be acknowledged internally or externally. We can imagine an agent for whom, though he has the idea of reasons and the rational 'ought', the fact that a particular course of action is recommended by reasons does

6. Note that even here we need to distinguish between someone who simply has the desire to act politely, viz., as the norms of etiquette require, and one who adopts the internal standpoint with respect to them in the sense that she is disposed to judge herself and others in terms of the norms. Both may be moved by their awareness of the norm, but the person who takes the internal point of view of the norms accepts their existence as justification for her conduct and for judgments of herself.

7. Also important, he is likewise possessed of a basis for similar attitudes and feelings toward others, even if these are not felt or expressed in the same way. The reasons for which we have etiquette, to live gracefully together, may militate against expressing such feelings to others and indeed against allowing oneself to dwell on or to encourage such feelings in oneself toward others.

not *itself* make any difference either to his motivation or to his attitudes. Such an agent will not himself act *for reasons* in the sense that his awareness of certain facts *as reasons* for him to act carries motivational weight. Still, we might imagine that he understands the idea of reasons and relative rationality even if he is not at all disposed to make normative appraisals of himself that bind internally, that make an independent contribution to his motivation and attitudes. To be sure, such a person is but barely imaginable. The very attribution of beliefs and desires to a being presupposes the attribution of *some implicit* rationality. Unless, for example, norms of relative rationality were to some degree *descriptive* of a being, we could make no clear sense of the idea that it believed or desired anything. Behavior cannot be taken as evidence of any particular beliefs or desires unless we suppose some disposition both not to hold simultaneously inconsistent beliefs and to choose acts believed to be effective in getting what is wanted most. Unless the principles of relative rationality are at least approximately descriptive of a being's behavior, we cannot conceive of such behavior as that of one whose acts express its beliefs and desires.

So the behavior of any agent will accord to some degree with the norms of the RNS. What may still be lacking is any internalization of the norms of the RNS as norms. For even if an agent is aware that he is subject to rational norms and that he is already, to some degree, disposed to act in accordance with them, he may still lack any disposition so to act *on account of* the norms. For example, although certain facts that he acknowledges as reasons for him to act are such that his awareness of them does indeed move him to act, he may lack the disposition to act on them because they are reasons for him. His acting may not be at all dependent on his view that they *are reasons*, on his taking his motivation to be the result of rational consideration. The self-identification of such a person as subject of the RNS is merely external.

By contrast, the agent who is internally self-identified as subject of the RNS is one for whom its norms have motivational and attitudinal weight. He is disposed to ask which course of action is best supported by reasons, to consider matters in certain ways because he believes it rational to do so, and to act on his judgment of what, all things considered, it is best to do. Although his reasons will themselves often provide him with motivation, especially when he judges their rationality for himself, his *judgment* of them as reasons is the controlling factor. Moreover, appraisals of himself that he makes from the intersubjective standpoint of a subject of rational norms figure prominently in his own self-esteem.

Since it will play a significant role in the argument of the next chapter, we shall want a shorthand way of referring to an agent who is internally self-identified as subject to rational norms. Let us call such a being an *ISIS* (short for internally self-identified subject) of the RNS.[8]

7. There is a tendency to think that an agent who is concerned with being rational and, therefore, with acting as required by the norms of the RNS, would either be constantly deliberating, always calculating reasons, or excessively concerned with such matters as consistency, to the impoverishment of his life. Because this picture of life is so unattractive, seeming to give no scope to our passions and spontaneous responses and to valued activities in which what is important is precisely that one *not* be calculating and deliberate, we may properly ask whether rationality and acting for reasons is rightly conceived by anyone as an ideal. Is not an ISIS of the RNS, therefore, someone whom we might admire at a distance, perhaps, but someone whom no one would want to *be*?

This objection contains its own reductio, for it implies itself that there are *reasons* against always making decisions on a case-by-case basis. To suppose that a fully rational person would always be deliberating is to suppose that what is suggested is false, that there are never good reasons for not constantly assessing the reasons for particular actions. To take a perfectly clear and uncontroversial example, a person who was concerned with being rational could make the decision to brush his teeth without having to decide before each stroke, or indeed even in midstroke, whether to con-

8. I am indebted to Jay Rosenberg for this suggestion.

tinue. Often, further deliberation frustrates the very activity it has been decided there is good reason to undertake.

Similarly, an ISIS of the RNS may choose to pursue certain activities, projects, or whole sections of life that will involve restricting deliberations, to more or less of a degree, within them, if he sees good reason for making such restrictions. By the same token, this will not mean completely sealing these areas off from further rational consideration. Background assumptions on which the basis of reasons for an activity depends may be challenged by particularly salient occurrences. The person who decides to brush his teeth is still in a position to decide to interrupt his tooth brushing in extraordinary circumstances, say, to put out a fire.

8. It is part of the very idea of the RNS that its norms are *finally authoritative* in settling questions of what to do. With respect to the dictates of law, morality, or etiquette we can always significantly ask *why* we should do what they require or recommend. But in asking this question we implicitly assume the role of subject of the RNS, for we ask what *reason* there is to act morally, legally, and so on. It may turn out, as many believe about morality, for example, that no *further* reason other than moral considerations themselves need be given for acting morally. But this does not mean that our question lacks significance. Its significance consists in the request to be shown that moral considerations *are indeed reasons* for us to act. Once we have established that a line of conduct is recommended by norms of the RNS, however, we put to rest the question of why we should do it. We cannot significantly ask whether there is reason to do what there is reason to do. We may, of course, ask whether we are right in *thinking* there is reason to do something. Or we may ask whether there is reason for us to act according to reason in the sense of living our lives in a very deliberate and calculating way as discussed above. These questions, and variants of them, are significant, but they gain significance not by challenging the authority of rational norms but by being posed from within the RNS itself.

It may be objected that the requirements of any normative

system can be criticized from the vantage point of any other, and therefore, that none can have any superiority. Certainly we may ask whether it is moral to act as reason recommends or whether it would be legal or polite to do so. But such questions do not challenge the authority of rational norms as would the question of *why* we should do what reason requires. And it is only in the case of rational norms that this question is unmeaning. With respect to any other norms we may sensibly ask why (that is, for what reason) we should do what they require of us. Only with respect to those norms in terms of which reasons are themselves understood, conceived as such, can we not meaningfully ask why we should follow them.

Because of the inherent final authority of reasons, an ISIS's commitment to act as reason recommends is, and is seen by him to be, *unconditional.* As noted above, he may restrict his own rationally deliberate activity and could even, at least conceivably, give up future rational action altogether by taking his life. But such an agent's willingness to undertake either would be conditional on his judgment that there were good and sufficient reasons for so doing. They would not, therefore, constitute any qualifying of his commitment to act on rational norms. For in his view that is what action on such norms would recommend. In internalizing a conception of the RNS as constituted by norms that are finally authoritative on matters of practice, he regards his own commitment to follow such norms to be unconditional.

9.   In addition to the idea of an internally self-identified subject of the RNS, we may introduce the notion of a *self-critical subject.* As Gauthier emphasizes, this is an exceedingly important idea. It is undeniable that one can engage in a sort of rational activity without any attempt to articulate and criticize the standards that are inherent in it. A conception of rationality may be only implicit in activity that we appraise as rational. And a person's assessment of the reasons for his acts may not extend to questioning whether what he takes to be reasons are so indeed. Nonetheless, the internal dynamic of rational activity naturally moves in this direction. Once we begin to move away from the immediacy of present

inclinations and take thought of the various alternatives before us, and of the reasons for and against each of them, it is but a further move along this same line of increasing abstraction to ask whether what we suppose to be reasons really are.

Since questions can obviously arise about whether certain considerations are indeed reasons and whether certain reasons really are, as we think, weightier than others, this next step is a natural one. The drive to system, and to critical reflection on it, therefore, is but an extension of a line of movement already begun when we move from behavior that may be characterized as simply purposive and sensitive to changes in awareness of information, to action that is undertaken for reasons. An ISIS of the RNS is, therefore, likely to become a *self-critical subject* as well.

In the next chapter, we shall consider rational norms as they would be viewed by subjects of the RNS who are *both* internally self-identified and self-critical. In order not to complicate our abbreviations unduly let us understand 'ISIS' to refer to a subject who is self-critical as well as internally self-identified.

CHAPTER 15

Impartial Reason

Now that the grounding of reasons in a system of rational norms has been described, we are in a position to bring that framework to bear on the substantive question of what reasons there are for agents to act. The hope is that reflection on formal aspects of the RNS can illuminate to some degree the more substantive question; that form can be at least somewhat fertile.

The grounding of reasons in universal rational principles is not a point of contention in the debate between those who hold moral requirements to give (overriding) reasons for all agents and those who defend an exclusively self-centered theory of practical rationality. It is agreed on all sides that the *universality* of rational principles does not by itself decide the debate. Universal principles may be subjective, as is the principle of informed individual utility maximizing, which was provided by our initial account.[1] Nor does Gauthier's requirement that rational principles be *self-supporting*

---

1. It is important to bear in mind that the objective reasons provided by considerations that would motivate an agent were he to be vividly aware of them (from an impersonal standpoint) are themselves grounded in the subjective principle of our initial account: if S would be motivated to prefer A, other things equal, were he to be vividly aware that *p*, then *p* is a reason for S to do A.

218

decide the issue. Unless we assume that everyone is always perfectly informed about each other's strategies, it may be equally rational, according to *each* respective theory, to choose to act on it.

Gauthier's requirement of self-support is not, perhaps, best regarded as restricting the *form* of acceptable rational principles. It addresses, rather, the role that principles must play in a system of rational norms. We may think of the requirement of self-support as anchored in the way that a rational norm would be regarded by a self-critical subject of the RNS, an agent inclined to assess critically even the norms he ordinarily takes as ultimate standards for rational choice. Faced with the impossibility of looking to some further standard in terms of which to assess the rationality of acting on his ultimate principles, he poses the self-referential question whether it would be rational according to a given principle to choose to act on it.

The more general approach that lies behind this way of grounding self-support is to consider what requirements are imposed on rational principles by the ways in which they must be regarded by ideally rational agents. If we take self-criticalness as one aspect of ideal rationality, the requirement of self-support is then seen to result as a consequence of the way in which an agent who is ideally rational must regard rational principles.

Self-support by itself is, as we have seen, fairly impotent as a basis for deciding between competing substantive conceptions of practical reason. It may be, however, that there are other aspects of ideal rationality that, when combined with self-criticalness, are more helpful. We may assume that another aspect of ideal rationality is internal self-identification as a subject of rational norms, that an ideally rational agent is an ISIS of the RNS. Consequently, we should consider whether, as with self-criticalness, requirements on acceptable rational principles can be formulated as a consequence of features that they must have to be regarded as norms of the RNS by an ISIS.

It is contended in the present chapter that as a result of the way in which rational principles must figure in the *motivation* of an ISIS, and of the way in which he must take his action on rational norms ultimately to be *justified*, we can derive a more stringent

Reason and Right

requirement of self-support. According to this criterion, which we shall call *universal impartial self-support*, it is a requirement of any principle that could be a norm of the RNS that it would be rational according to it to choose *all agents* to act on it, when this choice is made from an *impartial* standpoint. Not surprisingly, it will emerge that a principle of unconstrained individual utility maximizing does not meet this condition. On the other hand, if we think of principles of morally right conduct in some such way as Baier or Rawls suggests (as principles which are, in a suitable sense, in the interest of all alike, or choiceworthy from an impartial original position), it turns out that a principle of rationality counseling conduct in accord with moral principles does satisfy the condition of universal impartial self-support.

But that is not sufficient to validate the latter as a principle of rational conduct. There are presumably any number of possible principles that satisfy the universal impartial self-support condition. The final stage of the argument consists in showing that our initial account of rational consideration can be combined with the requirement of universal impartial self-support to generate a stronger condition on any reason-grounding principle: that it be a principle on which it would be (relatively) rational to choose all to act, were that choice made from a perspective in which one is motivated by a concern for one's ability rationally to pursue ends, as per our initial account, but is denied any information about oneself in particular—a perspective like Rawls's original position. This, I contend, is the intersubjective standpoint of a rational agent as such. Since it is (relatively) rational to choose, from this standpoint, that all agents act on principles of morally right conduct when they find themselves in the company of other agents with whom cooperation and conflict is possible, it follows that it is overridingly rational so to act.

1.   The general idea behind this approach is to reflect on the way in which rational principles function as norms of the RNS. Since any norm must be able to function as a *guide* for subjects, we may formulate what we shall call the *guidance principle*:

Impartial Reason

A principle is a rational principle only if an ISIS of the RNS could regard it as such. [2]

By definition, an ISIS is guided by principles he takes to be norms of the RNS. It is a necessary condition of any principle's actually being a guide for subjects of the RNS, therefore, that an ISIS could regard it as such. If a principle's having a feature is necessary for it to be regarded as a rational principle by an ISIS, then its having that feature is also a necessary condition of its actually being a rational principle.

We may think of the guidance principle as the rational analogue of Kant's idea that the concept of moral duty "contains that of a good will" (1785/1959, p. 13; Ak. p. 397). A Kantian good will is an ISIS of the system of moral norms, disposed to act, as Kant said, "from duty," that is, out of the sense that he morally ought. [3] Although the notion of the good will can be defined only in terms of moral duty, Kant thought that the notion of moral duty can itself only be understood in terms of its reciprocals within a system of moral norms. Something is a moral norm, then, if it is a principle on which a good will, an ISIS of moral norms, would be disposed to act. This means that it is a necessary condition of any norm that in fact grounds moral duties that it could be regarded as such by a good will.

2. To begin the argument, we must consider what is special about the way in which an ISIS regards principles she takes to be norms of the RNS. In order to preserve the distinction between an agent whose behavior simply accords with rational norms and an ISIS, whose conduct so accords because she sees it as what she rationally ought to do, let us suppose that *what* rational norms require or recommend can itself be specified in nonnormative terms.

2. Recall that we are using 'ISIS' to refer both to internal self-identification as a subject of the RNS and to self-criticalness.
3. Unless, Kant believes, like a holy will the person has absolutely no inclination to act otherwise. In that case there can be no constraining of the will and therefore no 'ought'. We need not worry about this complication.

Reason and Right

The general schema for such norms will then be "If p, then, ceteris paribus, do A," where substituends for 'p' and 'A' may be quite general and quite complex. According to an internalist account, 'p' will generally be something like 'after considering facts about A in ways x, y, and z, you are motivated to do A,' where 'x, y, and z' specify the process of rational consideration.[4]

Considering the content of rational norms in this nonnormative way, we can see how a person's behavior may accord with rational norms without her being an ISIS. A person may act in accordance with a rational norm, P, without following P. Indeed, she may even follow P without doing so because it is a rational principle.

In contrast, an ISIS is disposed to act as a rational norm directs *because* she thinks that is what she (and any other subject of the RNS) ought rationally to do. This involves two separable ideas. Since both are crucial, we must note each separately:

1. An ISIS judges her action on a rational norm to be *justified* by its being a rational norm: one on which agents ought rationally to act. (She supposes P's being a rational norm to justify her acting on P.)
2. An ISIS is *motivated* to act on a rational norm by her judgment that it is a rational norm. (Her judgment that P is a rational norm explains her acting on P.)

So an ISIS's action on what she judges to be a rational norm is explained by her judging it to be such, and it is justified, in her view, by its being such.

Number 2 is simply a reformulation of the characterization of an ISIS given in the last chapter. In being internally self-identified as a subject of norms, an agent is disposed to regulate her conduct by them because she sees them as normative for her. Number 1, however, introduces a distinct idea. It asserts that an ISIS of the

4. However, if there are substantive considerations that would be validated as reasons for anyone by a more fundamental internalist principle, then an internalist would recognize a universal rational principle referring explicitly to those considerations. I shall argue at the end of this chapter that considerations of moral requirement have that character.

RNS sees her conduct as conditional on rational norms, not simply in the sense that her awareness of rational norms actually motivates, and therefore explains, her conduct, but that she sees the rational justification for acting on the norms to be itself conditional on their being principles on which agents ought rationally to act.

Suppose, for example, that P is the principle of individual utility, and that an ISIS takes P to be a rational principle. Just as an ISIS's decision to perform specific acts is conditional on her judging them to be supported by reasons, so is her willingness to act on the underlying principles, including P, conditional on her judging them to be principles on which any agent ought rationally to act. And it is conditional in two ways. According to number 1, the rational justifiability of her acting on P is, in her view, conditional on P's being a rational principle: the latter, she believes, justifies the former. And according to number 2, her action on P is in fact conditional on, and motivated by, her judgment that P is a rational principle: the latter explains the former.

Now there is, of course, a sense in which the justification for acting on P, if P is a rational principle, is given by P itself (in our example, by the fact that it will maximize utility). And an ISIS will recognize that. But the ISIS is not simply motivated to act *in accordance with* P; nor even just to follow P out of a desire to act on P (for example, out of a desire to maximize her utility). As an ISIS, she is motivated to act on P by her judgment that P is a rational principle, one on which any agent ought rationally to act. Since this motivation is involved in being internally self-identified as subject to rational norms, and since reasons are (she understands) facts that motivate when considered rationally, she judges there to be a further justification for acting on P, namely, that P is a rational principle.

This may still seem a puzzling claim. How can a subject see her resolve to act on rational principles as rationally justified by their being such principles? Would not justification have to consist in the existence of further reasons? And would not further reasons require further principles, and so on, ad infinitum?

Principles of rational action obviously have to stop somewhere, but it does not follow that there could be a justification for acting on them (other than that given *within* the principles) only if there were *further* reasons and principles that grounded them. What, in the view of an ISIS, justifies action on the most ultimate principles is that they *are* the most ultimate principles on which agents ought rationally to act. There are no further reasons, grounded in yet further principles, for acting on them. But there is still a rational justification for doing so: their being principles that are rationally normative for agents.

The only alternative would be that while an ISIS is disposed to act on P *because* she thinks P to be a principle on which any agent ought rationally to act, 'because' expresses only a relation of causal or explanatory dependence. To see things in this way we must suppose that while the ISIS's acting on P is a result of her thinking P to be a rational principle, she need not view P's having that status as any *justification* for her acting on it. In this view, acting on rational principles is simply, from the ISIS's own viewpoint, an expression of her *desire* to act rationally and not *justified* by the rational principles' status as such. But while an ISIS's action on P is indeed an expression of her (personal) desire to act rationally, she cannot see it as *simply* so from her own viewpoint. That would rob her internalized conception of rationality of its normativity.

To understand this, consider how such an agent would ordinarily regard acts she sees as simply expressions of her desire and not as further justified. While she takes action on her desires to be presumptively rational as per our initial account, she regards the reasons to promote any particular desired state to be contingent on her having the desire, or on its being the case that she would have it were she adequately informed.

In order to regard action on her desire to act rationally similarly, she would have to think that the rational warrant for acting rationally is conditional on her having the desire to be rational; or on its being the case that she would so desire were she adequately informed. But this conflicts with what she internalizes in accepting her status as subject of the RNS. In accepting that role she accepts the idea that norms such as P ought rationally to be acted on by all agents, including herself, simply because they, and she, are subject to them. As an ISIS sees it, the desire to act on rational norms itself has a justification: their being rational norms. Like Butler's "principle of reflection," the ISIS's desire to act on rational norms implicitly claims its own authority.

3. Let us suppose, then, that an ISIS of the RNS judges P (again, the principle of individual utility) to be a rational principle. It follows from the previous discussion that his general resolve to act on P (that is, his desire to maximize his utility) is conditional in two ways. He judges that his desire to act on P is justified by P's being a principle on which all agents ought to act. And his desire to act on P is motivated and explained by his judging that P is such a principle.

Consider, now, the ISIS's *desire* to act on P. We may redescribe this as a desire (or preference) *that he act on P*. Putting it this way brings out the personal character of the preference. But now something interesting and important emerges. While the ISIS's action on P is proximately motivated by the personal desire that *he* act on P (that he maximize his utility, say), that desire or preference has a further explanation and, in his view, a further justification. What explains the ISIS's desire that he act on P is his judgment that P is a principle on which all agents ought rationally to act. It is this judgment, that P is a rationally normative principle, that motivates the ISIS's preference that he act on P. For example, if an ISIS judges that all agents ought rationally to maximize their individual utility, then this judgment motivates and explains his desire that he do so.

Now, as we noted in the last chapter, the judgment that a principle is a rational one is itself appropriately made from an impersonal, rather than the agent's own personal, standpoint. It properly concerns the agent himself only as one agent among others, all of whom are subject to rational norms. This means that insofar as an ISIS is motivated by his judgment that P is a principle on which any agent ought rationally to act, he is motivated from an impersonal standpoint. Any motivation he has, as an ISIS, for preferring that he act on P will be impersonal, therefore. He will be motivated to prefer that he, qua rational agent, act on P. Consequently, he will have the very same motivation to prefer that *any* agent act on P, indeed, that all do so. To return to our example, if an ISIS judges that all agents ought rationally to maximize their individual utility, he will be motivated *by that judgment* to prefer that he, as an agent, maximize his utility. But since the judgment is itself impersonal, any motivation it can provide will also be impersonal. Consequently, it will also motivate his preferring that all agents maximize their individual utility.

It follows, therefore, that a necessary condition of an ISIS's regarding P to be a rational principle is that he impersonally prefer that all agents act on P. Moreover, since his preference that all agents act on P is grounded in P's being a rational principle, it will not be conditional on anything not relevant to the latter judgment. This means that in addition to being impersonal, the preference will not be personally based. We may say, then, that if an ISIS takes P to be a rational principle, then he prefers from the impartial standpoint of an arbitrary rational agent that all agents act on P. This is the motivational consequence of the internal acceptance of rational norms.

4. An objection quickly suggests itself. Why should we suppose that an ISIS's preference that he act on P is motivated by his judging P to be a principle on which *any* agent ought rationally to act? Rather, why would he not see that preference as justified by P's being a principle on which *he* ought rationally to act? This latter justification is *subjective* and would not motivate, therefore, an impersonal preference for the similar conduct of others.

But the subjectivity here is only superficial. What is true is that he, *qua subject of the RNS*, ought rationally to act on P. No judgment that *he* ought rationally to act on P can be made independently of the judgment that *any* agent ought. Consequently, both judgments can be made only from the impersonal standpoint. The preference they motivate is, therefore, the impersonal one that all agents act on P.

Note how unlike the paradigmatic subjective consideration, 'that acting on P would promote his interest,' this is. Whether that judgment is true of an agent or not depends on *who he is*. And whether it is true of himself can be determined by an agent only from a perspective in which he has that information. Of course, it might be known that for any person, his acting on P would promote his interests. But that fact is, as it were, the sum of a number of logically independent facts: that it is in the interest of S, T, ... That one can judge whether P is in one's interest from the impersonal standpoint in this case is dependent on knowing there to be a true generalization of such logically independent facts. But the judgment of an ISIS that any agent ought rationally to act on P is not derivative as a sum of such logically independent judgments: that S, T, . . . , ought rationally act on P. To judge of any agent that he ought rationally to act on P, if P is an ultimate principle, is to judge of every agent that he ought rationally to act on P. The impersonal assessability of this judgment is fundamental and not derived.

It may also be objected that while an ISIS's preference that he, the ISIS, act on P is grounded in his judgment that P is a rational principle only if he would judge that any *other* agent's preference that he, the other, act on P is similarly justifiable, it does not follow that an ISIS would impersonally prefer that all agents act on P. But if what justifies *and* motivates an ISIS's preference that *he* act on P is (his judgment) that P is a principle on which all agents ought rationally to act, how can that judgment, taken by itself, motivate a preference simply for *his* acting on P? It could do so only if the judgment were essentially a judgment about his own conduct, made from his own standpoint. Since it is not, and since the judgment itself motivates the ISIS's preference that he act on P, it motivates equally his preferring that all agents do so.

I suspect that those inclined to make this objection have in mind a sort of rational egoist who is willing to admit that his preference for promoting his own interest is no more, but no less, rational than any person's preference for promoting his. What the egoist need not admit, they may think, is that an ideally rational agent would prefer that *everyone* promote his or her interest.

What this objection overlooks is the role that the judgment that a principle is a rational principle plays in the motivation of an ISIS. The rational egoist, as conceived by the objection, is an egoist first and a rationalist second. He begins with a concern for his own interest and accepts the rationality of the self-interested conduct of others as the price for maintaining the rationality of his own self-interested conduct. Such an agent is not an ISIS. An ISIS is concerned first and fundamentally to act rationally. Insofar as she is an ISIS, any preference she has for promoting her own interest will be motivated by her judgment that any agent ought rationally to do so. Since the latter judgment is impersonal, it will motivate the impersonal preference that all agents promote their own interest.

The preceding argument can be put intuitively in the following way. The motivation that an ISIS has for acting on rational principles is motivation qua subject of rational norms; that is, qua member of the community of rational beings. She identifies fundamentally with the standpoint of a subject of rational norms and is motivated *from that standpoint* to act on them. But that standpoint is an impersonal, intersubjective standpoint. Consequently, any motivation she has, qua subject, for her so acting she has equally for preferring any subject so to act. Therefore, if an ISIS regards something to be a rational principle it will be her will, from the impersonal, intersubjective standpoint of a subject of rational norms, that all agents act on it.

5.   Let us now reconsider the other aspect of ideal rationality that figures in the guidance principle: self-criticalness. We may think of self-criticalness as also implicit in the concern to act on rational principles. It is the readiness to consider whether principles that we suppose to be rational are so indeed.

We saw how Gauthier's requirement of self-support can be thought of as arising from the guidance principle by reflecting on how rational principles must be regarded by self-critical subjects. The question of whether an ultimate principle is a rational one cannot be settled by appeal to yet further principles, so a self-critical subject will be concerned to note whether the principle is self-supporting, whether it provides a standard of rational choices that recommends itself as the object of rational choice. Since a self-critical subject can suppose a principle to be a rational one only if it is self-supporting, it follows from the guidance principle that rational principles must *be* self-supporting.

Taken by itself, self-support is, *pace* Gauthier, impotent to settle the issue between exclusively self-centered and morality-regarding theories of practical reason. If, however, we combine the requirement of self-support with the conclusion of the last section, an argument comes into view. In asking the self-critical question, namely, whether a principle really is a rational one, an ISIS of the RNS asks, in effect, this question: *Does this principle have the property that would justify its being my preference from an impartial perspective that all agents act on it?* Although she cannot, we may suppose, answer the question by invoking a further principle, she can still ask the question of principles self-referentially. But the question she will now ask is not simply the question that Gauthier proposes—Is it rational according to this principle to choose to act on it? Rather the question she must ask is this one: Would it be rational according to this principle for a person who views matters from an impartial standpoint to choose that all agents act on it?

If an agent is an ISIS of the RNS, she will regard a principle as an ultimately rational one, then, only on the condition that it would be rational according to it for her to choose, from an impartial perspective, that all agents act on it. It follows from the guidance principle, then, that satisfying this requirement is a necessary condition of a principle's being a rational norm.[5] We may call this the requirement of *universal impartial self-support*.

Again, we may view passing this test only as a necessary, but not sufficient, credential for being a rational principle. There are presumably any number of principles having the property that it would be rational according *to them* to choose from an impartial standpoint that all agents act on them. But, like Gauthier, we have a special interest in whether the principle of maximizing informed individual utility satisfies this requirement. Not only is this principle well entrenched but we have already accepted on internalist

5. This is true only of reason-grounding principles and not of principles of relative rationality. The latter are not related to motivation in the same way as reasons. I take principles of relative rationality as being an articulation of the idea of coherence.

grounds that facts that motivate an agent to prefer an act when he attentively considers them are reasons for the agent to act. And this, together with considerations of relative rationality, entails that it is rational for agents to maximize informed individual utility, *other things equal.*[6] Like Gauthier, then, we have a special reason to consider the question of whether a principle counseling such action, and only such action, would be self-supporting in our special sense.

6. The issue before us, therefore, is whether, were we to choose from the impersonal, intersubjective standpoint of a rational agent (considered as such), it would be rational, according to the principle of maximizing individual utility, to choose that all agents act on that principle. But how are we to understand the impartial standpoint of an arbitrary rational agent? After Rawls's idea of the original position, I propose that we think of that perspective as defined by a *veil of ignorance,* though a somewhat "thicker" veil than characterizes the original position.

As Rawls conceives the original position, it is one in which the chooser is ignorant of any facts about himself and his circumstances in particular. He is assumed to know, however, whatever general truths there are about human beings, along with the fact that he is human. Furthermore, he knows that he is in what Rawls terms the "circumstances of justice": conditions of moderate scarcity that make cooperation both necessary and possible.

For our purposes we may understand the impartial perspective of a rational agent as one having an even thicker veil of ignorance than Rawls's. Whereas his original position is impartial with respect to human beings, let us imagine that our hypothetical chooser is ignorant of every fact about himself except whatever is involved in his being a rational agent. We may assume, therefore, that he knows that he has preferences, the capacity to revise his preferences in the light of information and experience, and, as per our initial account, the disposition rationally to realize his in-

---

6. To make matters simpler from here on, I will mean *informed* individual utility when I speak of individual utility.

formed preferences, other things equal.[7] Further, we may imagine that like Rawls's choosers, he is perfectly informed on general matters.

Actually, it is not sufficient even for Rawls's purposes that the veil be simply one of *ignorance*. After all, a person may be ignorant of desires and interests while these still affect choices.[8] What the veil of ignorance is supposed to accomplish is not just an abstraction from information regarding individual preferences and interests but from their motive power as well. So suppose that those behind our thicker veil are both ignorant of any preferences they may have that are not common to any rational agent as such and immune to their motive force. This means that there is in effect only one chooser behind the veil: an arbitrary rational agent.

7. Is the choice of everyone's acting on the principle of individual utility a rational one, as judged by that principle, when it is made from the perspective of an arbitrary rational agent? Put more perspicuously, would it maximize the expected utility of a person choosing behind a thick veil of ignorance to choose that all agents act on the unconstrained principle of individual utility? It seems clear that it would not.[9]

---

7. 'Other things equal' because we may suppose that such beings are also rational in the sense that they are willing, and able, to constrain their pursuit of informed preference by principles that would be chosen. (This is comparable to Rawls's assumption that his principles are chosen for beings with a sense of justice.) We also suppose that such a being is relatively rational. It is important to appreciate that Rawls supposes not simply that the parties know that they will have some conception of the good and that they desire to pursue it, whatever it is. He assumes also that some things are part of any *rational* conception of the good, most important, the freedom to criticize and revise one's ends that is required for one to be autonomous—for one's ends to be rationally self-chosen. On this extremely important point see Rawls 1974, p. 533, and 1975b, p. 94. See also Scanlon 1974, p. 178, and Buchanan 1975. I have treated these issues in Darwall 1980 insofar as they bear on Rawls's thesis that there is a Kantian interpretation of justice as fairness.

8. This point is made by Levin (1978).

9. As with Rawls's choice of principles from an original position, our arbitrary rational agent chooses principles on which all will act *once the veil of ignorance is lifted*. He is concerned, therefore, with how everyone's acting on a given principle will affect his own rational pursuits.

There are, of course, circumstances in which everyone's maximizing individual utility would maximize an individual's utility (relative to everyone's acting on some other principle)—if, for example, not even the suspicion of conflict of interest existed, or if that person had an extraordinary power advantage or the ring of Gyges. But the range of possible situations is not limited to these. Indeed, the circumstances in which all the rational agents of whom we are aware exist approximate rather more a Hobbes situation. And, as we have seen, everyone's maximizing individual utility in these circumstances leads to a worse situation for each. Each does better if all constrain their pursuit of individual preference by principles of morally right conduct. For example, each does better if all constrain their pursuit of individual utility by the principle of nonmaleficence than if all pursue individual utility without consideration of harm to others.

But if an agent behind a thick veil of ignorance cannot know that his actual situation is not a Hobbes situation, neither can he know that it is. So it does not follow directly from the considerations in the last paragraph that a choice, made in ignorance of actual circumstances, that everyone act on the principle of individual utility would not maximize expectable utility.

Since whether it would *in fact* maximize utility for all to act on the principle of individual utility depends on the actual circumstances in which rational agents are placed (once the veil is lifted), it seems only reasonable, when behind a thick veil, to choose principles sensitive to these circumstances. Consider the following pair of conditional principles which together may be thought of as forming a conjunctive principle.

If there are no other agents with whom cooperation or conflict is possible, then maximize informed individual utility.

If there are other agents with whom cooperation or conflict is possible, then constrain pursuit of informed individual utility by requirements of morally right conduct (for example, by the requirement of nonmaleficence).

Evidently, the choice behind the veil of every agent's acting on this conjunctive principle would have a higher expectable utility than would the choice of everyone's acting on the principle of individual utility. In situations in which there is no possible conflict or cooperation the two principles give identical guidance. But their divergence in situations of potential conflict or cooperation favors the principle that recognizes the overriding authority of moral requirements, since the expectable outcomes are better for all. For example, in Hobbes situations, all do better if they constrain their pursuit of self-interest by the principle of nonmaleficence than if they do not.

The significant possibility of Hobbes situations, then, makes it impossible for an exclusively self-centered theory of practical reasons to satisfy the condition of universal impartial self-support. It follows that reasons grounded in our initial account of rational consideration cannot be the only reasons to act. Indeed, it follows that a conception that recognizes moral considerations as reasons but that allows them always to be overridden by considerations of individual preference cannot be self-supporting in the required way, since it would give the same all-things-considered guidance in Hobbes situations as would the principle of individual utility. That is, it follows both that reasons grounded in our initial account are not the only reasons to act and that they cannot systematically override considerations of moral requirement.

We may take it, moreover, that the conjunctive principle does not lack its own support in the requisite sense. Nothing similar to the sorts of conflict created when everyone acts on the principle of individual utility seems to arise when everyone acts on the conjunctive principle. Choosing that everyone act on the conjunctive principle accords with the conjunctive principle itself. In circumstances of no potential conflict or cooperation the choice will maximize expectable utility, and in those of potential conflict and cooperation the choice appears to accord with principles of right conduct. It seems incontestable that if one could by one's own choice bring it about that everyone (oneself included) act as morality requires, morality would require one so to choose; especially if the only alternative, as in this case, is a choice that would bring about generally unethical conduct.

8.   A principle that directs agents to give greater weight to moral requirements than to reasons grounded in our initial account satisfies the condition of universal impartial self-support. And principles that claim that reasons grounded in our initial account are either the only reasons or always overriding reasons do not satisfy that condition. We may conclude from this that the latter must be rejected as rational principles. Since we have supposed universal impartial self-support to be a necessary condition only of principles of rationality, however, we cannot yet conclude that the conjunctive principle is a rational norm or that moral requirements do in fact provide overriding reasons for any agent in a Hobbes situation.

We have, nonetheless, the resources to draw this further conclusion, for the conjunctive principle is not simply *self*-supporting. In addition it has the property, we have supposed, of being the principle that would be chosen from a perspective of an arbitrary agent *concerned to be rational in the sense of our initial account.* [10] And we have good independent grounds for supposing our initial account to be at least a partial account of practical reason. This means that we have grounds, as I emphasized at the beginning of Chapter 9, to embrace a conception of the rational person as having a "highest order interest," as Rawls puts it, in revising her ends by reflection on reasons she finds compelling and as being committed, at least tentatively, to our initial account of reasons as facts that motivate one to prefer certain ends when such facts are reflectively considered.

An agent who accepted as tenable our initial account of rational

10.   As I shall make clear in the next chapter, the sense in which the conjunctive principle *would* be chosen is that in which the *rational* choice would be *relative to* promoting the end of maximizing an arbitrary rational agent's ability rationally to pursue his informed preferences. Since principles of relative rationality are not themselves grounded by such a choice test, no circularity is involved.

consideration and the theory of reasons it generates, *other things equal,* and who considered what principles it would be rational for him to choose all to act on, supposing the choice to be made from the intersubjective standpoint of an arbitrary agent concerned to be rational in that sense, would choose the conjunctive principle. So, not only is that principle self-supporting in the required way, it also has the property of being the principle that would be impartially chosen for all to act on when that choice is made for agents who are concerned to be rational in terms of our independently grounded initial account. We may see it, therefore, as an extension of our initial account required by the normativity of reasons.

We may appreciate this point, and see its relation to an internalist account of reasons, by thinking along more explicitly internalist lines. The ground for our initial account of reasons is its internalist character—the way it explains the close connection between judging there to be reasons to do something and being motivated to do it. But the initial account is not necessarily a complete theory, for reasons also have a normative aspect. They are guides to what we rationally ought to do. This compels us to say that reasons are facts the *rational* consideration of which motivate (where 'rational' has normative force). We accept our initial account as one form of rational consideration, but the question arises, is it the only one?

Now how is an internalist to think of the property of being a *rational* way of considering things? Is that not as likely a candidate for being a nonnatural metaphysical property as the property of being a reason? And what about the ISIS's desire to consider matters rationally (so that then he might be directly motivated by facts that are reasons)? Does that not threaten to be the same superadded desire which the internalist thought to make a mystery of rational motivation, reappearing at a new level? The same arguments that the internalist finds compelling for thinking of the property of being a *reason* as a complicated motivational property seem also to apply to the property of being a *rational* way of considering things. This means that, as the internalist sees it, the ISIS's desire to be rational cannot be a superadded fascination with a metaphysical property. Rather, it is a concern to act in ways, and

235

to consider matters in ways, that themselves have a certain motivational attraction for the ISIS. But the argument of this chapter enables us to see in precisely what that motivational attraction must consist. In regarding a way of considering things as rational the ISIS regards it as normative for any agent. Consequently its attraction for him is not simply personal but one he apprehends from the impartial standpoint of an arbitrary rational agent. The ISIS is concerned to act on principles that he would *choose*, from that standpoint, all to act on.

Consider now an internalist who accepts our initial account of rational consideration, other things equal. What he wants to know is whether the initial account is adequate as it stands or whether it must be extended—in short, whether there are ways of rationally considering things other than simply making oneself vividly aware of facts about alternative acts. As dictated by the argument of the present chapter, he assumes the position of an arbitrary agent concerned to be rational as per our initial account and considers the state of affairs of everyone's acting exclusively on the initial account. If he reasons as in the preceding section, he will prefer the state of affairs of everyone's acting on the conjunctive principle to the state of affairs of everyone's acting exclusively on the initial account. Actually, since an internalist compares ways of considering things, we should strictly say that he prefers the state of affairs of everyone's acting on principles they would be led to adopt were *they* rationally to consider from the impersonal, intersubjective standpoint of a rational agent everyone's acting on them *and* that it would be (relatively) rational for them (and him) to choose the conjunctive principle on so considering. This fact demonstrates to him that the initial account cannot be a complete account of rational consideration. It *also* shows the way in which it must be completed: to consider rationally a fact as related to someone's doing something, one must consider whether one (anyone) would choose from the standpoint of an arbitrary agent concerned to be rational in the terms of our initial account that everyone act on a relevant principle.

There are two ways in which a principle might be relevant to a fact's relating to some act. A principle might, like a principle of right conduct, *specify* facts that are relevant. Principles of right conduct are overriding reasons in the extended internalist account because, first, from the standpoint of an arbitrary rational agent, anyone would rationally choose that all act on principles that they would rationally choose from an impartial standpoint everyone to act on, and, second, the principles anyone would rationally choose all to act on from that standpoint include principles of right conduct.

Or a principle may be relevant not in the sense that it specifies the fact as a reason for or against the act but in the sense that it directs an agent to perform the act *if* he is motivated by his awareness of the fact so to act (as in the initial account). Reasons grounded in this way in the initial account are also grounded in the extended account, since the principles that would be impartially chosen direct one to pursue informed individual preferences except when constrained by requirements of right conduct.

Since, if the argument of the preceding section is sound, it would be rational for any agent to choose, from the standpoint of an arbitrary agent concerned to pursue his ends rationally, that all agents act on the conjunctive principle, we may suppose that an internalist account of reasons, while basically procedural, will establish certain substantive considerations as overriding reasons for all agents. So even though what the internalist is fundamentally concerned with is whether ways of considering things are rational or not, he will end up with certain specific considerations, the requirements of right conduct, as reasons for any agent in a Hobbes situation.

Internalist considerations enter at two places in our construction, therefore. They enter initially as support both for a general account of reasons as facts that motivate when rationally considered and for the initial account of rational consideration itself. Their second point of relevance is as support for our idea that the judgment of whether a principle is a rational one, or whether a way of considering things is a rational one, itself involves a condition of will. Since these judgments can be made only from the impersonal, intersubjective standpoint of a subject of rational norms, the *relevant* condition of will is whether one would choose from that standpoint that all act on a given principle.

9. We have taken many steps in this chapter, and since by this point the exact path must be somewhat unclear, a summary is in order.

The normativity of reasons led us to investigate their grounding in principles on which all agents ought rationally to act—norms of a rational normative system. From a purely systemic conception of such norms, guides for the conduct of subjects of the RNS, we derived the guidance principle: something is a rational principle only if it can be so regarded by an ISIS of the RNS.

In considering a principle to be rational, and therefore one on which all agents ought rationally to act, an ISIS takes herself to have a justification for acting and for desiring to act on it: that it is a principle on which any agent ought rationally to act. And in being motivated by that impersonal judgment to prefer that she act on it, she is motivated also to prefer that any agent do so. When she judges a principle to be rational, therefore, and is motivated by that judgment to act on the principle, she takes the principle to have a property that justifies her impersonally preferring that all agents act on it.

Moreover, as a self-critical agent she is disposed to consider, of those principles she supposes to be rational ones, whether they are so indeed. When she cannot appeal to further principles to decide this, she must ask of particular candidates whether they are self-supporting. Consequently, she approaches the question of whether a principle has that property that would justify her impartially preferring every agent to act on it, through the question of whether it would be rational according to a given principle to choose, from an impartial perspective, that all agents act on it. It follows from the guidance principle that something can be a rational principle only if it satisfies this requirement of universal impartial self-support.

Although perhaps many principles have the required property, our having an independent argument for the rationality, other things equal, of pursuing one's own informed preferences gives us a special reason to ask whether the principle counseling *only* such action supports itself in the right way. It does not, and therefore it cannot be a principle on which all agents ought rationally to act.

Among those principles that can provide their own universal impartial support, the presumptive rationality of action that promotes the agent's own informed preferences warrants our asking which principles would be chosen by an agent who is concerned to pursue his informed preferences and who chooses from behind a thick veil of ignorance. Whatever principles would be so chosen have a claim on us as principles on which all agents ought rationally to act. The effectively unanimous verdict of writers in this area is that the object of rational choice under such circumstances includes principles that direct the constraining of individual utility maximizing by the requirements of morally right conduct, at least for agents who, like us, live in circumstances of potential cooperation and conflict. Moral considerations of this sort provide, therefore, overriding reasons for any agent who finds himself in these circumstances.

These same conclusions are confirmed by a more explicitly internalist argument as well. In an internalist view, not only the rationality of specific facts but also that of a procedure of consideration must consist in the capacity of each to motivate preference under certain conditions. In this case, since the relevant principles purport to have intersubjective validity and because our initial account has independent grounding, it turns out that principles that adequately define rational consideration must be those on which one, from the intersubjective standpoint of an agent concerned to be rational as per our initial account, would choose all agents to proceed. The initial account is proved not fully adequate by this test. Rather, the process of rational consideration that would be chosen is the procedure of universal impartial choice just described. Moreover, there exist substantive principles recommended for all from that standpoint, and they direct agents to act on moral requirements in Hobbes situations.

CHAPTER 16

Caveats and Consequences

With the general outlines of our theory of reasons sketched in, many questions regarding the theory's details and implications suggest themselves. In this chapter we shall consider a few of these, but only a few.

1. The argument of the last chapter concluded that principles of rational action are those that *would* be chosen for all to act on by a person concerned to pursue his informed preferences but lacking any knowledge about himself in particular. However, if 'would' here is simply predictive, what reason is there to think that different individuals would in fact make the same choice from behind the veil?

It may seem that we cannot deal with this problem by Rawls's method of considering what principles it would be *rational* for individuals to choose, concluding that since everyone is in the same position, what is rational for one must be rational for all. That path seems closed, since what is at issue is what the principles of rational action themselves are. Would it not be viciously circular to say that principles that ground reasons are those that it would be rational for one to choose in one's interest for all to act on from behind a thick veil of ignorance?

Caveats and Consequences

The perhaps surprising answer is that it would not. In considering what it would be rational for a person behind the thick veil to choose *in order to* enhance his ability to pursue informed preference, we are considering a question not of substantive reasons for acting, but of means-end or *relative rationality*. Consequently, we can bring to bear the appropriate theories of relative rationality: the hypothetical imperative, Rawls's principles of rational choice, and the theory of decision in circumstances of uncertainty. These theories can be thought of as articulating a concept of *coherence* and do not themselves require grounding in principles that would be impartially chosen for all. Since they articulate the very notion of coherent choice, they cannot themselves be subject to a test of choice, hypothetical or actual. No problem arises, therefore, in using the notion of relative rationality to ground a theory of substantive reasons for acting.

It is notorious that the theory of decision under uncertainty has yet to generate a single received paradigm, so it may be questioned whether there is a single set of principles that it would be rational to choose from behind a thick veil. The mixed reception of Rawls's argument from the original position for his principles of justice makes clear that people have very different views on just what it would be rational to choose from behind a veil of ignorance. Perhaps there is no single solution. Were this the case, our theory would dictate that there is no single correct answer to the question of what reasons there are for a given person to act in a given situation. Not only might people reasonably disagree about reasons; there might be no rational method of settling their disagreements.

I think that it is fair to say that at this point no one knows the truth about these matters. Should it turn out that there are no single solutions to problems of rational decision in conditions of uncertainty, and consequently, to what to choose from behind the thick veil, then it seems not an unwelcome consequence that our theory requires us to accept a similar indeterminacy regarding reasons for acting. At the very least, we may still be able to specify a *range* of principles that it might be rational to choose. Even if, for example, we cannot specify precisely which principles of morality

241

it would be rational to choose for all to act on in Hobbes situations, we will still be able to see that it is rational to choose one within the range rather than, say, any principle of an exclusively self-centered theory of reasons.

2. This latter point raises the issue of the *conditionality* of rational principles. There are a number of points connected with this general matter.

To begin with, it should be pointed out that even if rational principles are conditional, that does not undercut their grounding as rationally choiceworthy from behind a thick veil for *all* to act on. Indeed, as we have seen, it is their very conditionality that makes them most eligible. Conditional rational principles still *apply* to all agents even if they are not in the relevant conditions. They are valid for all in the plain sense that it is true of all agents that were they in the appropriate conditions the principles would provide rational guidance for them.

It is noteworthy that this very same conditionality attaches to Rawls's principles of justice. Although they are requirements for social institutions that are stated in unconditional terms, they can be thought of as conditionally applicable to all persons. If Rawls is right about what justice requires, then of all persons it is true that *if* they are in the circumstances of justice, then they (as a collectivity) are to satisfy his two principles. The principles give no direct guidance to individuals who are not in those circumstances, but the conditional principles are still applicable to them.

Our veil of ignorance is thicker than that of Rawls's original position. Nonetheless, if a principle would be chosen from the Rawlsian original position, we may suppose that an associated conditional principle would be chosen from behind the thicker veil: one that holds social institutions accountable to the Rawlsian principles, conditional on the existence of the circumstances of justice. The question of just who is to be considered a member of a society in deciding, for example, whether the difference principle has been satisfied, is a problem that arises both for Rawls's principles and for whatever correlates would be chosen from behind a thicker veil.[1] How are boundaries to be drawn? Or should they be drawn at all? What does it matter if a society satisfies a principle of justice if it is set within a large potential social order that does not satisfy it?

These are serious problems. The key to seeing a way through them is to realize that customs, conventions, and understandings affect reasons to act.[2] Consider an extreme instance of Prisoners' Dilemma.[3] Since each prisoner does better if both do not confess, it seems plain that this is the strategy that one would choose each to act on from behind a thick veil. It appears to follow in our theory that each prisoner has a reason not to confess that overrides his reason of self-interest to confess. Moreover, it appears to follow that each has an overriding reason not to confess *even if* the other is going to confess, for it is still true that for both to follow the strategy of nonconfession would be better for each. Our theory seems to commit us to the untoward result that it is rational to sacrifice oneself to others who have no intention of cooperating in joint action for mutual benefit, but there actually is no such implication. If the other will in fact confess, regardless of whether it is rational to do so, then that is itself one of the fixed conditions of the situation. And what we must consider, therefore, is what principle it would be rational to choose all to act on in *that* kind of situation. Even if it would be better if both did not confess, that cannot possibly happen, since it is one of the givens of the situation that the other will in fact confess. Since the other's behavior is already set, we must simply regard it as though it were a part of the (nonrational) world in which the action takes place. Accordingly, we consider only what principle one could impartially recom-

1. The Difference Principle, Rawls's second principle of justice, requires that "social and economic inequalities are to be arranged so that they are both: (a) to the greatest benefit of the least advantaged, . . . and (b) attached to offices and positions open to all under conditions of fair equality of opportunity" (Rawls 1971, p. 302).

2. I am indebted here to conversations with and to the writings of Conrad D. Johnson, especially his "Moral Legislation," presently unpublished. The classic work on convention is Lewis 1969.

3. The description of Prisoners' Dilemma is given in Chapter 13.

mend to *actors* in this kind of situation. The principle most in one's interest, from behind the thick veil, would recommend confession if it is given that others will confess.[4]

What it is rational to choose depends on what others will in fact do. If their conduct is unalterable it must simply be regarded as a condition of action, and rational principles will take such conditions into account. Another clear example of rational principles' including conditions regarding the actual conduct of others is the circumstance in which each person's interest, considered behind a veil, is best served by any of a number of different *coordinated* patterns of conduct. The classic example is provided by rules of the road. If rational principles could not take into account circumstances concerning actually existing understandings and conventions, they could give no guidance, for example, to motorists regarding what side of the road to drive on. Since it is equally in an arbitrary person's interest either that everyone drive on the right or on the left, there would *seem* in our theory to be equal reason for a motorist to drive down either. But once we take into account as a circumstance of action the existence of an understanding that people will drive on the right, it is plain that there is reason for motorists to drive on the right and *not* on the left. The principle one would impartially choose all to act on in circumstances in which this understanding exists is to follow the understanding.

This example raises a general and very important point about the role of convention in rational action. Consider Rawls's principles of justice. These principles structure an *ideal* in that they say what a society *most* in the rational interests of an arbitrary human person would be like. But we, of course, find ourselves in societies that are less than ideal. Even if we should work for the actualization of that ideal, that cannot be our sole guide. Claims on us arise

4. Note that it follows from this that, for example, the principle of nonmaleficence will be rationally binding on all only if others do not flout it. Principles of the right, binding on all rational agents, differ in this way from considerations of intersubjective *value*. There is a sense in which the former articulate a conception of fair or reasonable cooperation.

from *existing* customs, laws, contracts, and the like; while they are not ideally just, they are nonetheless what we in fact have.

One instance of this general difficulty is the vexing problem of worldwide justice. If we believe, for example, that a just society will satisfy Rawls's difference principle, then we may well believe that justice on the planet will not be achieved until the difference principle is satisfied by the world society, not just each particular society. One major obstacle to achieving such worldwide justice is that there is no world society in the same sense that we have different societies. For that to exist we would have to have worldwide custom, law, and conventions with de facto authority sufficient to serve as a vehicle for worldwide justice.

What does justice require of particular nation-states in the present situation? If it is parochial in the long run for them to concern themselves solely with the justice of their own societies, how can they be justified in doing so? But how can they concern themselves simply with what would be ideally just on a worldwide basis if there exists no political scheme for achieving it and if other nations are not similarly concerned?

Again, it would seem that we should consider what policy or strategy could be chosen for all from an impartial standpoint for situations in which these complications exist. Seen in this way, the existing understandings and conventions are a crucial and ineliminable part of the situation to be addressed from behind the veil. Accordingly, it may be rational and just, for example, for a nation to give some greater concern to achieving justice within its own society than to solving the problem of worldwide justice. But from a genuinely impartial perspective it will also be evident that it should be actively working to form the coalitions necessary ultimately to achieve such coordinated worldwide efforts.

The general moral is that what there is reason to do will partly depend on actually existing conventions for conduct. Even if those conventions are at odds with others that would be more in a person's rational interest, considered from behind the veil, it does not follow that they may be rationally disregarded. For what conduct one could recommend to all, *given their existence*, may be quite different from what would be desirable if they did not actually exist. Even if the present tax laws cannot be embraced from behind a veil of ignorance, that does not mean there is no reason to respect them given their existence.

3. The argument of the last chapter may be regarded as providing the cash value for one version of the claim that there is a *Kantian interpretation* of Rawls's theory of justice. This is a matter about which I have written at greater length elsewhere (Darwall 1980), but because the present work provides an argument for one of the main claims of the Kantian interpretation, it is appropriate to make some remarks here.

In *A Theory of Justice*, Rawls writes: "Within the framework of justice as fairness we can reformulate and establish Kantian themes by using a suitably general conception of rational choice" (1971, p. 584). It is his view, then, that there is a broader conception of practical reason, other than the "economic rationality" assumed to characterize the parties to the original position, which is expressed in our willingness to regulate conduct by principles we could impartially choose for all. This is, of course, one of Kant's most famous doctrines. Principles of morality are principles of pure practical reason.

In the explicit discussion of his claim to a Kantian interpretation, however, Rawls focuses his remarks more on the connection between the original position and the Kantian ideas of autonomy, the categorical imperative, and the realm of ends, and less on practical reason itself (1971, pp. 251–257). Since he does not attempt to sketch, as did Kant, the relation between autonomy and reason, this leaves one rather unsure why it is that practical reason has anything at all to do with action on principles that could be willed for all from an impartial standpoint.

David Richards (1971) has propounded a theory of practical reason that attempts to fill this gap.[5] He maintains that there is a distinction within practical reason between the *rational* and the *reasonable*. Being rational, he believes, is a matter of acting in

5. This view evidently owes a great deal to Rawls's own work.

ways that are rational relative to one's interests. This makes rationality identical with what Rawls calls economic rationality. To be reasonable, however, is to be willing to give and accept reasons that are compelling from an impartial or intersubjective standpoint. The reasonable person is willing to regulate conduct by principles that would be chosen for all from an impartial perspective. [6] His willingness to be fair and just in his dealings with others and to live in societies that satisfy the principles of justice is an expression of practical reason even if it is not required by rationality. It is what is necessary to be reasonable. The basic problem with this view, which Rawls himself embraces in his recent Dewey lectures (1980, pp. 528–533), is that it leaves unexplained why rationality and reasonableness are both aspects of practical reason. Why, we may ask, should we not regard reasonableness, so characterized, as simply a category of *moral* appraisal? Why, other than by simple assertion, is it associated with practical reason at all?

These are, of course, the questions that the arguments of the last two chapters are intended to settle. If we conceive of reasonableness in the above way, these arguments show why reason requires us to be reasonable as well as to be rational.

Rawls has been criticized by Kantians who argue that the attempt to derive principles of justice from the original position is not at all Kantian in spirit. They maintain that according to Kant any principle that is based on a desire must be heteronomous. So they see Rawls's assumptions that the parties in the original position are motivated by self-interest and by a desire for primary goods as incompatible with the principles of justice being categorical imperatives, or Kantian "laws of freedom."

Two replies are appropriate. First, it is not plausible to regard primary goods simply, as one critic has put it, as "transhistorical human wants" (Levine 1974, p. 51). If primary goods are considered as what it would be rational for an agent to prefer in his own pursuit of informed preferences from behind the veil, it is difficult

---

6. As I noted in Chapter 1, note 4, the distinction between the rational and the reasonable is made by a number of writers.

to see what ties them in particular to the *human* condition. Liberties, opportunities, command over resources, and self-respect are all presumably of value to any agent with the desire rationally to pursue ends. Second, the principles of justice are not conditional on desire in a way that Kant would have thought to be evidence of their heteronomy. They are to be adopted not because they are a means to desire-satisfaction but because they would be chosen behind a veil of ignorance by any rational agent (who may be presumed, as rational, to prefer primary goods) for all to act on.

It is particularly myopic to complain that the principles of justice must be heteronomous because they are chosen by parties to the original position *in their own interest*.[7] The veil of ignorance makes the original position not a position of self-interest at all. It is more appropriate to characterize it as a standpoint that expresses an interest in *selves*, or individual rational agents, as such. To understand this, suppose that the parties are not directed to pick principles of justice in their own interest but are assumed to be utterly unconcerned about themselves and consumed with concern for the (rational) interests of a single *other* person. Suppose, that is, that they are *trustees*, each for one other.[8] Because the veil of ignorance makes it impossible for them to consider specific individuals in their deliberations, there is no operative difference at all between this situation and the one Rawls constructs. All of the arguments that a person would find compelling behind the veil for favoring a principle in his own rational interest would be likewise compelling for favoring a principle in an arbitrary *other* person's rational interest.[9] The assumption that the parties are self-interested, therefore, does not show that the principles are heteronomous. Quite the contrary, that they would be chosen for all from a perspective expressing a concern for the ability of an arbitrary individual agent rationally to pursue his ends is perhaps the best argument that they express the Kantian ideal of autonomy.[10]

7. As do Wolff (1977, p. 115) and Johnson (1974, p. 62).
8. Rawls has suggested this term to me in correspondence.
9. I am indebted for this point to Terry Moore and Arthur Kuflik.
10. I accept Jean Hampton's interpretation of Rawls's theory as based on a hypothetical choice in the original position rather than an agreement or bargain. See Hampton 1980.

Kant's idea that moral principles would be the object of will for all in a realm of ends ties them to the more abstract perspective provided by our thick veil. In discussing his notion of such a realm he wrote: "By 'realm' I understand the systematic union of different rational beings through common laws. Because laws determine ends with regard to their universal validity, if we abstract from the personal difference of rational beings and thus from all content of their private ends, we can think of . . . a whole of rational beings as ends in themselves" (1785/1959, p. 51; *Ak*. p. 433). This abstract perspective is the intersubjective standpoint of a rational agent considered as such.

I have argued that the fullest expression of practical reason is to act on principles we could choose for all from this point of view.

Works Cited

Abelson, Raziel. 1969. "Doing, Causing, and Causing to Do." *Journal of Philosophy* 66.

Aristotle. 1968. *De Anima*, in *The Basic Works of Aristotle*. Edited by Richard McKeon. New York. Random House.

Aune, Bruce. 1977. *Reason and Action*. Dordrecht, Holland: D. Reidel.

Austin, J. L. 1961. *Philosophical Papers*. Oxford: Oxford University Press.

Baier, Annette. 1978. "Hume's Analysis of Pride," *Journal of Philosophy* 75.

Baier, Kurt. 1958. *The Moral Point of View: A Rational Basis of Ethics*. Ithaca: Cornell University Press.

——. 1973. "Reason and Experience," *Nous* 7.

——. 1978a. "Moral Reasons and Reasons to Be Moral." In *Values and Morals*, edited by Alvin I. Goldman and Jaegwon Kim. Dordrecht, Holland: D. Reidel.

——. 1978b. "Moral Reasons." In *Midwest Studies in Philosophy, Volume III, Studies in Ethical Theory*, edited by P. French, T. Uehling, Jr., and H. Wettstein. Morris: University of Minnesota, Morris.

——. 1978c. "The Social Source of Reason," *Proceedings of the American Philosophical Association* 51.

Becker, Lawrence C. 1973. "The Finality of Moral Judgments: A Reply to Mrs. Foot," *Philosophical Review* 82.

Benditt, Theodore M. 1976. "Egoism's Inconsistencies," *The Personalist* 57.

Binkley, Robert. 1965. "A Theory of Practical Reason," *Philosophical Review* 74.

Blum, Lawrence. 1981. *Friendship, Altruism, and Morality*. London: Routledge & Kegan Paul.

Works Cited

Brandt, Richard. 1969–1970. "Rational Desires," *Proceedings of the American Philosophical Association* 43.

——. 1972. "Rationality, Egoism, and Morality," *Journal of Philosophy* 69.

——. 1976. "The Psychology of Benevolence and Its Implications," *Journal of Philosophy* 73.

——. 1979. *A Theory of the Good and the Right*. Oxford: Oxford University Press.

Brandt, Richard, and Kim, Jaegwon. 1963. "Wants as Explanations of Actions," *Journal of Philosophy* 60.

Bratman, Michael. 1981. "Intention and Means-End Reasoning," *Philosophical Review* 90.

Brock, Dan. 1977. "The Justification of Morality," *American Philosophical Quarterly* 14.

Buchanan, Allen. 1975. "Revisability and Rational Choice," *Canadian Journal of Philosophy* 5.

——. 1977. "Categorical Imperatives and Moral Principles," *Philosophical Studies* 31.

Butler, Joseph. 1950. *Five Sermons*. New York: Liberal Arts Press. Originally published, 1726.

Churchland, Paul. 1970. "The Logical Character of Action-Explanations," *Philosophical Review* 79.

Daniels, Norman. 1979. "Wide Reflective Equilibrium and Theory Acceptance in Ethics," *Journal of Philosophy* 76.

Darwall, Stephen L. 1974. "Nagel's Argument for Altruism," *Philosophical Studies* 25.

——. 1977–1978. "Two Kinds of Respect," *Ethics* 88.

——. 1980. "Is There a Kantian Foundation for Rawlsian Justice?" In *John Rawls' Theory of Social Justice*, edited by H. Gene Blocker and Elizabeth Smith. Athens: Ohio University Press.

——. 1982a. "Scheffler on Morality and Ideals of the Person," *Canadian Journal of Philosophy* 12.

——. 1982b. "Reply to Scheffler," *Canadian Journal of Philosophy* 12.

Davidson, Donald. 1963. "Actions, Reasons, and Causes." *Journal of Philosophy* 60.

——. 1970. "How Is Weakness of the Will Possible?" In *Moral Concepts*, edited by Joel Feinberg. Oxford: Oxford University Press.

——. 1978. "Hume's Cognitive Theory of Pride," *Journal of Philosophy* 73.

Davidson, Donald, McKinsey, J. C. C., and Suppes, Patrick. 1955. "Outlines of a Formal Theory of Value, I," *Philosophy of Science* 22.

Edwards, Ward. 1954. "The Theory of Decision-making," *Psychological Bulletin* 51.

Falk, W. D. 1952. " 'Ought' and Motivation." In *Readings in Ethical Theory*, edited by Wilfrid Sellars and John Hospers. New York: Appleton-Century-Crofts.

——. 1956. "Moral Perplexity," *Ethics* 66.

——. 1975. "Hume on Practical Reason," *Philosophical Studies* 27.

——. 1976. "Hume on 'Is' and 'Ought,'" *Canadian Journal of Philosophy* 6.

Foot, Philippa. 1967. *Theories of Ethics*. New York: Oxford University Press.

——. 1969. "Moral Beliefs." In *Ethics*, edited by Judith J. Thomson and Gerald Dworkin. Cambridge: M.I.T. Press.

——. 1972a. "Morality as a System of Hypothetical Imperatives," *Philosophical Review* 81.

——. 1972b. "Reasons for Action and Desires," *Proceedings of the Aristotelian Society*, supp. vol. 46.

Frankena, William. 1958. "Obligation and Motivation in Recent Moral Philosophy." In *Essays in Moral Philosophy*, edited A. Melden. Seattle: University of Washington Press.

Frankfurt, Harry G. 1971. "Freedom of the Will and the Concept of a Person." *Journal of Philosophy* 68.

Friedman, Milton. 1962. *Capitalism and Freedom*. Chicago: University of Chicago Press.

Gauthier, David. 1967. "Morality and Advantage," *Philosophical Review* 76.

——. 1974. "The Impossibility of Rational Egoism," *Journal of Philosophy* 71.

——. 1975. "Reason and Maximization," *Canadian Journal of Philosophy* 4.

Gergen, Kenneth. 1971. *The Concept of Self*. New York: Holt, Rinehart, & Winston.

Gewirth, Alan. 1971. "The Normative Structure of Action," *Review of Metaphysics* 25.

——. 1978. *Reason and Morality*. Chicago: Chicago University Press.

Goldman, Alvin. 1970. *A Theory of Human Action*. Englewood Cliffs: Prentice-Hall.

Gosling, J. C. B. 1969. *Pleasure and Desire*. Oxford: Clarendon Press.

Grandy, Richard E., and Darwall, Stephen L. 1979. "On Schiffer's Desires," *Southern Journal of Philosophy* 17.

Grice, Geoffrey Russell. 1967. *The Grounds of Moral Judgment*. Cambridge: Cambridge University Press.

Grice, H. P. 1974–1975. "Method in Philosophical Psychology," *Proceedings of the American Philosophical Association* 48.

Hampton, Jean. 1980. "Contracts and Choices: Does Rawls Have a Social Contract Theory," *Journal of Philosophy* 77.

Hare, R. M. 1968. *The Language of Morals*. New York: Oxford University Press.

——. 1971. "Wanting: Some Pitfalls." In *Agent, Action and Reason*, edited by Robert Binkley, Richard Bronaugh, and Ausonio Marras. Toronto: University of Toronto Press.

Harman, Gilbert. 1975. "Moral Relativism Defended," *Philosophical Review* 84.

——. 1976. "Practical Reasoning," *Review of Metaphysics* 29.

Works Cited

Harrison, Jonathan. 1971. *Our Knowledge of Right and Wrong*. New York: Humanities Press.

Harsanyi, J. C. 1976. *Essays on Ethics, Social Behavior, and Scientific Explanation*. Boston: D. Reidel.

Hart, H. L. A. 1961. *The Concept of Law*. Oxford: Oxford University Press.

Held, Virginia. 1977. "Rationality and Reasonable Cooperation," *Social Research* 44.

Hempel, Carl G. 1965. *Aspects of Scientific Explanation*. New York: Free Press.

Hill, Thomas E., Jr. 1973. "The Hypothetical Imperative," *Philosophical Review* 82.

Hobbes, Thomas. 1957. *Leviathan*. Edited by Michael Oakeshott. Oxford: Basil Blackwell. Originally published, 1651.

Hudson, Stephen D. 1977. *Self-Respect and Character*. Ph.D. dissertation, University of Pittsburgh.

Hume, David. 1957. *An Inquiry Concerning the Principles of Morals*. Edited by Charles W. Hendel. Indianapolis: Bobbs-Merrill. Originally published, 1751.

——. 1967. *A Treatise of Human Nature*. Edited by L. A. Selby-Bigge. Oxford: Oxford University Press. Originally published, 1739.

Hutcheson, Francis. 1964. "Illustrations upon the Moral Sense." In *British Moralists*, edited by L. A. Selby-Bigge. Indianapolis: Bobbs-Merrill. Originally published, 1728.

Johnson, Oliver. 1974. "The Kantian Interpretation," *Ethics* 85.

Kant, Immanuel. 1956. *The Critique of Practical Reason*. Translated by L. W. Beck. Indianapolis: Bobbs-Merrill. Originally published, 1788.

——. 1959. *Foundations of the Metaphysics of Morals*. Translated by L. W. Beck. Indianapolis: Bobbs-Merrill. Originally published, 1785.

——. 1964. *The Critique of Pure Reason*. Translated by Norman Kemp Smith. London: Macmillan. Originally published, 1781; revised 1787.

Körner, Stephan. 1973. "Rational Choice," *Proceedings of the Aristotelian Society*, supp. vol. 47.

Levin, Margarita. 1978. "The Problem of Knowledge in the Original Position," *Auslegung* 5.

Levine, Andrew. 1974. "Rawls' Kantianism," *Social Theory and Practice* 3.

Lewis, David. 1969. *Convention*. Cambridge: Harvard University Press.

——. 1979. "Prisoner's Dilemma Is a Newcomb Problem," *Philosophy and Public Affairs* 8.

Locke, Don. 1974. "Reasons, Wants, and Causes," *American Philosophical Quarterly* 11.

Lovejoy, Arthur O. 1961. *Reflections on Human Nature*. Baltimore: Johns Hopkins University Press.

Luce, R. Duncan, and Raiffa, Howard. 1957. *Games and Decisions: Introduction and Critical Survey*. New York: Wiley.

Mead, George Herbert. 1934. *Mind, Self, and Society.* Chicago: University of Chicago Press.

Meikle, Scott. 1974. "Reasons for Action," *Philosophical Quarterly* 24.

Milgram, Stanley. 1974. *Obedience to Authority.* New York: Harper & Row.

Milligan, D. E. 1974. "Reasons as Explanations," *Mind* 83.

Moore, G. E. 1962. *Principia Ethica.* Cambridge: Cambridge University Press.

Morgenbesser, Sidney, and Ullmann-Margalit, Edna. 1977. "Picking and Choosing," *Social Research* 44.

Nagel, Thomas. 1970. *The Possibility of Altruism.* Oxford: Oxford University Press.

———. 1979. *Mortal Questions.* New York: Cambridge University Press.

Neely, Wright. 1974. "Freedom and Desire," *Philosophical Review* 83.

Nell, Onora. 1975. *Acting on Principle.* New York: Columbia University Press.

Perry, R. B. 1926. *A General Theory of Value.* New York: Longmans, Green.

Pitcher, George. 1958. "On Approval," *Philosophical Review* 67.

Rawls, John. 1971. *A Theory of Justice.* Cambridge: Harvard University Press.

———. 1974. "Reply to Alexander and Musgrave," *Quarterly Journal of Economics* 88.

———. 1975a. "Fairness to Goodness," *Philosophical Review* 84.

———. 1975b. "A Kantian Conception of Equality," *Cambridge Review.*

———. 1980. "Kantian Construction in Ethics, the Dewey Lectures, 1980," *Journal of Philosophy* 77.

Raz, Joseph. 1975. "Reasons for Action, Decisions and Norms," *Mind* 84.

Reid, Thomas. 1969. *Essays on the Active Powers of the Mind.* Cambridge: M.I.T. Press. Originally published, 1788.

Rescher, Nicholas. 1954. "Reasonableness in Ethics," *Philosophical Studies* 5.

Richards, David A. J. 1971. *A Theory of Reasons for Action.* Oxford: Oxford University Press.

Sartre, Jean-Paul. 1975. "The Wall." In *Existentialism from Dostoyevsky to Sartre,* edited by Walter Kaufmann. New York: New American Library.

Savage, Leonard. 1954. *The Foundations of Statistics.* New York: Wiley.

Scanlon, T. M. 1975. "Rawls' Theory of Justice." In *Reading Rawls,* edited by Norman Daniels. New York: Basic Books.

Scheffler, Samuel. 1979. "Moral Skepticism and Ideals of the Person," *Monist* 62.

———. 1982a. "Ethics, Personal Identity, and Ideals of the Person," *Canadian Journal of Philosophy* 12.

———. 1982b "Reply to Darwall," *Canadian Journal of Philosophy* 12.

Schiffer, Stephen. 1976. "A Paradox of Desire," *American Philosophical Quarterly* 13.

Schwartz, Thomas. 1972. "Rationality and the Myth of the Maximum," *Nous* 6.

Works Cited

Sen, Amartya K. 1974. "Choice, Orderings, and Morality." In *Practical Reason*, edited by Stephan Körner. New Haven: Yale University Press.

Sibley, W. M. 1953. "The Rational vs. the Reasonable," *Philosophical Review* 62.

Sidgwick, Henry. 1967. *The Methods of Ethics*, 7th ed. London: Macmillan.

Simon, Herbert A. 1957. *Models of Man*. New York: Wiley.

Smith, M. B. E. 1972. "Indifference and Moral Acceptance," *American Philosophical Quarterly* 9.

Stevenson, Charles. 1963. *Facts and Values*. New Haven: Yale University Press.

Strang, Colin. 1960–1961. "What If Everyone Did That?" *Durham University Journal* 53.

Sturgeon, Nicholas. 1974. "Altruism, Solipsism, and the Objectivity of Reasons," *Philosophical Review* 83.

———. 1982. "Brandt's Moral Empiricism," *Philosophical Review* 91.

Suppes, Patrick. 1966. "Some Formal Models of Grading Principles," *Synthese* 16.

Taylor, Paul. 1978. "On Taking the Moral Point of View." In *Midwest Studies in Philosophy, Volume III, Studies in Ethical Theory*, edited by P. French, T. Uehling, Jr., and H. Wettstein. Morris: University of Minnesota, Morris.

Thomas, Laurence. 1980. "Ethical Egoism and Psychological Dispositions," *American Philosophical Quarterly* 17.

Tversky, Amos. 1969. "Intransitivity of Preferences," *Psychological Review* 76.

Wallace, James. 1978. *Virtues and Vices*. Ithaca: Cornell University Press.

Watson, Gary. 1975. "Free Agency," *Journal of Philosophy* 72.

Wertheimer, Roger. 1972. *The Significance of Sense*. Ithaca: Cornell University Press.

Wheeler, Samuel G, III. 1974. "Inference and the Logical 'Ought'," *Nous* 8.

Williams, Bernard. 1976. "Persons, Character, and Morality." In *The Identities of Persons*, edited by Amelie O. Rorty. Berkeley: University of California Press.

Wills, Gary. 1978. *Inventing America*. Garden City: Doubleday.

Wolff, Robert Paul. 1977. *Understanding Rawls*. Princeton: Princeton University Press.

Wright, G. H. von. 1963a. *The Logic of Preference*. Edinburgh: Edinburgh University Press.

———. 1963b. *The Varieties of Goodness*. London: Routledge & Kegan Paul.

256

Index

Abelson, Raziel, 37n
Agency, unity of, 90–96, 98, 101–113
Agent, conception of rational, 101, 102, 231n, 234
Agent, ideally rational, 219
Agent's reasons, 27–29, 32, 34–42, 205
Aristotle, 75–76, 206n
Aune, Bruce, 47n
Austin, J. L., 205
Authority of reason, 215–216

Baier, Annette, 154–155
Baier, Kurt, 17, 19, 30–32, 51n, 90n, 175n, 180–191, 198–199, 202, 220
Becker, Lawrence C., 175n
Benditt, Theodore M., 190n
Binkley, Robert, 45n
Blum, Lawrence, 132n, 160n, 167n
Brandt, Richard, 81n, 90n, 95n, 134n, 202n
Bratman, Michael, 47n
Brock, Dan, 176n

Buchanan, Allen, 102n, 173n, 231n
Butler, Joseph, 134, 173n, 183n, 191, 225

Caring, 160–164
Categorical imperative, 172–173, 246
Choosing, 68–77
Churchland, Paul, 90n
Coherence:
  of intention and belief, 43–48
  of preference, 63, 67–77, 109–112
  and relative rationality, 14–16, 44–49, 66–67, 68n, 79, 104, 207, 213, 241
Community, 140, 144, 166–167
Conflicting preferences, 89–98, 108–112
Consideration, rational, 81, 85–86, 222, 235–239
Conventions, 243–246

Daniels, Norman, 109n
Davidson, Donald, 27, 36, 66, 72, 154–155

Index

DBR Thesis, 25–28, 33–80, 106
  version I, 33, 37, 78–79
  version II, 33–34, 37, 78–80
  version III, 38, 78–80
  version IV, 58–61, 78–80
Decision, formal theory of, 14–16,
  28, 48–49, 62–77, 101–102,
  195, 207
Desires, 26, 35–37, 39–41, 46, 48,
  66
  second-order, 91–95
Difference principle, 243–245
Dispassionate consideration, 93–96,
  99, 107–108
Dray, William, 30n, 201

Edwards, Ward, 76n
Egoism, 184, 188–190, 194–198,
  227–228, 231–233
Explaining reasons, 28–30, 34,
  201–202
Externalism, 51–52, 79–80

Falk, W. D., 37n, 51n, 56n, 95n,
  139n, 142n, 175n
Foot, Philippa, 38, 90n, 183n
Formal theory of decision, 14–16,
  28, 48–49, 62–77, 101–102,
  195, 207
Frankena, William, 51n
Frankfurt, Harry G., 91, 93n
Friedman, Milton, 140
Future-regarding reasons, 106–108

Gauthier, David, 17, 19, 182–183,
  192–199, 202, 218, 228–230
Gergen, Kenneth, 154n
Gewirth, Alan, 18–19, 118n
Goldman, Alvin, 90n
Good, intersubjective, 113,
  140–167, 171–172
Good, personal, 103–113
Gosling, J. C. B., 26n, 37n

Grandy, Richard E., 93n
Grice, G. R., 180n
Grice, H. P., 90n
Guidance principle, 220–221,
  228–229, 238

Hampton, Jean, 248n
Hare, R. M., 15n, 54
Harman, Gilbert, 27, 43–45, 48
Harrison, Jonathan, 18n
Harsanyi, J. C., 100n
Hart, H. L. A., 211
Held, Virginia, 18n, 180n
Hempel, Carl G., 30n, 90n,
  201–202
Hill, Thomas E., Jr., 14n
Hobbes, Thomas, 176–185,
  191n–194n
Hobbes situation, 176–198,
  232–239
Hudson, Stephen D., 153n
Hume, David, 41, 51–61, 94–95,
  138, 141–143, 154–155, 157,
  162, 173, 196
Hurwicz, Leonid, 64–65
Hutcheson, Francis, 30n
Hypothetical imperative, 14–15,
  44–46, 79, 207

Ideally rational agent, 219
Imagination, 94–99, 107–108
Impartial standpoint (and rationality), 210–211, 225–242,
  246–249
Impersonal preference, 132–167,
  225–226
Impersonal standpoint, 112,
  120–129, 130–167, 210–211,
  225–249
Impersonally basable preference,
  137–145, 146–167
Individual utility, principle of,
  194–198, 229–233, 239

Initial account of rational consideration, 85–100, 102, 107–108,
  111, 117, 135–136, 195, 218,
  220, 230, 233–239
Intentions, 45–48
Internal self-identification, 211–217
Internalism, 20, 42, 51–61, 80–82,
  124, 128–129, 135, 206, 222,
  229, 235–239
Internalist account of reasons,
  80–82, 128–129, 135, 185,
  206, 222, 235–239
Intersubjective value, 113, 140–167,
  171–172
ISIS, 213–217, 219–229, 235–238

Johnson, Conrad D., 243n
Johnson, Oliver, 248n
Justifying reasons, 28–34, 51,
  201–202

Kant, Immanuel, 14, 44–46,
  111–112, 172–175, 196, 200,
  221, 246–249
Kantian interpretation of Rawls,
  246–249
Kim, Jaegwon, 90n
Körner, Stephan, 91
Kuflik, Arthur, 248n

Levin, Margarita, 231n
Lewis, David, 179n
Locke, Don, 32n, 37n
Lovejoy, Arthur O., 153n
Luce, R. Duncan, 28n, 64n, 177n

McKinsey, J. C. C., 72
Mead, George Herbert, 161n
Meaningful life, 164–166
Means/end rationality, 14–15,
  44–46, 104, 207
Meikle, Scott, 28n
Milgram, Stanley, 95

Milligan, D. E., 32n
Money pump, 72–76, 109
Moore, G. E., 55–56, 122n, 146
Moore, Terry, 248n
Morality, 172–176, 180–200, 220,
  232–239, 241, 246
Morgenbesser, Sidney, 68
Motivational aspect of reasons, 20,
  41–42, 51–52, 56–58, 80–82,
  128–129, 199, 206, 235–239
Motivational content, 52n, 124–129

Nagel, Thomas, 17–19, 31–32,
  38–39, 51n, 106–108, 112,
  118–132, 136–137, 145, 159n
Neely, Wright, 91–93
Nell, Onora, 202
Normative aspect of reasons, 19–21,
  31, 80–81, 113, 199, 201–239
Normative system, 203–204,
  211–212

Objective reasons, 118–129,
  130–167
Original position, 17n, 220,
  230–231, 240–249
Otto example, 89–96, 99n

Perry, R. B., 103n
Personal preference, 132–133, 225
Personal standpoint, 112, 120–129,
  133, 157–161
Picking, 68–71
Pitcher, George, 149n
Postema, Gerald, 47n
Preferences, 66, 68–77
  conflicting, 89–98, 108–112
  extrinsic, 86–88
  impersonal, 132–167, 225–226
  impersonally basable, 137–167
  informed, 99–100, 138n
  intrinsic, 86–88
  mutually supporting, 109–112

Index

Preferences (*cont.*)
  personal, 132–133, 225
  transitivity of, 63, 67–77
Pride, 154–155
Prisoners' dilemma, 177–180, 243

Raiffa, Howard, 28n, 64n, 177n
Rational agent, conception of,
  101–102, 231n, 234
Rational consideration, 81, 85–86,
  222, 235–239
  initial account, 85–100, 102,
  107–108, 111, 117, 135–136,
  195, 218, 220, 230, 233–239
Rational egoism, 184, 188–190,
  194–198, 227–228, 231–233
Rational normative system (RNS),
  204–239
Rationality, relative, 14–16, 44–49,
  66–67, 79, 104, 207, 213, 241
Rawls, John, 17, 101–105, 190n,
  207, 220, 230–231, 241–249
Rawls's principles of justice,
  242–249
Raz, Joseph, 47n
Reason, authority of, 215–216
Reasonableness, 18, 244n, 246–247
Reasons:
  agent's, 27–29, 33, 34–42, 205
  explaining, 28–30, 34, 201–202
  future-regarding, 106–108
  general internalist account,
  80–82, 185, 222, 235–239
  initial account, 86, 99, 102,
  107–108, 111, 117, 135–136,
  195, 218, 220, 230, 233–239
  justifying, 28–34, 51, 201–202
  motivational aspect of, 20, 41–42,
  51–52, 56–58, 80–82,
  128–129, 199, 206, 235–239
  normative aspect of, 19–21, 31,
  80–81, 113, 199, 201–239
  objective, 118–129, 130–167

subjective, 118–129, 132–133
universality of, 88, 117–118,
  121–122, 131–132, 145,
  207–208
Reflection (in rational considera-
  tion), 85–86, 91–93
Reflective awareness, 85–86
Reid, Thomas, 183n
Relative rationality, 14–16, 44–49,
  66–67, 68n, 79, 104, 207,
  213, 241
Rescher, Nicholas, 18n
Respect, 148–152
Richards, David, 17–18, 31n, 246
Right, principles of, 17, 172–176,
  180–200, 220, 232–239, 241,
  246
  and fairness, 173, 244n
RNS, 211–239
Roberta example, 39–41, 58, 97
Rosenberg, Jay, 71n, 214n

Sartre, Jean-Paul, 160
Savage, Leonard, 69n
Scanlon, Thomas M., 102n, 231n
Scheffler, Samuel, 102n
Schiffer, Stephen, 91
Schwartz, Thomas, 75n
Second-order desires, 91–95
Self-concern, 160–161
Self-criticalness, 216–217, 219,
  221n, 228–229, 238
Self-esteem, 152–161
Self-identification, internal,
  211–217
Self-respect, 151
Self-support (and rational princi-
  ples), 195–200, 218–219, 228,
  238
Sen, Amartya, 65, 180n
Shaftesbury, Anthony, Earl of, 173n
Sibley, W. M., 18n
Sidgwick, Henry, 103, 207n

Simon, Herbert A., 65
Smith, Adam, 167n
Smith, M. B. E., 51n
Star Trek, 144n
Stevenson, Charles, 81n
Strang, Colin, 173n
Sturgeon, Nicholas, 81n, 120,
 121n, 126n
Subjective reasons, 118–129,
 132–133
Suppes, Patrick, 66, 72
Sympathy (and teleological ethics),
 162–163, 173–174

Taylor, Paul, 175n
Teleological ethics (and sympathy),
 162–163, 173–174
Teleological theory of reasons,
 185–186, 199
Thomas, Laurence, 183n
Trianosky-Stillwell, Gregory, 186n
Tucker, A. W., 177n
Tversky, Amos, 74

Ullman-Margalit, Edna, 68
Unity of agency, 90–96, 98, 101–113
Universal impartial self-support,
 220, 229–234, 238
Universality of rational principles,
 88, 208–210, 218–239
Universality of reasons, 88,
 117–118, 121–122, 131–132,
 145, 207–208
Utilitarianism, 101–102

Veil of ignorance (thick), 230–249
Vulcans, 144

Wallace, James, 176–177
Watson, Gary, 76n, 93, 107n
Weakness of will, 205–206
Wertheimer, Roger, 209
Wheeler, Samuel G., III, 30
Williams, Bernard, 108n
Wills, Gary, 167n
Wolff, Robert Paul, 248n
Wright, G. H. von, 76n, 103n

Library of Congress Cataloging in Publication Data

Darwall, Stephen L., 1946–
   Impartial reason.
   Bibliography: p.
   Includes index.
   1. Reason.   I. Title.
BC177.D37 1983   128'.3   82-22046
ISBN 0-8014-1560-8